Pɪ

Living the

"*Living the Asian Century* is a well-written and thoroughly engaging book by Kishore Mahbubani which captures the highs and the lows of his amazing and curious life. He describes his personal crises and career with surprising openness and frankness, which will surprise many readers who are exposed only to his political and strategic thinking in his many books and articles. This is a story of fierce survival and grit on borrowed optimism. Mahbubani weaves analyses of realpolitik and geopolitical dynamics in his account of the international power play and negotiations he witnessed and experienced in bilateral diplomacy in national capitals and in multilateralism at the United Nations and the UN Security Council. Public officials and diplomats can draw many sharp insights from this memoir to deepen their understanding of how to navigate when faced with similar challenges in foreign policy."

—Chan Heng Chee, Singapore's former
ambassador to the United States (1996–2012) and
ambassador at large, Ministry of Foreign Affairs

"To have travelled from 'poverty to plenty' and lived in an eventful time in history would endow any life with rich complexity. Mahbubani's journey through our Asian century, from childhood deprivation to adult eminence, reflects his brave, intrepid, and fearless spirit. He offers a kaleidoscopic view of the cut-and-thrust of world politics as he experienced it as a diplomat in the US, alongside a local and intimate bird's eye view of Singapore's political struggles, and those of its founding fathers, especially the inimitable Mr. Lee Kuan Yew. Zooming out of global crises and into poignant personal moments and difficulties, this is an absorbing memoir of unflinching honesty. It is a pleasure and an education to read it."

—Meira Chand, recipient of Singapore's Cultural
Medallion and author of *A Different Sky*

"Mahbubani's memoir tells the remarkable story of his rise from poverty to a distinguished career in diplomacy and academia. This deeply personal account also captures the incredible transformation of Singapore and Southeast Asia. This is an inspiring story, beautifully written, that I just could not put down. A must-read."

—Indra Nooyi, former chairman and CEO, PepsiCo

"The arc of Mahbubani's remarkable life and career tracks the birth and rise of Singapore as an independent nation. Through insightful and amusing stories, always told with his trademark candor, this distinguished diplomat and public intellectual also provokes us to think hard about 'the Asian century.'"

—Anne-Marie Slaughter, CEO, New America

"Having known Mahbubani for fifty-nine years, I never expected to learn new things about him in his memoirs. But he surprised me by revealing so many details about his life in this no-holds-barred account that I finished within a day. His seductive writing skills and his excellent storytelling ability make this one of the best memoirs I've read of a Singapore public servant."

—Eddie Teo, chairman, Council of
Presidential Advisers, Singapore

"I first met Mahbubani as a fiercely bearded and rather combative, though undeniably brilliant, mid-level official of the Singapore foreign ministry in 1981. Thereafter, I have had the pleasure of watching him rise to an outstanding permanent representative of Singapore at the United Nations, the founding dean of the Lee Kuan Yew School of Public Policy, and a public intellectual of coruscating intelligence and insight who has carved a niche for himself in the world of geopolitical ideas. His memoirs are a beguiling glimpse into his fascinating journey from very humble beginnings to the highest echelons of international diplomacy. Punctuated with eclectic anecdotes across continents, anchored in the warmth and affability of Mahbubani's personality, this is a must-read for all those enthused by a diplomatic career and those driven to understand the lessons it can teach for life."

—Shashi Tharoor, author, parliamentarian,
former UN Under-Secretary-General, and
former government minister in India

"The rise of Asia is the great economic and political story of our age. Nobody's life story could illuminate better than

Mahbubani's—a man of Indian heritage, a product of multiracial Singapore, and someone with deep knowledge of Western ideas and achievements—how and why this transformation happened. This book, then, is far more than the fascinating autobiography of a man who is arguably Asia's most influential thinker on today's transforming global order. The experiences and achievements of his life as student, diplomat, and commentator also provide important lessons for Westerners. Not least, it will help them understand how an informed and favorably disposed outsider judges both their historic achievements and recent follies."

—Martin Wolf, chief economics commentator, *Financial Times*

"When I once mused to a senior European journalist that Mahbubani must be the most well-known Singaporean internationally, she agreed emphatically. Apart from Lee Kuan Yew, no other Singaporean has achieved a wider reach through his writings and speeches. In his short but fascinating memoirs, Mahbubani gives the reader an insight into what drove him. Rooted in different cultures, he rejoices in a new Asia re-emerging on the global stage. His non-Chinese view of China opposes a widespread western perception that China's actions somehow threaten peace and stability in the world. Mahbubani's analysis of the role of raw power in global politics is sobering. He watched and experienced it at close range. Mahbubani freely admits that he had detractors, both in Singapore and outside, and tries to understand their criticisms of him. One can sense the pain he must have felt writing those paragraphs. As the

Founding Dean, Mahbubani was hugely responsible for the exceptional success of the Lee Kuan Yew School of Public Policy. Yet, even here, he faced many criticisms. Happily, he emerged stronger and more energized after each of life's challenges. He had more than his fair share. Mahbubani's memoirs are not only about foreign affairs, but also about an individual life in the Singapore story which would not be put down by misfortune or hardship. His story will inspire a younger generation of Singaporeans."

—George Yeo, former foreign minister, Singapore

Also by Kishore Mahbubani

Beyond the Age of Innocence: Rebuilding Trust between America and the World

The New Asian Hemisphere: The Irresistible Shift of Global Power to the East

The Great Convergence: Asia, the West, and the Logic of One World

Has China Won? The Chinese Challenge to American Primacy

Living the Asian Century

AN
UNDIPLOMATIC
MEMOIR

Kishore Mahbubani

PUBLICAFFAIRS

New York

PublicAffairs

Hachette Book Group

1290 Avenue of the Americas, New York, NY 10104

www.publicaffairsbooks.com

@Public_Affairs

Printed in the United States of America

First Trade Paperback Edition: August 2024

Published by PublicAffairs, an imprint of Hachette Book Group, Inc. The PublicAffairs name and logo is a registered trademark of the Hachette Book Group.

The Hachette Speakers Bureau provides a wide range of authors for speaking events. To find out more, go to hachettespeakersbureau.com or email HachetteSpeakers@hbgusa.com.

PublicAffairs books may be purchased in bulk for business, educational, or promotional use. For more information, please contact your local bookseller or the Hachette Book Group Special Markets Department at special.markets@hbgusa.com.

The publisher is not responsible for websites (or their content) that are not owned by the publisher.

Print book interior design by Amy Quinn.

Library of Congress Cataloging-in-Publication Data

Names: Mahbubani, Kishore, author.

Title: Living the Asian century : an undiplomatic memoir / Kishore Mahbubani.

Other titles: Undiplomatic memoir

Description: First trade paperback edition. | New York : PublicAffairs, 2024. | Includes bibliographical references and index.

Identifiers: LCCN 2024000847 | ISBN 9781541703049 (trade paperback) | ISBN 9781541703056 (ebook)

Subjects: LCSH: Mahbubani, Kishore. | Diplomats—Singapore—Biography. | Sindhi (South Asian people)—Singapore—Biography. | Singapore. Ministry of Foreign Affairs—Officials and employees—Biography. | United Nations—Biography. | Singapore—Foreign relations.

Classification: LCC DS610.73.M34 A3 2024 | DDC 327.59570092 [B]—dc23/eng/20240409

LC record available at https://lccn.loc.gov/2024000847

ISBNs: 9781541703049 (paperback), 9781541703056 (ebook)

LSC-C

Printing 2, 2024

*With gratitude to
my late mother,
Mrs Janki Mahbubani,
and
my late father,
Mr Mohandas Detaram Mahbubani,
for making Singapore my birthplace*

Contents

CHAPTER 1

Born Poor

B LAME IT ALL ON THE DAMN BRITISH.

After effortlessly colonising the Indian subcontinent for a century or more, they royally screwed up their departure in 1947. The partition of British India into Muslim-majority Pakistan and Hindu-majority India triggered a mass migration, with Muslims fleeing India to go to Pakistan and Hindus and Sikhs fleeing Pakistan to go to India. Riots and terrible communal violence accompanied these flights, resulting in a mass wave of killings. Up to eighteen million people were displaced, and two to three million people died as they tried to flee Pakistan and India.[1] My mother could easily have been among them.

As a young Hindu woman, she grew up in Hyderabad, Sind, where she was born on August 8, 1925. She was twenty-two when partition happened. Like many Hindus, she had to flee Pakistan. She managed to get on a train to India with my elder sister, Duri, who was just one year old. She was in the last car of the train with a few dozen other Hindu women, also with children. They were protected by a single Sikh guard with a single-shot rifle. In the middle of the night, their car was decoupled from the train, stranding all these Hindu women in the middle of the desert. If a Muslim mob had come along, they would have been raped and killed. It was a terrifying night. Fortunately, the next morning, another train came along and literally pushed her stranded car across the border into India. It was a close shave.

After her narrow escape from Pakistan in August 1947, she first ended up in Mumbai (then called Bombay), as she had many relatives there. These relatives helped to arrange a passage by ship to Singapore in January 1948, as my father had already moved back there, which was why I was conceived in Singapore and born there in October 1948. All this happened only because my father had been sent to work as a peon for five cents a day in Singapore in 1933, when he was thirteen years old. Hence, my being born in Singapore was an accident. I could just as easily have been born in any corner of the British empire, where the sun never set in 1948.

As independence approached in the Indian subcontinent in the 1940s, and as troubles between Hindus and Muslims increased (partly stoked by British divide-and-rule policies), my Hindu Sindhi ancestors began to flee from Hyderabad and

Karachi, where they were an imperilled minority. The killings began before partition. My father told me that a Muslim mob had brought the dead body of his brother to his family home in Hyderabad to ask if he was a member of his family. Wisely, the family had denied that the dead body belonged to them. If they had accepted it, they could all have been slaughtered. Given this violence (and it must be emphasised that both Hindus and Muslims carried out these killings), it's not surprising that my relatives fled to all areas of the earth to seek safety and prosperity.

One little-known fact about Sindhis is that they are remarkably entrepreneurial. When the Hindu Sindhis began to flee from what became Pakistan in 1947, they went to all corners of the world (often to cities where Sindhi merchants had already been operating since the late 1800s) and, amazingly, succeeded in many different environments. I can say this with confidence since I have first cousins sprinkled all around the globe: in Guyana and Suriname in South America, in Nigeria and Ghana in Africa, in Hong Kong and Tokyo in East Asia, and of course in Mumbai and Calcutta. I could just as easily have been born in any of these places.

The first stroke of good luck in my life was to be born in Singapore. I am absolutely sure that if I hadn't been born in Singapore, I wouldn't have had the life I have enjoyed. The accident that led to my being born in Singapore was a result of my father, Mohandas Mahbubani, having been orphaned soon after he was born in 1920. He was brought up by his sisters, who couldn't spare time for him as they had their own children to take care of. This was why his sisters sent him from Sind at the age of thirteen to "Wild West" Singapore, where he worked as a peon in a Sindhi textile shop. One reason Singapore was chosen was that one of his elder sisters had moved there with her husband. In theory, it was her responsibility to take care of him. In practice, she had little time to do so. She was focused on her own children and adjusting to a new country herself. As a result, my father grew up as an unsupervised young teenager in Singapore. Inevitably, he acquired many bad habits. He began to smoke, drink, and gamble. With these rough foundations, he ended up having a rough life. I discovered these facts only after I had become an adult. Hence, even though my sisters and I resented (and sometimes hated) our father when we were young, I came to forgive him when I understood that life had dealt him a very bad hand.

My father's life must also have been affected by the turbulence in Southeast Asia. Fortunately, he left Singapore just before World War II broke out and thus did not live there under the harsh Japanese occupation from 1942 to 1945. He returned to Sind to live with his relatives. While he was there, his relatives arranged a marriage with my mother, following traditional Hindu Sindhi customs. My mother had no clue that she was being married to a young man who had accumulated many self-destructive habits. Her Kirpalani family, a respectable clan, was happy that she was marrying into the supposedly prestigious Mahbubani clan. Almost all Asian societies are hierarchical. The Sindhis were no exception, and in the hierarchy of surnames, the Mahbubanis ranked high.

Having been brought up in a stable and conservative home, my mother had no idea of the turbulent life that awaited her after her marriage to my father. All her siblings, three brothers and three sisters, ended up in stable and successful marriages; she was the exception. Since she ended up in Singapore, she was far from sibling support. There were no close relatives she could turn to (except that preoccupied sister-in-law), even though she experienced a great deal of turbulence as we were growing up.

We were poor. I first became aware of this at the age of six when I was put on a special feeding programme when I first enrolled in school.[2] All the Primary 1 boys were weighed when they joined Seraya School, and about a dozen of us were deemed to be underweight. At recess, we assembled in the principal's office, where a big pail of milk with a single ladle awaited us. Each of us drank from the ladle, happily sharing our germs and inadvertently boosting our immune systems. Being underweight was obviously not a positive state, yet I was lucky to be alive at six. My mom told me that when I was six months old, the doctor told her that I would not survive a bad case of diarrhoea. I could have become an infant mortality statistic in Singapore.

Our poverty was a direct result of my father's inability to hang on to a job for very long. At one point or another, his bad habits, especially drinking and gambling, would get in the way. He would also become violent, getting into fights after heavy drinking. My memory has erased some of my more dramatic encounters with my dad. Yet my oldest childhood friend, Jeffery Sng, whom I have known since the age of six since he lived less than a hundred metres from my home, remembers one of them vividly:

During the hot afternoon, we gathered inside the high-ceilinged living room to enjoy the cool air under the hanging fan. In the evening, the family would move out to sit on rattan chairs in the veranda of our Peranakan-style[3] bungalow to enjoy the natural breeze coming from outside. One day when we were on the veranda, shouts suddenly rang out from the street, accompanied by the sound of footsteps of people running. When I looked down, I saw the neighbours and our kampong[4] boys running past our big gate towards the Crane Road junction at the head of Onan Road. I could not help being infected by the sudden burst of excitement from the street below and rose from my chair to rush out from my house and follow the neighbourhood boys running ahead towards Crane Road. As I approached the junction, a crowd was building up in front of the corner kopitiam.[5] There was a large crowd, which spilled into the street, blocking off motor traffic. I pushed my way through the crowd, asking the onlookers in Malay and Hokkien dialect, "What's happening?" "It's a fight!" someone replied. As I nudged my way, body against body, to the front row, a police car arrived. A policeman was already walking past the tables on the shop floor towards the large counter where the shirtless Hylam Chinese owner was standing. People's attention was directed to a particular spot next to the large counter. They were looking at an Indian man standing by a table with a broken Tiger Beer bottle and a broken beer mug. His white shirt, wet with beer, was torn and spattered with blood. He had an unshaven square face and neatly pomaded shining black hair parted in the middle. It suddenly struck me that he was Kishore's father. The shirtless coffee-shop owner was standing nearby but hesitated to approach. Kishore's father, the object of attention, looked drunk and fiercely defiant. Meanwhile, the policeman who came from the patrol car made his presence felt and started asking questions and waving his notebook. I couldn't hear what was said. Then I suddenly noticed that Kishore had shown up next to the policeman and was calling out loudly, "Dad, Dad!" He went up to his father and took his arm lightly, with an anguished expression. "Please come home, Dad," said Kishore. The Indian man with his torn shirt let himself be led by his son out of the kopitiam. The crowd parted to let the father and son pass through. I watched them cross the street together. Kishore's house was almost right across from the kopitiam. Kishore walked his father up the front steps leading to the door of the house. The door opened, and they disappeared inside.

The person most traumatised by this event must have been me, not Jeffery. Logically, I should be the one who remembers it and Jeffery the one who has forgotten it. Instead, the opposite happened. This episode made me aware of how faulty our memories are. We remember some traumatic events. We also forget a lot. Nonetheless, I recall similar events. One night, our neighbours knocked on our door to say that my father had fallen into a nearby drain while walking home drunk. I vividly remember pulling him out to bring him home. I have even more frightening memories of going to the door of our house to tell some Chinese gangsters (and debt collectors) that my father was not home while he quickly rolled under the bed to escape detection. I don't recall how the gangsters looked, but I'll never forget the look of absolute fear in my father's eyes.

He knew that he would be beaten very badly if the Chinese gangsters got hold of him. In some ways, we lived on the edge in many phases of my childhood.

While my father was often involved in violent incidents, he was not violent at home. If he became angry, he would take it out on objects, not people. My three sisters and I remember one incident well. For Hindu families, the main celebratory event of the year (similar to Christmas) is Diwali, the festival of lights. That's when we clean the house, buy new clothes, and indulge in eating a lot of sweets. One year, as Diwali approached, my father was prospering, and so he showered us with new clothes. He even bought a massive TV set that must have been five feet wide. A real luxury.

Unfortunately, he got into one of his usual drunken spats on the eve of Diwali and returned home angry. In his drunken anger, he took away all the new clothes he had bought us. He also carried the TV set out of the house. He piled up all the new luxuries in front of our home and set them alight, creating a huge bonfire that attracted the attention of the whole neighbourhood. Everyone came to witness it. Our then neighbours still speak about this memorable event today: the festival of lights, done rather differently.

Incidents like this were traumatic for us children. They must have been even more traumatic for my mother. Her reaction to these domestic troubles was to pray—a lot. She would wash little silver idols of Hindu gods such as Krishna and Ganesh first in milk, then in water. I would sit by her as she prayed in front of our little family altar. Given the many hours I spent praying with my mother in my childhood, I should have emerged as a devout Hindu. Instead, the opposite happened. I felt restless and bored as she prayed, yet, as I sensed that the prayers helped her, I suppressed my boredom.

My father got into debt mostly because of his gambling, especially on horse races. Foolishly, he would take money (collected on behalf of his employer) and use it to gamble in the hope of striking it rich. He never did. He would lose the company funds, and as a result, he would lose his job as one Sindhi employer after another dismissed him for losing their money. Nevertheless, those Sindhi employers were kind and generous: they only fired him. The big mistake my father made was to accept a job from a respectable British firm, China Engineers. Initially, things went well. He earned more money from this more prosperous British outfit. Then the inevitable happened. He gambled away some funds he had collected on behalf of the firm.

The British, being British, played by the rules and reported this theft to the police, who arrested my dad. On October 30, 1962—six days after my fourteenth birthday—he was sentenced to nine months' imprisonment for criminal breach of trust. He was jailed in Outram Prison, which had been built by the British in 1847. As the only other male in the family, I was designated to visit him. These were not happy occasions. I had to take several buses to travel to the prison, which was far from our home. We often had to wait outside the prison until the visiting hours arrived. During our visits, I could not touch or hold him. We could speak to each other only through a window. He said little. I said little too. But the ritual of visiting seemed to help him. All I remember is feeling sad whenever I visited him.

While my father was in jail, my mother took the brave step of going to the government's Legal Aid Bureau—which had been set up just a few years earlier, in 1958—to initiate proceedings for a legal separation from my father. It must have taken a great deal of courage, as she had no legal experience or knowledgeable friends to help her out. Fortunately, her brothers in Suriname and Guyana were doing well in business and sent money to keep us going when my father had none. However, my mother had no relatives in Singapore to help her with practical matters or provide psychological support. Hence, at the age of fourteen, I became the second senior adult in the house. I accompanied my mother to the Legal Aid Bureau to obtain the separation papers.

My father was informed of the separation while he was in jail. Legally, he had no place in our home after the end of his prison term. Still, we dreaded the day of his release, fearing that he would forcibly try to enter our house. Our house in Onan Road had once had very attractive colourful glass windows facing the street. However, one year, in one of his usual fits of rage, my father had thrown stones at them and shattered them. We had no choice but to replace them with ugly metal grilles. We felt comforted by those metal grilles on the day of his release from prison.

Sure enough, straight out of jail, my father appeared in front of our Onan Road home. He didn't try to force his way in. He sat in the coffee shop opposite for several hours and then left. We all breathed a sigh of relief.

The legal separation turned out to be a blessing. My father rented a room and earned just about enough to keep himself going. We survived with the support of welfare payments from the state and the checks we received from my mother's brothers in Guyana and Suriname. It was always a pleasure to accompany my mother to the post office to cash a banker's draft that had come in the post. The money would be sent in British pounds. In those days, we got 8.5 Singapore dollars for each British pound. Today, you can get barely 1.7 Singapore dollars for each British pound.

The poverty that my family, as well as our Malay neighbours, experienced created many challenges and handicapped us in many ways. It prevented the full education of my sisters. My elder sister, Duri, left school at the age of twelve; my younger sister Vimu left school at sixteen; and my youngest sister, Chandra, left at eighteen. All our Malay neighbours also dropped out before they could graduate from secondary school.

I believe Jeffery Sng and I were the only two children from our section of Onan Road who ended up in university. Why were we the exceptions in our poor neighbourhood? At that time, university was not considered a necessary or even useful preparation for many occupations. We both had strong mothers who protected and nurtured us. We both accidentally discovered the Joo Chiat Public Library in our childhood and became voracious readers from a young age. Indeed, many of our childhood peers ridiculed Jeffery and me for the time we spent reading books.

While these personal factors were important, there were also larger national forces at play. If Jeffery and I had grown up in one of the British colonies that became either a failing or failed Third World nation, we wouldn't have completed our studies. Unbeknownst to us as children, Singapore had miraculously begun to enjoy relatively good governance (by Third World standards), which created a favourable ecosystem that enabled us to grow and develop. From the daily ladle of milk in the principal's office at the age of six to the trained teachers who always greeted us in the clean, functional classrooms; the constant bursaries that I received as a poor student; and the President's Scholarship I received after finishing high school in 1967, my life was improved by the benign national environment that was developing around me.

Looking back to my childhood, I can clearly see how a well-governed state affected my life. Since my parents had several siblings who had scattered to all corners of the earth after the partition of India and Pakistan in 1947, I could compare my growth and development with those of many first cousins in Guyana and Suriname, Nigeria and Ghana, Mumbai and Calcutta, Hong Kong and Japan. Since my father hadn't done well, my family was clearly the poorest compared to all my first cousins, some of whose parents became millionaires. Yet, with the exception of my two first cousins in Suriname (whose father, Jhamat Kirpalani, did exceptionally well in business by any standards), none of my first cousins completed a university education.

Therefore, Singapore played a key role in my ability to escape from the clutches of poverty and enjoy a rich life of diplomacy and learning.

CHAPTER 2

Still Poor

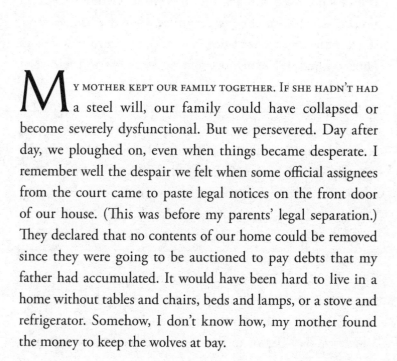

My MOTHER KEPT OUR FAMILY TOGETHER. IF SHE HADN'T HAD a steel will, our family could have collapsed or become severely dysfunctional. But we persevered. Day after day, we ploughed on, even when things became desperate. I remember well the despair we felt when some official assignees from the court came to paste legal notices on the front door of our house. (This was before my parents' legal separation.) They declared that no contents of our home could be removed since they were going to be auctioned to pay debts that my father had accumulated. It would have been hard to live in a home without tables and chairs, beds and lamps, or a stove and refrigerator. Somehow, I don't know how, my mother found the money to keep the wolves at bay.

In my life, in which I have experienced many ups and downs, if ever I was tempted to give up, I would remember my mother. She never melted, even under pressures greater than anything I experienced. My resolve was further strengthened by a troubling incident that occurred when I was thirteen years old, in Secondary 1 at Tanjong Katong Technical School (TKTS). One of my classmates was a South Indian boy, probably Tamil. His family situation seemed to be similar to mine: a dysfunctional father, an unemployed mother, several sisters. Clearly, he was under great stress. Unfortunately, he didn't share his stress with any of us. He looked calm most of the time, though a troubled, anxious expression crossed his face once in a while. Certainly, we had no clue that he was close to the brink. Hence, when we came to class one day, we were deeply shocked to learn that he had hanged himself. I remember well the deep horror I felt when the teacher told us what had happened to him.

Giving up was never an option for me. I could not possibly let down my mother after all that she had been through to protect us during our childhood. It would have been hard enough to cope with all of our travails in the familiar environment of her youth, with the support of the Hindu Sindhi community that she had grown up in. Instead, she was parachuted into an alien place called Singapore, into a society where she had no close relatives or close friends to turn to.

However, while she was alone in one sense, she was not alone in another. Quite surprisingly, despite the remarkable religious and ethnic diversity surrounding our little home on Onan Road, we had begun to develop some kind of community.

14

Looking back now, I feel that I grew up in a small village with many supportive neighbours, many of whom were as poor as we were, if not poorer. We were, however, the only Hindu family.

My mother professed a deep antipathy towards Muslims due to her traumatic experiences during partition. She would repeat well-known insults that were common among Hindus from India, such as "What do you expect? He's Muslim, isn't he?" Her prejudices against Muslims ran deep. Yet, on a person-to-person level, she was able to set them aside so that we could become very close to two wonderful Muslim families, the Haniffas and the Maricans, who lived in the houses on either side of us on Onan Road. Unlike my father, neither Mr Haniffa nor Mr Marican went to jail. They had precarious jobs that paid little. Like our family, they lived on the edge. Our house seemed small for the five of us after our father left us. However, I remember that they had even more people crammed into the tiny single-bedroom terrace houses that we lived in. For the first twenty-five years of my life, our three families lived and grew up as one extended family, visiting each other's kitchens and exchanging food all the time. All of us were poor. All of us had travails. And we all supported one another.

I have never been quite sure how my mother reconciled her in-principle hatred for Muslims with her deep and sincere love for our Muslim neighbours. Perhaps she made a distinction between Pakistani Muslims and Malay Muslims. To us as children, what mattered was that we had neighbours whom we loved and trusted, and who loved and trusted us. We were absolutely at home with them, as they were with us. We would celebrate Muslim festivals with great joy, just as they would celebrate Diwali.

Malay therefore became a second language for me (after English), especially because I also learned it in school. In my soul, my Southeast Asian identity is as strong as my Indian identity. I feel equally at home culturally in Indonesia and in India. The Hindu-Muslim divide that my mother insisted on never prevented me from seeing our Malay neighbours and other Malay Muslims as members of my tribe. Indeed, I remember with some bitterness that when my family needed help, few members of the Sindhi community stepped forward, even though many were wealthy. Instead, the opposite happened. As soon as the *Straits Times* reported that my father had gone to jail, a member of the Sindhi community drove up to our house in a Mercedes-Benz—not to offer sympathy but to ask for the repayment of $100 that my father had borrowed from him.

I retain a powerful visual memory of this incident, which drove home a key life lesson for me. When a poor family experiences problems, it is more likely to receive solidarity and support from fellow poor families, as we did from our equally poor Malay neighbours.

One thing we and our neighbours had in common was that Indian Hindus and Malay Muslims were minorities in Singapore. The largest population was (and still is) Chinese. The neighbours who lived on the other sides of the Haniffas and Maricans were Chinese. We got along well with them, especially the Peranakan Chinese family at 175 Onan Road, who also spoke Malay at home. Yet it would be misleading to suggest that this harmony among Indians, Malays, and Chinese in our immediate neighbourhood reflected a natural national condition. I lived through two Malay-Chinese riots in 1964 and 1969. After the first days of rioting in 1964, when one of my Malay neighbours at 177 Onan Road thought that the situation had improved, he tried to go to work downtown. I saw him return home barely ten minutes later, battered and bruised, having been beaten by a Chinese mob barely a hundred metres from our home. Not far from where my neighbour was beaten, a Malay bus conductor lost his life during a riot when a Chinese mob killed him by driving a long, sharp pole into his body.

Such violence was not uncommon in poor Third World cities, such as Singapore in the 1950s and 1960s. Another vivid childhood memory is of sitting on the steps of my home one afternoon and seeing a bloodied Chinese gangster fleeing from another bloodied Chinese gangster who was attacking him with a broken beer bottle. However, despite all these bursts of violence so close to my childhood home, Singapore was primarily a peaceful place, and the Indian, Malay, and Chinese communities lived harmoniously most of the time. No one except police officers had guns.

Despite having been brought up by a fervent Indian nationalist—my mother—and living and eating in Malay Muslim homes, my best friends for most of my life have been Chinese Singaporeans, including my oldest friend, Jeffery Sng. We have known each other since we were six years old. We both became passionate readers. As children, we took long walks together, often to the East Coast Beach. And Jeffery, who went on to become a young state gymnast, protected my frail body from bullies in our neighbourhood.

Jeffery's memory of Onan Road when we were children is of

a time when a low-rise urban collection of kampong houses, compound houses, and bungalows had already given way to medium-rise flats, terraced town houses, and large Peranakan stilt bungalows. When we were children, itinerant hawkers selling Hokkien mee,[1] coconut pickers, travelling Indian milkmen, and Chinese kopitiams were still around, though many of these were disappearing from the neighbourhood. There was still a lingering kampong atmosphere in our street; some houses still sported an attap roof and had hedges of hibiscus flowers and large potted pomegranate plants.

Since I had experienced poverty all through my childhood and youth, for a long time, I associated this period of my life with deprivation. Looking back now, it's clear that while I lived with material deprivation, I was absorbing cultural richness. Unknowingly and unwittingly, I was inhaling the vapours of three of the most dynamic and resilient Asian civilisations: Indian, Islamic, and Chinese. This was an extraordinary privilege. Through this direct exposure, I could intuitively and unconsciously absorb the deeper thought patterns and cultural drives of these rich cultures, which together make up half of the world's population.

Growing up in Singapore, it felt perfectly natural to live with other cultural and religious traditions and enjoy their festivals. Since our immediate neighbours were Muslims, the young boys had to be circumcised before puberty. Once, when my neighbour was circumcised at around the age of ten, I was invited to lift the net to see the bloody physical results of the procedure, probably carried out by a cleric, not a medical doctor. I shuddered. Nevertheless, we enjoyed the festivals. During the fasting month, our Muslim neighbours would end their fast with sumptuous meals. Some of the food flowed into our home. Barely thirty metres from our home was a large Chinese bakery with a large empty yard in front of the building that was an ideal location at Chinese New Year for lighting a massive number of firecrackers, which were both deafening and uplifting. We felt proud that our Chinese bakery had the loudest firecrackers in our entire neighbourhood.

This sense of living in a village provided a psychological buffer that helped us cope with poverty. We weren't the only family struggling. Across the road from our house was a Tamil family living in a bungalow within a huge compound that probably measured about forty thousand square feet. In theory, they should have been prosperous. In practice, they seemed to have more problems than we did. Several of their children suffered from mental illness. One of them, Pakiri, would wander aimlessly around the neighbourhood and was occasionally confined to a mental institution.

We suffered other inconveniences. The houses in Onan Road had no flush toilets. Instead, we were provided with large metal cans. Each morning, the night soil men (as they were called) went around the neighbourhood. When they got to our house, they opened a small door in the wall, pulled out a metal can filled with twenty-four hours' worth of faeces and urine from a family of five, and replaced it with a clean, empty metal can. Using the toilet in the morning wasn't too bad, but by afternoon, after the tropical heat and humidity of Singapore had enveloped the toilet, the stench was terrible.

The arrival of the first flush toilet at 179 Onan Road was a transformational moment in my childhood. It wasn't just about the physical experience, pleasant as it was. It was also about the sense of improved dignity. I had always felt ashamed of living in a house without a flush toilet. The psychological relief was as important as the material or physical improvement.

I thought that my childhood experience with metal-can toilets was bad until I visited my relatives in Jakarta in my late teens. Their household had at least a dozen people, and their metal cans were removed once a week. By the third or fourth day, the stench was nauseating. I could hardly breathe. This Jakarta experience made me even more aware of how much my life had improved and how far Singapore had developed.

As a child, I somehow created my own coping mechanisms to insulate myself from many of the dramatic events unfolding around me. Like any other family, we had our fair share of intra-family disputes. Here too, Jeffery Sng recalls better than I do how I shielded myself from some of the more disturbing ones:

> I approached Kishore's house. A short flight of steps led up from the street to the door. As I walked up, the sound of loud voices broke out of the doorway. I heard Vimu's voice protesting loudly in Indian dialect about something. I couldn't understand what she was wailing about. The other voice was Kishore's mother's. They were fighting about something.

Kishore's younger sister Vimu was the Wednesday child of the family. She felt that her mother and elder sister, Duri, were always picking on her. Her wishes were always denied or over-ruled. She was not one to take it lying down; she was quick to protest against her perceived treatment. When I looked through the doorway, Vimu was hurrying away teary-eyed down the corridor with emphatic steps. As she disappeared into the house with her agonised voice trailing behind, I saw Kishore in the living room to the right of the doorway. He was seated on the sofa, bent over his school math exercise book. He seemed to be unaffected by and oblivious to the high-decibel noise that filled the house like a burst of malevolent energy. He didn't notice me coming in and looked up from his math exercise book to find me standing by his homework table. I asked, "What happened?" He answered, somewhat distractedly, "I don't know, lah!"

According to Jeffery, "Nothing could shake his formidable concentration on his book or his homework, be it TV blar-ing, loud Bollywood Indian music playing, sisters' shouting or his mother's constant attempts to lecture him about life." My mother complained exasperatedly to Jeffery, "My son never lis-tens to me. Whatever I say goes in one ear and comes out the other ear. When I get upset, he just says, 'What, what did you say?'" In this, she was only partly right: in fact, her words never got as far as one ear and certainly did not escape the other. I just blocked everything out.

Jeffery was absolutely right about the books, though: during my childhood, I was completely absorbed in them. They provided a place of safety, a place to satisfy my curiosity and fire my imagination. When I asked the Haniffas and the Maricans what they remember about me as a child, the first thing they said was that I was always immersed in a book while all the other children were busy playing marbles, fighting with spiders, flying kites, or kicking a football on some hard ground nearby. I didn't participate in these activities. Instead, I took long walks with Jeffery.

Both Jeffery and I loved books. Our love of books was the result of a lucky accident: our discovery of the Joo Chiat Public Library, which was about one kilometre away from our neighbourhood. It was not inevitable that we would find our way there since neither of my parents had studied beyond primary school. They were not well-educated, and we had no books in our house. Indeed, as far as I can recall, no one in our neighbourhood except Jeffery and me frequented this library. Somehow, we happened upon it. And thus began a passionate love affair with reading that completely transformed my life.

The word "library" has only positive connotations for me. Today, most people associate libraries, especially in Singapore, with some kind of well-equipped modern building. The Joo Chiat Public Library, which opened in 1949, was by contrast a very modest outfit. It was housed in the Joo Chiat Community Centre, which could best be described as a large shed with brick walls. It had no air-conditioning, only ceiling fans to cool us in the hot, humid Singapore weather. Despite the heat, Jeffery and I spent hours there browsing through books. The uncomfortable physical environment didn't matter. The books transported us to magical places.

My other main occupation as a child was, of course, going to school. My primary school, Seraya School, was a typical neighbourhood school. It was a three-storey building crammed with classrooms and with no indoor places for play. Instead, we shared a football field with a neighbouring school. Since it was an English-language primary school and I attended from the age of six, English became my first language. My mother spoke to me primarily in Sindhi, even though she spoke reasonably good basic English, but I replied in a combination of English and Sindhi. Similarly, my "aunties" (all adults in Singapore are referred to as "uncles" or "aunties" by those who are younger) in the neighbouring houses spoke to me in Malay, and I replied in a combination of English and Malay.

Why did I cling so strongly to the English language? The only honest answer is that my mind had been fully colonised when I was a child. When I was born, Singapore was a British colony. My birth certificate described my citizenship (or lack of it) as "British subject." As a child, I unquestioningly believed that Asians were inherently inferior to "white" people, especially the British. I remember few stories from the time when I was six or seven years old, yet I will never forget a conversation I had with an Indian schoolmate called Morgan. I vividly remember asking him where he would like to live when he grew up. He replied, "London." I asked, "Why London?" He replied, "Because in London, the streets are paved with gold."

In 1959, when I was eleven, Lee Kuan Yew was elected the first prime minister (PM) of the new "self-governing" Singapore, while the British retained control of Singapore's defence and foreign affairs. I should have welcomed this first step towards political decolonisation. Instead, I vividly remember feeling great apprehension because Singapore's dominant English-language newspaper, the *Straits Times*, which was pro-British, convinced me that a dangerous "leftist" leader had taken over. This reckless man was trying to kick out the safe and wise British rulers of Singapore! The English-language education that I'd had throughout my life only reinforced this pro-British mentality since the curriculum had obviously been designed by Singapore's British colonial rulers. Directly or indirectly, we Asians imbibed the belief that Western societies were superior to Asian ones and became more and more distanced from our own cultures.

My mother did try to nudge me towards my Sindhi destiny. As children, my sisters and I were made to study Sindhi. There is a building known as Sindhu House on Mountbatten Road, not far from our house on Onan Road, that is the home of the Sindhi Merchants Association. The way the building was used in the early days illustrated the conflicted soul of the Sindhis. On the second floor there was, and still is, a temple where my mother used to pray regularly. I often went there with her. On the ground floor, some rooms were set aside for gambling tables. The Sindhis loved to gamble. It was part of their mercantilist streak. The worship of gods and money went hand in hand.

Even though the wealthy Sindhis (and there were many) didn't help our family in our hour of need, there's no doubt in my mind that the ecosystem that the Sindhi community had built in multiracial Singapore provided a great deal of emotional support to my mother. Before coming to Singapore, she had spent her entire life in the monocultural Hindu Sindhi environment in Sind (since she had little or no interaction with Muslim Sindhis). Even though she could speak, read, and write English (although not fluently), she was more comfortable speaking Sindhi and reading and writing in the Sindhi script.

She loved to participate in the Satsangs (prayer services) in Sindhu House on Mountbatten Road. She sang well and played the harmonium and was often asked to be the lead singer. My sisters and I sometimes accompanied her. When I was a child, the Sindhi businesses occupied most of the shophouses on High Street, especially between Hill Street and North Bridge Road. When my father was working in Sindhi shops on High Street, I visited him from time to time, taking a long bus ride from Onan Road.

It was also a treat to visit the homes of a few better-off Sindhi families where the woman of the house was a friend of my mother's. We used to visit the Gulabrai family in the Capitol flats and the Nanwani family on Joo Chiat Road, within walking distance of our home. Uncle Shankar, as we called Mr Nanwani, gave us one of the biggest treats of our childhood by driving us to the Kota Tinggi waterfalls in Johor, a neighbouring state. The waterfalls were not large, but to the eyes of a child, they were massive. One of our trips to Kota Tinggi left me with one of my most vivid childhood memories: being chased by a pack of dogs when I strayed too close to the gate of a tin mine.

I also retain happy memories of spending Diwali evenings on High Street. Each Sindhi shop would open its doors and lay out a wide array of Sindhi savoury and sweet treats. We would go from shop to shop, savouring all kinds of treats. These happy encounters with Sindhi families were important for me, but the Sindhi community was much more vital for my mother. It was the root of her resilience and gave her a sense of who she was. One reason was that it allowed her not to feel completely lonely and isolated in "foreign" Singapore. Participating in Sindhi events, either prayer services or card games with other Sindhi women (which she did regularly after we grew up), gave her a sense of community.

I ended up with ambivalent and conflicted feelings about my Sindhi identity. On the one hand, I carry some resentment over the local Sindhis' lack of support in our family's darkest moments. On the other hand, they provided an ecosystem that nurtured my mother's belief in herself. Moreover, without the worldwide diaspora of her Sindhi relatives, many of whom supported us, we would have suffered much more.

I am also glad that even though we were poor, my mother found the money to send me to language classes to learn both Sindhi and Hindi. My command of the Sindhi language has diminished significantly, but I have managed to retain a greater comprehension of Hindi, as I continue to listen to the Hindi songs that I heard regularly as a child. Indeed, I am writing this book in English while listening to Hindi songs sung by famous Bollywood playback singers, such as Mohammed Rafi, Kishore Kumar, Lata Mangeshkar, and Asha Bhosle. I couldn't even begin my writing without playing their songs. The neurons of my brain are triggered by Hindi songs, not English ones.

This is why I view the disappearance of the Sindhi community's sense of cultural identity with some sadness. While my mother was fluent in Sindhi, most of her eight grandchildren barely speak it, if they speak it at all. The same is true of the larger Sindhi community. Many of the children of my Sindhi contemporaries don't speak Sindhi either. They live in multi-cultural, multiracial Singapore, feeling more comfortable using English as a first language, as I do.

As a child, I did not value my mother's efforts to keep me connected to the Sindhi language and culture. Instead, as I read more and more books by Western writers such as Bertrand Russell and H. G. Wells during my frequent trips to the Joo Chiat Public Library, I felt that I was gradually being transported out of the dark caves of Asian superstition and idol worship into a new and modern shining world that was ruled by logical reasoning and the scientific method. I began to understand the big truth of Western civilisation. It was the first civilisation to successfully modernise and strengthen itself by liberating itself from medieval prejudices. As I plunged deeper into the writings of Western civilisation, I felt that I was being pulled out of a dark cave into a bright, shining room where everything worked better. As a result, I became a passionate believer in the power of the scientific method as well as the power of the ruthless razor of reasoning. Bertrand Russell argued that "Western Europeans, and men in the New World whose ancestors, whatever their racial origin, had lived in Western Europe, had for about three centuries a virtual monopoly of science, and acquired thereby a supremacy throughout the world such as neither they nor anyone else had possessed at any earlier time."[2] I felt that power and potential viscerally.

When I came home from the library and tried to explain to my mother why the West was much more advanced, she wasn't impressed. For example, when I told her that the modern aeroplane was an amazing invention, she replied that in the Hindu epics, there were many stories of Hindu gods who flew great distances. Anything that the West achieved had been achieved before in ancient Indian times. Similarly, even though our lives improved significantly when we began to acquire modern appliances, such as the refrigerator and TV set, she wasn't impressed by the almost magical power of electricity. She claimed that ancient India had also had all this. It was difficult for me to believe in the glorious *past* of India, as my mother did, since to me it seemed that it had not prevented India's subjugation or our continuing poverty. The glorious *future* that Western writers envisioned for the West and the world was far more alluring. Now, later in life, I see that in some ways, my mother was not wrong about her faith in India. She would have been thrilled by the dynamism that PM Narendra Modi has injected into the Indian spirit.

All this voracious reading helped me to do well in primary school. Often, I would end up at the top of the class, coming home at the end of each term with some award or another. This good performance also resulted in my receiving bursaries for my studies, which helped our family financially. In 1960, I sat for the Primary School Leaving Examination (PSLE), the national examination for all twelve-year-olds in Singapore. Before receiving our results, we were asked to list our secondary schools of choice. If we passed, we would be placed in these schools based on our performance on the PSLE. The first PSLE was held in 1960, and of the 30,615 of us who sat for the inaugural exam on November 2–4 that year, only 13,736 (or 45 percent) passed.[3] (In contrast, 98.4 percent of PSLE candidates passed the exam in 2022.)

Somewhat ambitiously, I selected the top school in Singapore, Raffles Institution, as my first choice. Despite my good academic performance, I didn't get in. Instead, I was assigned to my second choice, TKTS, which was a neighbourhood school literally next door to Seraya School. As it was so near my home, I was able to walk. To get to school, I took a shortcut along a drain that ran behind a block of flats where British servicemen lived with their wives. The kitchens were at the back, facing the drain. Hence, each morning when I walked past these kitchens, I often saw the wives cooking breakfast for their husbands. Sometimes the British women found the heat and humidity of Singapore hard to handle, especially with the added heat and humidity of the kitchen, and some of them would strip down in their kitchens, not expecting any scurrying teenage schoolboys to be passing by along the drain outside. It was naturally exciting for a teenage boy to spy their beautiful breasts. I felt slightly guilty about this pleasure, but I justified it to myself as an act of anticolonial rebellion. It was a Sikh history teacher at TKTS who first alerted me to the fact that British accounts of colonial rule in India were false and hid many painful truths. He wasn't fiercely anti-British, but he was the first to sow doubts in me about the "benevolence" of British colonial rule that the British-dominated media at the time fed us relentlessly.

I had selected TKTS as my second choice because I assumed that a "technical" education, which would provide me with skills such as woodworking, metalworking, and technical drawing, would equip me for a job. I was a solid student in Secondary 1 and Secondary 2, which led to my being assigned to Secondary 3B, the second-highest class of the grade. Our class specialised in metalworking. For the final examination around October or November 1963, we were asked to produce a metal hinge with two flat pieces of metal. I worked hard on these two pieces, cutting and filing both with the materials assigned to us. I had to make one piece with three prongs and the other with two prongs so that they would fit into each other. Instead, I meticulously produced two pieces of metal, each with three prongs. Clearly, they couldn't fit into one unit. I completely failed my metalwork examination.

This failure (like many others to follow) was one of the best things to happen in my life. I was, in theory, demoted from Secondary 3B to Secondary 4G, the class where all the weakest academic performers were sent. In Secondary 4G, we didn't do any technical subjects. Instead, we studied only the humanities, such as English literature, history, and geography. In this class, it became clear where my natural affinity was. I did very well. For the first time in the history of TKTS, the student with the highest examination marks in the school didn't come from Secondary 4A or 4B. Instead, he came from Secondary 4G, a class in which most students did poorly in the critical O-level examinations.

One episode in the final O-level history examination taught me a valuable life lesson. It was the tradition for Singaporean students to "spot," or predict, likely questions for this examination by studying the transcripts of previous years' examinations.

Most years, the predictions came true. Hence, I prepared for the history examination by developing answers for six likely questions, giving me a safety cushion, as we would have to answer four questions in the assigned time. To my absolute horror, none of my six questions appeared on the actual examination. I hadn't prepared for any of the questions in front of me. I panicked. I could have given up on the examination in despair. Instead, after the panic subsided, I told myself that I was clearly going to fail this history paper. Since I was going to fail anyway, I saw no harm in relaxing and just trying to answer four questions using distant memories of classroom lessons and my imagination. My imagination must have worked well that day. Instead of failing, I got an A. This unexpected success taught me never to give up hope.

As the top student of TKTS, I once again applied to join the top school, Raffles Institution, for pre-university. Once again, I was rejected. And once again, this rejection turned out to be a blessing. I ended up spending my two pre-university years at St Andrew's School. I knew nothing about this school, and I still have no idea why I put it as my second choice. I didn't even know where it was when I applied for it.

I soon discovered that it was far from my home. I couldn't walk there but had to take two buses. This meant getting up very early to reach school before classes began at 7:30 a.m. But it was worth it. Having studied in two drab government-built school buildings for Seraya School and TKTS, I was enchanted when I walked into the famous "pink" building where I was going to study for two years. Its walls were covered in a carnation-pink fish-scale pattern. For the first time in my life,

I learned that studying and working in beautiful buildings can enhance one's sense of well-being. I began my two bus journeys from a small, drab home in Onan Road. When I arrived at St Andrew's School, I felt that I was entering a magical environment. Many years later, when I first heard the description of Harry Potter entering Hogwarts, I couldn't help feeling that the building of St Andrew's had enchanted me in the same way. I particularly loved the quiet green courtyard that the pink building enclosed. It was an oasis of peace.

Since I was put into the arts and humanities stream rather than the science or premedical stream, I enjoyed all the subjects I studied: economics, history, geography, English literature, and general paper (which tested general knowledge). I still remember well, after sixty years, the teachers I had: Molly Goh for economics, Ronald Chan for history, Robert Yeo for English literature, and Cheong Hock Hai for geography. Ms Cheong was older. She was a tyrant and a strict disciplinarian. But her harsh methods worked, and her students always did well. Since I read more than the writings assigned by her, I actually finished reading a very thick geography textbook, *Principles of Physical Geography* by Francis J. Monkhouse. And in history, I read a thick textbook, *An Advanced History of India* by R. C. Majumdar, H. C. Raychaudhuri, and Kalikinkar Datta.

While the academic education was excellent (and I felt intellectually challenged in the classrooms), it wasn't what made St Andrew's School unique. Since it was a "mission" school affiliated with the Anglican Church of Singapore (which had been the preferred church of the British ruling classes when Singapore was a colony), the school had a value system of integrity and compassion that seeped into our veins. It helped that the principal, Francis Thomas, was an inspirational leader. He was an Englishman, but he had become a citizen of Singapore. He was a strong, authoritative figure, but he also exuded kindness. Hence, in addition to the aura of physical well-being that we received from the beautiful premises, we were blessed with a spiritual aura emanating from the values and kind personality of Francis Thomas. Looking back, I rate these two years as among the happiest of my life.

Yet the same two years, 1965 and 1966, were among the most tumultuous years of Singapore's history. Singapore had gained its independence from Britain and joined the Federation of Malaysia on September 16, 1963. Since the leaders of Singapore, Lee Kuan Yew, Toh Chin Chye, Goh Keng Swee, and S. Rajaratnam, were convinced that the tiny island could not possibly survive without its natural Malayan hinterland, they had persuaded the then reluctant PM of Malaysia, Tunku Abdul Rahman, to accept Singapore into the federation, together with the distant states of Sabah and Sarawak. Wisely, Brunei, which had also been invited to join this federation, declined.

Singapore's entry into Malaysia began with high hopes. Tunku Abdul Rahman depicted a glorious future for Singapore, declaring that it would become the New York of Malaysia, while Kuala Lumpur (KL), the capital, would become its Washington, DC. However, the high hopes of a harmonious relationship between KL and Singapore were dashed soon after Singapore's entry into Malaysia. The elites of KL and Singapore were like the proverbial couple who slept in the same bed with different dreams.

The main priority of the dominant Malay elite in KL was to preserve the Malay domination of the political system and particularly to ensure that the Chinese minority, who already dominated the economic system, didn't take over the political system too. By contrast, the Singaporean political elite declared that they believed in the principle of a "Malaysian Malaysia" where all races were treated equally and the leader was chosen on the basis of merit, not race. There couldn't have been two more contrasting visions. Hence, the whole experiment of Singapore joining Malaysia was doomed to failure almost from the beginning.

As a fifteen-year-old when Singapore joined Malaysia in 1963, I wasn't aware of these enormous political tensions. We were too preoccupied with our domestic travails. However, in 1964, the negative effects of all these political and racial tensions affected our neighbourhood. Racial riots broke out in Malaysia in 1964 and spread to Singapore in July of that year. The riots were ostensibly instigated by activists from the Malaysian political party United Malays National Organisation (UMNO), which launched a campaign accusing the Singaporean People's Action Party (PAP) of oppressing Malay people in Singapore. As a result, Malay-Chinese riots broke out in the aftermath of disturbances during a twenty thousand–strong procession on Prophet Muhammad's birthday. The riots led to the deaths of twenty-three people, and over four hundred more were injured.

The Singaporean government sensibly imposed a curfew to prevent further loss of life. I remember being confined to home at the time. However, since we needed to eat, my mother made me crawl along the drains (to avoid police detection in the deserted streets) to the Indian bakery, about two hundred metres from our home, to buy bread. The drains weren't very big. They were V-shaped and deep and were a metre wide at their widest point. I remember lying flat in the drain when I saw a police car suddenly approach. Fortunately, I wasn't caught. I did not feel in physical danger, but our Malay neighbours did in Chinese-majority Singapore during this period (although our immediate Chinese neighbours protected them).

In the end, Malaysia and Singapore separated on August 9, 1965, when I was in my first year of pre-university at St Andrew's School. I remember the day well. I happened to be home when the Singaporean radio station incessantly repeated the announcement that Singapore was separating from Malaysia. I remember walking around aimlessly in my neighbourhood, seeing the depressed, even frightened faces of our neighbours. We all had a common feeling: Singapore was doomed after separation since a city couldn't possibly survive alone without any hinterland. Many countries celebrate their independence with parades and massive fireworks. There was absolutely no sense of celebration on the day that Singapore became independent in 1965. The despondency was shared equally among all the ethnic groups.

Yet school carried on as normal, and so did our lives. Despite all the turbulence of that time, I still remember 1965 and 1966 as happy years in my life. Two separations had brought calm to my life: my mother's from my father in 1962 and Singapore's from Malaysia in 1965.

My years at St Andrew's School led to some lifelong habits and attachments. Although I was a well-established book lover before I joined St Andrew's, my emotional and symbolic attachment to books was reinforced when I was appointed first as a librarian and then as chief student librarian of the school. As chief librarian, I, along with the other student librarians, was assigned the major task of reclassifying all the books in the library, as the teacher in charge of the library had decided to implement the Dewey Decimal System. I wrote an article for the 1966 *St Andrew's School Magazine* documenting that "a suitable classification system—the universally-adopted Dewey Decimal System—was for the first time adopted by the library" and that the librarians "had to classify in a single stage five thousand books" as well as build up a suitable card catalogue. The process of classifying five thousand books was a good learning experience. It made me aware of the breadth of knowledge that humankind had accumulated. My lifelong love of books became even stronger.

I also developed deep friendships with my classmates at St Andrew's School. I left St Andrew's School in 1966, yet at least five of us from that class still meet regularly: Laurence Chan, Basskaran Nair, Eddie Teo, Wong Meng Meng, and I. We all had a wonderful experience at St Andrew's School and share a common nostalgia for the happy years there.

I came close to migrating to the United States at the age of seventeen when I was offered a scholarship from the American Friends Service Committee to spend a year in a high school there. If I had gone to the United States at that impressionable age, I would have believed that I had entered a far more advanced society, and I probably would not have returned to Singapore. Unfortunately (or fortunately), my mother was experiencing many domestic difficulties, and even though she had separated from my alcoholic father, he continued to present challenges. So I stayed home to protect her.

Nevertheless, the conviction that someday or somehow I would end up living in the West was firmly planted in my mind. By the end of my teenage years, as a result of all my education and reading, I had become a passionate disciple of Western civilisation. Slowly and steadily, my Asian mind was questioning some of the fundamental assumptions that I had absorbed during my childhood. As a young child, I had happily bathed the tiny idols of Krishna and Ganesh in milk. As a young teenager, I accepted a fundamental premise of Western thought: that worship of idols was primitive and symptomatic of a defective culture. I also began to believe that the polytheistic Asian religions, such as Hinduism, were backwards, while the monotheistic Western religions, such as Christianity, were advanced. Hence, as my teenage years progressed, I became convinced that the only way for me to progress was to steadily shed my primitive Asian prejudices and replace them with the advanced thought of Western civilisation.

For a young Asian like me, encountering Western thought was a liberating experience in many ways. Asian culture and thinking encouraged respect for tradition and acceptance of authority. Indeed, as a young Sindhi boy, I was expected to touch the feet of older male relatives as a sign of submission and respect. As a young teenager, influenced by Western thought, I rebelled against this submissive practice and stopped touching the feet of older male relatives. My mother was shocked. However, I retained the strong Indian/Hindu belief that my most important moral obligation was to take care of my mother.

Similarly, I questioned the worship of idols. As a teenager, I discovered Bertrand Russell's famous book *Why I Am Not a Christian* (1967) in Joo Chiat Public Library. I don't remember exactly what Russell said, but I remember that he made me sceptical of all religious beliefs. On rereading the book, I rediscovered strong statements such as these: "Religion is based, I think, primarily and mainly upon fear. . . . Fear is the parent of cruelty, and therefore it is no wonder if cruelty and religion have gone hand-in-hand. It is because fear is at the basis of those two things."[4]

Russell also documented at some length how religion impeded the "progress" of societies. He said,

> You find as you look around the world that every single bit of progress in humane feeling, every improvement in the criminal law, every step towards the diminution of war, every step towards better treatment of the coloured races, or every mitigation of slavery, every moral progress that there has been in the world, has been consistently opposed by the organised Churches of the world. I say quite deliberately that the Christian religion, as organised in its Churches, has been and still is the principal enemy of moral progress in the world.[5]

Some aspects of Asian thought can also cripple human agency in many subtle ways. For example, my mother, as a devout Hindu, believed that everything in life was "fated." Hence, it was pointless to struggle to escape one's destiny. Acceptance of "fate" may have made it easier for her to accept the many trials and tribulations in her life. But the more I steeped myself in Western thought and traditions, the more I believed that I could shape my own destiny. Directly or indirectly, I may have been influenced by great Western thinkers such as Jean-Paul Sartre, who famously said, "Man is nothing else but that which he makes of himself."

If anyone had said to me that within a few decades, some Asian societies would eventually succeed and outperform Western societies in economic productivity and development, I would have reacted with scorn. I would have characterised such a statement as wishful thinking. My lack of confidence in the possibility of Asian societies succeeding was accompanied by a belief that the only glorious future for a young Asian like me was to migrate and live in a Western society.

One curious lapse in my memory of those two years is that I don't recall whether I was preparing, psychologically and formally, for going to university. My classmate Eddie Teo certainly was. He studied French and Latin in those two years to qualify for admission to Oxford University, where he enrolled in the legendary philosophy, politics, and economics (PPE) course. I didn't even know then that Latin was available for study in Singapore. Laurence Chan went on to study law in Cambridge and went into accountancy in London after he graduated. Wong Meng Meng and Basskaran Nair—who, like me, came from poorer families—applied to study law and the arts at the University of Singapore, respectively.

As far as I can recall, I never thought of going to university. Certainly, my mother had little idea of what a university was since none of her relatives or friends had attended one. When I finished at St Andrew's School, she made me do what most Sindhi boys did when they finished school: start working as a textile salesman. Since most of the Sindhi stores were on or around High Street in Singapore, I immediately started working there, earning a small salary. I learned to roll and unroll large reams of cloth and sell them by the yard (we did not use metric measurements then). Since we also sold shirts and other clothing, I learned to carefully unwrap shirts and wrap them back in their plastic folders so that they looked as good as new. In early 1967, I thought that this would be my destiny: remaining as a textile salesman, starting with the initial monthly salary of S$150 (around US$50 then), all of which went to my mother. This money brought much-needed financial security to our family.

Then one of the greatest miracles of my life happened. The Singaporean government offered me a President's Scholarship, offering to pay me S$250 a month to study at the then University of Singapore (now the National University of Singapore [NUS]). To the best of my knowledge, I hadn't applied for this scholarship, nor had I applied to the University of Singapore since I couldn't afford to study there. So when the scholarship came, I had to scramble and apply to join the Faculty of Arts and Social Sciences (FASS). My mother encouraged me to go to the University of Singapore for one simple reason: the S$250 a month I would get from the President's Scholarship was more than the S$150 I was earning as a fabric salesman.

There's no doubt in my mind that if the blessing of the President's Scholarship hadn't happened, I wouldn't have gone to university, and all of my subsequent life would have been very different. It remains a mystery to me why or how I received the scholarship. My academic results were good—I got three As in my main subjects—but not outstanding. Since I had never succeeded in being accepted to Singapore's premier school, Raffles Institution, it's surprising that my academic results led to my getting an even higher honour, the President's Scholarship.

Why did I receive the scholarship? My mother would have offered me a single answer: I was "fated" to receive it. In the end, she may have been right. I have been extraordinarily lucky in my life. It's easy to believe that divine forces were shining benevolently on me.

CHAPTER 3

Lighting
Firecrackers

T HE FIRECRACKERS THAT THE CHINESE BAKERY SET OFF JUST A FEW
doors from our home each Chinese New Year were matched
by the intellectual firecrackers that were set off in my brain
during my four years at the Bukit Timah Campus of the University of Singapore (from 1967 to 1970) as I learned one new thing
after another, and particularly after I fell in love with the study
of philosophy. Plutarch was right—education isn't about filling a
bucket; it's about lighting fires.

Perhaps this was the result of my low expectations when I
enrolled. As I had never planned to study at a university, I had
no clue what a university education entailed. When I enrolled,

I thought that it would just be another three years of school with exam after exam, and I knew by then that I was good at taking exams.

Still, I remember that I felt excited when I first entered the campus after the long walk up the hill from the bus stop. The campus had been commissioned in 1919 as a memorial for the centennial anniversary of Sir Stamford Raffles's arrival in Singapore. Raffles had founded colonial Singapore by negotiating for the British East India Company to be allowed to set up a trading post there in 1819. The colonial administrators felt that it would be fitting to establish a tertiary institution, Raffles College, in his honour. Raffles College later merged with other schools and eventually became the University of Singapore.

The university was housed in a set of white colonial buildings with wide arches. This stately design was chosen through an architectural competition that spanned the British Empire, and it won an award for being the best-designed campus in the British Empire after it was built. Once I entered the two courtyards of the campus, I felt that I was once again in a beautiful learning environment, just as the internal courtyard of St Andrew's School had charmed me. I found it strange that I was going to "school" for the first time in my life without wearing a school uniform. That was a clue that I was going to enjoy some special years of "freedom" at a university, and I certainly took advantage of them.

When I enrolled in the FASS, I was told that there was a clearly established pattern of studies for the three-year programme. In the first year, students chose three subjects. This would provide an opportunity to assess which subject, or subjects, was most appealing to them. They would then concentrate on either one or two subjects for their second and third years. Somehow—I don't know why—I enrolled in economics, sociology, and philosophy in my first year. My only certainty was that I had to study economics since it was considered the most "practical" subject and could lead to a good job. During my first year, I was virtually certain that when I had to choose my one subject or two subjects for my second and third years, economics would be one of them.

Unfortunately for me, at the end of my first year, the University of Singapore, in a nod to the principle of a broad-based liberal arts education, decided to try out a reform. It declared that students no longer needed to enrol in one subject or two subjects. It was well known that the top students always chose one subject so that they could specialise. I probably should have specialised in economics in my second and third years, but instead of following this conventional wisdom, I became the only student in the entire faculty to take advantage of the offer of a broad-based education by enrolling in three subjects in the second and third years. No other FASS student was so diffuse! Since we were expected to enrol in eight courses each year, I chose to do four courses in economics, two courses in sociology, and two courses in philosophy.

A few months into my second year, I began to realise that I had made a serious mistake. Clearly, I wasn't studying any field in depth. More importantly, I began to realise that the courses in economics didn't interest me. In part, this was because they were badly taught and depended on memorising concepts and principles that we would then regurgitate in tutorials and exams. There was little questioning of any of the fundamental concepts. By contrast, I was captivated by the two courses on philosophy. I was particularly entranced by a course on metaphysics, which raised big fundamental questions about the human condition.

By the middle of my second year, as it became clear that my three-subjects option was a mistake, I approached the head of the Department of Philosophy, Roland Puccetti, to ask whether I could repeat my second year and switch back to a one-subject track, specialising in philosophy. Fortunately for me, Prof Puccetti was a wise and shrewd man. He had observed that Toh Chin Chye, who had become the vice-chancellor of the university in April 1968, was rigid and doctrinaire. No one dared to challenge his authority. As Prof Puccetti later wrote in a paper about the University of Singapore, "I cannot recall a single senate 'decision' which went against the vice-chancellor's expressed view."[1] Hence, Prof Puccetti decided to charm him instead. Dr Toh, who was a physiology scholar, had published several papers on the brain.[2] Prof Puccetti specialised in the mind-brain connection and was indeed a leading global authority in the field. He was also a jovial person with a constant twinkle in his eye. He unleashed his full charm on Toh Chin Chye during the university senate meeting at which the question of whether I could (somewhat unusually) repeat my second year was discussed. Miraculously, despite his rigidity and unwillingness to compromise, Dr Toh agreed to this deviation. This turned out to be doubly miraculous for me because the next year, in June 1969, the Public Services Commission told the university that philosophy was no longer an approved subject for first-year students on government scholarships. If I had been part of the next cohort of students and made my request a year later, it would certainly not have been approved.

Although I was overjoyed when I heard that I could repeat my second year, I had to pay an economic price. First, as my father told me, I was delaying my entry into full-time employment, thereby sacrificing one year of earnings. Second, my President's Scholarship was suspended while I repeated my second year, so I had to earn enough money to pay the university fees, cover my expenses, and support my family for that year. Fortunately, I was able to get a job teaching night classes for students preparing for their A-level examinations. Studying in the day and teaching at night was exhausting, but I had no regrets. The sheer excitement and joy of doing eight philosophy courses for two years running erased all other discomforts. It was a foundational time for me, and I have never regretted making the critical switch to studying philosophy full-time. What it taught me, more than anything, was that you can ask fundamental probing questions in any area.

In the mid-1960s and early 1970s, as Singapore was still a developing country and most of us came from poor or lower-middle-class families, most students opted for "practical" subjects such as economics or business administration. Consequently, these departments had hundreds of students. By contrast, in my first year, the Department of Philosophy had only seven one-subject students. It also had seven full-time professors. This teacher-student ratio was probably even more favourable than that at universities such as Oxford and Cambridge.

I became particularly close to one of my philosophy professors, Colin Davies, for both intellectual and social reasons. Intellectually, the philosopher with whom I was most enchanted in my studies was Ludwig Wittgenstein. Indeed, like all other philosophy departments in the Anglo-Saxon world, our department had been captured by the linguistic-analytic school of philosophy that Wittgenstein had launched with his *Philosophical Investigations*. I was genuinely awed that both major schools of philosophy of the twentieth century (including the previous one based on his *Tractatus Logico-Philosophicus*) had been launched by Wittgenstein. As an Austrian-born British Jew, he had done all this while Europe was convulsed by the threat created by an Austrian-born German, Adolf Hitler. As the eminent philosopher John Searle put it,

> Wittgenstein, in my opinion, is the greatest philosopher of the 20th century. . . . In the middle decades of the 20th century, he was by far the most influential philosopher in the English-speaking world. Although he had both followers and critics, he could not be ignored. No philosopher today has anything like the stature or influence that Wittgenstein had in the 20th century, especially after the publication of the *Philosophical Investigations* in 1953.[3]

Colin Davies was absolutely enchanted with Wittgenstein. And I inherited his enthusiasm.

I must have learned well under Davies's guidance. For the final examinations, which I took at the end of my fourth year, our degree was determined by how well we did in eight three-hour examinations. In one of the papers, we had to answer a single question. The one question I chose to answer over three hours was "Can a stone feel pain?" From my exam results, I gained a first-class honours degree, which was rare in the Department of Philosophy. Since our final examination papers were also sent to Peter Winch, one of the leading scholars on Wittgenstein in the world, I felt honoured that my first-class honours had been endorsed by him.

Colin Davies deserves the credit for my fascination with and passion for Wittgenstein. Somehow, through his lectures, he drew out the genius of Wittgenstein. He also used to smoke (yes, smoking was allowed in classrooms then), and while he was lecturing and smoking, he would become so engrossed in his train of thought that he would forget that he was holding his cigarette close to his head while speaking. Then the inevitable would happen: his hair would catch fire. I remember at least two or three occasions when we students rushed forward to put out the fire in his hair, which he seemed oblivious to. He was the quintessential absent-minded professor.

Colin Davies was as generous socially as he was intellectually. He and his then wife, Barbara, who was also English, used to invite students to their comfortable traditional black-and-white bungalow at the top of a hill near campus. It was when I walked up this hill at around 4 p.m. one day in the hot and humid weather of Singapore that I experienced my first clash of civilisations.

When I arrived at the doorstep, Barbara took one look at me, drenched in sweat, and asked, "Kishore, would you like a glass of water?" Obviously, I would. However, my mother had taught me that all polite Sindhi boys and girls would never say yes immediately when offered food or drink. This would be uncouth, as it signalled greed. We could say yes only after we were asked a third time. Hence, as a result of my mother's training, I said no to Barbara and waited for her to ask me a second and third time. She never did. Instead, she looked puzzled by my answer and just walked away. On my next trip to their home, I said yes immediately.

My philosophy classmates and I spent countless evenings in Colin and Barbara Davies's home. Having lived all my life with various Asian communities, I accepted the essential principle of Asian social order: all societies are, in one way or another, hierarchical. Each of us was supposed to know our station in life. Certainly, teachers were superior beings. The role of students was to sit at the feet of their teachers and learn from them. We were not supposed to treat them as peers.

But Colin Davies and the other Western or Western-educated professors in the Department of Philosophy insisted that we talk as equals. They asked us to address them by their first names. This alone was shocking. It was inconceivable in most Asian societies to address any elder, much less a respected philosophy teacher, by his or her first name.

All these changes were intellectually liberating. Most importantly, what I learned in the Department of Philosophy had an explosive impact on my thinking. To use a familiar German expression, there was a total revolution in my Weltanschauung as a result of studying Western philosophy. Plato, who lived from 428 or 427 BCE to 348 or 347 BCE, is usually acknowledged to be the greatest philosopher of all time. He said that truth exists in the realm of ideas rather than in the "sensible" world of human sensory experience. Humanity cannot see the ultimate reality because it exists in perfect forms, or "Platonic ideals." All we can see with our eyes are the imperfect forms of things such as chairs, tables, beds, and cupboards. None of the tables that we can see and touch are able to encapsulate the full concept of a "table," as there are many different kinds of tables. How is it that we are able to understand all of them as "tables"? It is because in the realm of ideas, there exists a perfect, "true" form of a table. When we see a table, we recognise in it the shadow of the "perfect" reality that exists in that realm.

Wittgenstein overturned this fundamental Platonic view by saying that there are no perfect forms. Instead, what we see is conditioned by the language and concepts we use. There is no perfect "table" out there. The table we see is the result of our decision to use the word "table" to describe an object with a flat surface and one or more legs. Hence, there is no ultimate "truth" to find. All we can try to understand is the language and concepts we have chosen. Philosophical problems arise when we start to abuse language. There is a simple reason why we cannot answer the question "What is the meaning of life?" The word "meaning" is used in specific situations and contexts when we try to understand concepts. Take words such as "dancing" or "singing," for example. We can describe these activities to explain the "meaning" of these terms. But the word "meaning" is not meant to apply to words such as "life," at least not beyond a mere definition of the term, which describes the condition opposite to death. I could write eight pages over three hours in response to the question "Can a stone feel pain?"

because Wittgenstein's ideas allowed me to deconstruct the meanings of the words in this apparently simple question.

The process of focusing on the language we use came in very handy when I joined the Ministry of Foreign Affairs (MFA) in April 1971 and embarked on my long career in the study of geopolitics. Our understanding of "objective reality" is clearly conditioned by the language we use. The first major war that I had to analyse as a Foreign Service officer was the Vietnam War. The "facts" were clear: soldiers from North Vietnam were fighting soldiers from the United States. We could see this. But what were they fighting about? The US leaders, Johnson and Nixon, had no doubt: they were fighting against a global push by the Soviet Union and China to expand communism. But the North Vietnamese soldiers also had no doubt: they were fighting for "national liberation" from the "imperialist" US forces. So who was right? What is the truth here? Adding to the elusiveness of an absolute "truth" is the fact that fifty years after the United States withdrew ignominiously from Vietnam, one of the best friends of the United States in Southeast Asia will be the Communist Party of North Vietnam—the United States wants to upgrade its ties with Vietnam to a strategic partnership.

Another course at the University of Singapore that generated lifelong lessons for me was on moral philosophy, also taught by Colin Davies. The moral philosopher who was in vogue then was R. M. Hare. His slim book *The Language of Morals* had a profound effect on me. By a strange geographical coincidence, many of the ideas that flowed into his book, which was published in 1952, were generated when Hare was a prisoner of war of the Japanese in Changi Prison, Singapore (which is not far from my current home). If the legend is true, he wrote his ideas on toilet paper there.

Hare's ideas proved to be powerful and durable. One of his principles became deeply etched into my mind: the principle of universalisability, which essentially states that every moral statement can and must be universalisable. We would all agree with the statement that it is wrong for Russia to invade Ukraine. If we accept this statement, then, based on the principle of universalisability, we should also accept that it is wrong for one country to invade another country. Such moral statements are in harmony with the sense of moral intuition that we develop as human beings.

One of the strengths of Western philosophy is that the laws of logic are ironclad. They allow no exceptions. Hence, if it was wrong for Russia to invade Ukraine, it was also wrong for the United States to invade Iraq. Since the principle of universalisability is as easy to recognise as ABC, it's surprising how often this principle is violated. I found the principle of universalisability to be a wonderful and powerful weapon when I engaged in debates in various diplomatic fora. In 1985, I participated in a meeting of the Non-Aligned Movement (NAM) in Luanda, Angola, six years after the invasion of Afghanistan by the Soviet Union in late December 1979. At this meeting, the Soviet invasion of Afghanistan was defended by Cuban diplomats. There were sound geopolitical reasons for Cubans to defend the Soviet Union, as they depended on it to protect them from the United States. But their defence of the Soviet Union wasn't logical.

Using the principle of universalisability, I said at the NAM meeting that if Cuba defended the right of the Soviet Union to invade Afghanistan, then it was defending the universal principle that it was right for a great power to invade a neighbouring small state. If Cuba defended this universal principle, it was also stating effectively that it would be right for the United States, a great power, to invade a neighbouring small state, Cuba. The Cuban diplomats were naturally furious, yet they couldn't refute the logic. They could also see that most members of the NAM quietly nodded in agreement when I made the case.

I first learned of the principle of universalisability around 1968, and since then, fifty-five years have passed. Yet it has always stood me in good stead. I have no doubt that I couldn't have been as productive as I have been in the intellectual arena without the four explosive years of learning in the Department of Philosophy at the University of Singapore and a further year of learning at Dalhousie University in Halifax, Nova Scotia. The learning came from the lectures in classrooms and from constant, often late-night discussions with my classmates. But it also came from the total enchantment I felt sitting on the floor between the stacks of philosophy books in the university library. I would often pick up a book at random. It might be about social justice. Or beauty. I could dive for hours into understanding the forces of language that created a concept like beauty. We use it every day, but do we have any clue to how that word originated? Four years of constant questioning transformed my mind fundamentally.

It would be misleading to suggest that I engaged only in intellectual activities in my four years on the campus. There were some exciting social activities, most of them with a group of friends who were also studying philosophy: Tom Thekathyil, Balbir Singh, and my childhood friend Jeffery Sng. We were joined by an American exchange student, Dean Swift, who has remained a lifelong friend.

Like all young men, we soon discovered the joys of alcohol, especially cheap alcohol like vodka. We scouted around for good drinking places. On the beautiful Bukit Timah campus of the university, we discovered that the rooftop of the science block was a great place to drink under the stars at night. There was one catch: the only way to get there past the locked door of the science block was to take the lift up the adjoining block. There was a small gap of three feet or so between the two buildings. Any able-bodied person would have had no difficulty jumping across it, but a misstep would have ended in certain death. I am not surprised that we survived this jump at the beginning of the evening; however, I'm amazed that we managed to jump back at the end of the night.

The escapades of those years (1967 to 1971) were not confined to the campus alone. One day, I told Dean Swift that I had a dream of visiting Kathmandu. Dean remembered this. A few months later, just before the end of the school year, he handed me US$2,000 in cash. This was an extraordinarily generous gift. Since Dean had often come to my home in Onan Road for meals, he could see how poor we were. He knew that I couldn't travel without his financial assistance. He said that the gift was for me to fulfil my Kathmandu dream.

So off I went. I travelled by road to Penang, a trip of about five hundred miles. In Penang, I boarded a train to Bangkok. It was a long trip that left behind two indelible memories. First, I managed to finish reading Dostoevsky's *The Brothers Kara-mazov*. Second, as we were travelling on the day of Thailand's water festival, Songkran, the Thais we passed tried to douse us with water as a gesture of goodwill. Hence, we closed the windows of the train when we passed towns and villages and then opened them when we went through the countryside. I was sitting across from some young Australian students, including some women. As we crossed a stream, some young Thai children managed to throw some water from the stream into our compartment. We laughed it off until one of the Australian students screamed when she discovered that the stream water contained some tadpoles that were wriggling in her bra.

From Bangkok, I took a plane to Calcutta, where fortunately my mother's elder sister, Aunty Lakshmi, lived with her pretty daughters. I then decided to travel overland to Kathmandu. Within India, I could take trains to the border with Nepal. However, when I reached the border town, I discovered that the cheapest way to reach Kathmandu was to sit in the back of a lorry carrying sacks of potatoes. The driver allowed me to sit on the sacks of potatoes for a small fee. This perch on top of the sacks without guard rails seemed comfortable and safe in the flat lowlands. However, as we climbed up the mountain roads, I found myself staring at vertiginous drops without anything to stop my fall if I were to slip off the sacks of potatoes.

More hazards awaited me when I arrived in Kathmandu. Since I was travelling very cheaply, most of the people I met were young people from the United States and Europe. In Kathmandu, some Americans told me that the US Embassy in

Kathmandu had wanted them to receive a vaccination against hepatitis, which was rampant in Nepal then. The US Embassy was providing the jabs free of charge to American citizens. Since I wasn't an American citizen, I couldn't get one. Mercifully, I didn't get hepatitis, even though I couldn't afford to buy bottled water on this trip.

When I was in Kathmandu, I heard from my new Western friends that it was possible to walk to Nagarkot, a mountain about seven thousand feet high, to enjoy the brilliant night sky. Once again, I found a lorry to take me to the base of Nagarkot before I walked up alone. On this walk, I discovered that young Nepali children could be entrepreneurial. To avoid getting lost on the way up, I decided to walk up on the main road, which zigzagged up the mountain. After a while, a very young Nepali boy, perhaps ten or twelve years old, approached me. He said that for twenty rupees, he could show me a shortcut that could get me to the top faster. I agreed. When we were about halfway up the shortcut, in the middle of wild countryside, he turned to me and said that he would charge one hundred rupees instead. He and I both knew that I had to pay him.

When I reached the top, I realised that I would have to stay in a wooden hut. There wasn't much food available. After a simple meal of Nepali food, which I shared with some young travellers from the United States and Europe, we were offered cookies, and I bought some. As the night darkened, the view outside was stunning. There were thousands of stars. For me, it was particularly gratifying to see so many stars since the city lights of Singapore prevented a view of most stars in the night sky. After I lay on the ground for a few minutes, I found something strange happening. The stars began to move and go around in circles. Gradually, they began to move faster and faster. I remember pressing myself tightly to the ground to avoid getting dizzy. The next morning, my fellow occupants of the wooden hut explained what had happened. Unwittingly, I had had my first taste of hashish in the cookies.

It was clearly unwise for me to travel alone, with little money and no backup, to those remote regions. At several points, things could have gone wrong. What made this adventurous trip to Nepal even more strange was that for most of my life, I had been a bookworm. I had indulged in adventures by reading novels, remembering, for example, how Pierre, the hero of *War and Peace*, perched himself precariously on a windowsill while taking a shot of vodka. Before I went to university, I had never participated in many physical activities. My mother thought sweating was unhealthy and discouraged such pursuits. I was a typical nerd, not inclined to physical adventures.

I had another close shave trekking up a mountain when I went to visit Chandrasekaran Pillay, a friend living in Kedah, a state in northwestern Malaysia, in 1968 or 1969. Tom Theka-thyil, Jeffery Sng, and I hitchhiked together from Singapore to Kedah. Chandra had unfortunately been stricken with polio as a child and had limited mobility. When we arrived at his home, he told us that we were not far from the highest peak in Kedah, a 3,992-foot mountain called, appropriately, Kedah Peak. These days, it is known as Mount Jerai. He told us that we could climb up and down within a day.

It was sunny when we took a bus to the base station of Kedah Peak. From there we walked, following the zigzagging road. We made it to the top comfortably. On the way down in the afternoon, we thought that it would be faster to walk down in a straight line.

Since Tom, Jeff, and I had grown up in urban Singapore, we had no idea how dense and impenetrable a Malaysian forest could be. Inevitably, within an hour or two, we were lost. We also had no idea which direction to head in. Then the sun began to set. A Malaysian jungle isn't like a temperate forest, where there's often enough space to walk between trees. Instead, the dense vegetation made movement difficult. In World War II, the Malaysian resistance fighters who fought the Japanese occupation carried long knives called parangs to slash through the thick vegetation. We had none. Eventually, it became so dark that we couldn't even see our hands. Since we had assumed we were on a day trip, we had no equipment, no extra layers of clothes, no blankets, no torches—and in those days, there were no mobile phones. Since none of us smoked, we didn't even have a cigarette lighter.

As we stumbled along, we felt our way with our hands until we thought that we had come across a massive boulder. Since the boulder had no vegetation on it, we decided to sleep on top of it, away from the snakes, insects, and leeches that densely populated the jungle floor. We were happy that we had found a safe haven and slept the night away.

When the sun rose the next morning, we discovered that the three of us had been sleeping just a few feet away from a precipice with a drop of several hundred feet. If we had moved the wrong way in our sleep or woken up to pee, we could easily have gone over the cliff!

No campus story is complete without a dash of romance. Since I was busy studying and happily engaged with my circle of friends, I made little effort to date any of the many beautiful women on campus. I don't know why I took no initiative in this regard. It's possible that I had assumed at that age that, as for all my Sindhi relatives, my marriage would eventually be arranged by my mother. I respected that custom in my younger days.

Fortunately for me, a beautiful young woman on campus decided to take the initiative. Her name was Marilyn Girvin. Her family was English. Her father worked as an engineer for the Public Utilities Board (PUB), Singapore's national water agency. She was studying English literature. Even many decades later, I still remember the magical moment when she approached me at a party. The room was dark, and there was loud music—the beautiful songs of the '60s, from the Beatles to the Rolling Stones, Procol Harum, and Blood, Sweat and Tears. Many couples were dancing. Since I had no girlfriend, I was standing on the sidelines, probably drinking beer. Suddenly, out of the blue, Marilyn approached me, took my hand, and pulled me to the dance floor. My heart exploded with happiness.

For the next few years, I was enchanted with Marilyn. The definition of happiness was to spend time with her. Unfortunately, I discovered that I couldn't spend much time with her, as she was always surrounded by an inseparable group of close friends. I resented them at first but later became good friends with all of them. Still, since they rationed very little time for me to spend with Marilyn, it made those few opportunities even more precious. Having read a great deal of Shakespeare and many novels, I was well acquainted with literary descriptions of the enchantment of romantic encounters. Until I fell head over heels in love with Marilyn, I had no idea how powerful and magical falling in love could be. I thought that I had gone to heaven.

My most visible contribution to university life as a whole came when I was appointed as the editor of the student newspaper, the *Singapore Undergrad*. As editor, I discovered that I had a provocative streak. The politically apathetic students of my time had no interest in student newspapers. Hence, I tried to increase interest in the paper and to encourage greater debate and reflection by choosing provocative headlines. The most memorable editorial decision I made was to leave the entire front page of the paper blank and print in the middle of the white page a headline in small print: "Are we really this blank?"

That was perhaps the boldest headline, but the article that many years later I came to believe changed the course of my life appeared after PM Lee Kuan Yew was invited to visit the campus and deliver a lecture in June 1969. During the Q&A session, one of the philosophy professors declaimed at length against the government's proabortion policy. When the student moderator of the lecture refused Lee's request that he move things along, Lee pushed him aside and took charge. I wrote an article protesting this indecorous act and suggested that Lee could well be heading down a path towards dictatorship. Initially, I floated this article as an editorial representing the views of the paper. While the other editors liked the piece, they suggested that I publish it in my own name instead. I agreed.

It was an act of folly. My fellow editors were obviously smarter than I. They knew well that the PAP government of that time was not tolerant of dissent or criticism and that there could be serious consequences for writing such strong and direct criticism of the PM. If I had been squashed, in one way or another, after publishing this article in my name, my fellow students would not have been surprised. Indeed, some time after I published this article, I was told that Vice-Chancellor Toh Chin Chye—who had been the founding chairman of the PAP and had only recently stepped down as deputy prime minister (DPM)—had said, "Tell Kishore not to take me on. If he does, I will crush him."

Instead of being squashed, I became a celebrity after publishing the article. The *New York Times* (*NYT*) correspondent in Singapore, Anthony Polsky, came to interview me on campus. The BBC followed suit. Equally importantly, my fellow students began to treat me with greater respect. I was no longer an obscure philosophy student, as everyone knew who I was.

My celebrity status was further enhanced when I decided to shave my head. My bald head had a kind of electrifying effect, and the campus began speculating about why I had staged a major protest against the government by adopting the shaven appearance of a monk. Actually, it was a complete accident. As I was turning twenty-one in October 1969, my mother decided that I should undergo an important Hindu ceremony symbolising the transition from boyhood to manhood. When I asked my mother how to prepare for this ceremony, she said that I had to go for a haircut and told me that the tradition was for boys to be shaved completely bald. So when I went to the barber on East Coast Road, I told him to shave everything. When I made the request, I assumed (quite foolishly) that he would cut my hair down slowly and I could stop him if I felt uncomfortable. Instead, he took out an electric shaver and immediately created a bald strip through my hair. There was no turning back. So I arrived bald on campus, creating a memory that many of my fellow students still speak about.

My growing reputation as a public critic of the Singaporean government didn't hurt me. It may even have helped me because the Singaporean government had an unusual policy of recruiting dissenters. Tommy Koh, who preceded me as Singapore's ambassador to the United Nations, and Chan Heng Chee, who succeeded me in that post, had both challenged government policies before joining the MFA—Tommy in his capacity as a member of the University Socialist Club and president of the University of Malaya Students Law Society and Heng Chee by writing a book arguing that the PAP's consolidation of power had weakened democracy in Singapore. Another outspoken critic was David Marshall, the founder of the Worker's Party, Singapore's second major political party after the PAP. He was recruited as Singapore's ambassador to France and served in that post for fifteen years.

This big-tent policy may have been the reason why Goh Keng Swee, who was then the minister of defence, invited me to join his team of "whiz kids" in the Defence Ministry and promised that I would have a great career there. This was obviously an amazing offer for a recent graduate. However, I foolishly told him the truth: that I could not take up his offer, as I was a pacifist. He gave me a look of total contempt and threw me out of his office.

For better or worse, my four years on the Bukit Timah campus had given me the confidence to live as a free and independent spirit. Given my conservative Hindu parents, who believed that our first duty in life was to obey ancient Hindu traditions, and the conformist culture of the colonial population of Singapore, which believed that the best way to survive was to subjugate oneself to authority, I could have ended up with a conformist and cautious soul. Instead, after four years on campus, I was ready and willing to question conventional wisdom on all counts. Various factors contributed to this spirit of fierce intellectual independence: my studies in philosophy, which questioned everything; the iconoclastic spirit of all my philosophy professors; the nonconformist streak in my group of friends; and the "student radical" image I fell into on campus.

This free and independent spirit could have been a liability when I made the abrupt transition on April 22, 1971, to the life of a bureaucrat. Instead, it proved to be a major asset. In the course of my thirty-three-year career in the Singaporean Foreign Service, I interacted often with three key founding leaders of Singapore: Lee Kuan Yew, Goh Keng Swee, and S. Rajaratnam. As I grew to know them, I discovered that intellectually and spiritually, they were also free and independent spirits. They had succeeded because they had rebelled against much more powerful forces than I had: a more powerful and pervasive British colonial authority, a brutal Japanese occupation, a hostile Malaysian government, and an inauspicious start as an independent country. They couldn't have defied the odds if they hadn't been prepared to take bold and unconventional leaps. They also fiercely questioned everything. I found myself in very good company.

I didn't know all this as I prepared to work for the government in 1971. Instead, I dreaded it, as I thought that the PAP government was an oppressive force suppressing freedom in Singapore. Since I had fallen in love with the study of philosophy in my undergraduate years, I told myself that I would quit working for the government as soon as I finished the five-year "bond" I was obliged to serve under the terms of the President's Scholarship I had received. My goal was to return to my intellectual studies in philosophy. I have many debts of gratitude to pay off in my life. One of my greatest debts is to the University of Singapore (now NUS). The university unleashed my free spirit, which propelled me forward into a rich, eventful, and colourful life.

CHAPTER 4

Explosive Lessons in Geopolitics

B ARELY THREE TO FOUR WEEKS AFTER I JOINED THE MFA ON August 22, 1971, I contracted chicken pox. There was no quick cure for it, nor were there any medicines to take. All I could do to recover was spend three weeks at home, where I marvelled at the thought that I could be earning S$30 (then US$10) a day while lying in bed.

Thirty dollars was a lot of money for me and my family then. For the first time in my life, I felt a sense of financial security.

We had enough money to pay all our bills each month. Out of the S$900 a month I earned, I gave my mother S$800 and kept S$100 for my personal expenses.

The MFA offices were on the second floor of the City Hall building. (Today, this space has become the second floor of the National Gallery.) We could enter them by walking up the grand steps facing the Padang on St Andrew's Road. There were absolutely no security barriers then. Any stranger could walk in and not be stopped. In some ways, we enjoyed real freedom of movement then.

In 1971, most of City Hall had no air-conditioning. Ceiling fans kept us cool, but in the cavernous two-storey-high hall that served as our office, they didn't work well. I remember sweating from time to time while sitting at my desk. Given Singapore's hot and humid weather, this wasn't surprising. This experience made me realise the wisdom of Lee Kuan Yew's comment that air-conditioning was "the greatest invention of the 20th century." When asked what his dream invention would be, he said, "Air-conditioned underwear."

The new hires, like me, were made "desk officers" of several countries. On our desks were piles of newspapers from the countries we were assigned to. We could easily have been mistaken for a newspaper store. Indeed, when auditors from the Ministry of Finance came to the MFA, they reported that MFA desk officers didn't do enough work to justify their monthly salaries since they spent all day reading newspapers. I confess that I enjoyed reading newspapers as part of my job.

Many of my fellow desk officers became lifelong friends, and I am still in touch with them. Geoffrey Yu was the best man at my wedding in 1985. Tan Siok Sun became the god-mother of our eldest son when he was born in 1986. In 1971, Singapore still had many street-side stalls, most of which have disappeared today. As young desk officers, we often ate at these hawker stalls. We bonded over char kway teow.[1] From the back door of City Hall, we could easily reach Hock Lam Street. Many street-side stalls filled this short, narrow street. We would sit on stools parked precariously near a drain and gobble down our char kway teow, which was delicious and cost slightly more than thirty cents a dish. Thus began my lifelong love affair with this quintessential Singaporean dish.

The MFA was a very small ministry then. Essentially, there were three very senior people there: the minister, S. Rajarat-nam; the permanent secretary, Stanley Stewart; and the deputy secretary, Lim Kim Kuay. All of us, including newly arrived junior officers like me, could join the minister around a long rectangular table in a relatively small air-conditioned confer-ence room. Minister Rajaratnam sat at the head of the table.

Initially, meetings followed a set script. Minister Rajarat-nam would hold forth on the state of the world. Since he was intellectually brilliant and read a great deal, his presentations were insightful and stimulating. When he finished, he would ask whether we had any comments. True to Asian form, we would all remain silent. Then Stanley Stewart, who had prob-ably been well trained in the British Colonial Service, would say that we all agreed with the minister's brilliant presentation. The meeting would then end with little or no discussion.

This script ended when my fellow desk officers and I decided to trust that Minister Rajaratnam would really like to hear the

MFA officers' views. We conspired to "break ranks" and make some comments. My friend Siok Sun, who joined the MFA a month after I did, recalls that at first, Stanley Stewart glared at us for daring to speak. However, he was a nice man. He didn't punish us and allowed us to carry on making comments and asking questions during these Monday meetings with the minister. And it turned out that open dialogue was just what Minister Rajaratnam wanted. His face lit up whenever we made comments. He was happy to engage in discussion, as he loved the back-and-forth of a good argument. Indeed, he was a skilled debater, as I would learn in the course of my career in the MFA. Whenever I spoke to Minister Rajaratnam, either at these meetings or elsewhere, I felt that I was talking to a fellow free spirit.

The central paradox of his character and personality was that while he could be a fierce debater (especially when he was taking on either the procommunist forces in Singapore or the pro-Soviet forces internationally), he was also a remarkably warm and kind soul at the person-to-person level. He was very generous with his compliments, even to us junior officers. We felt very proud when he praised our analyses of international situations.

Even though I was enjoying my work at the MFA in 1971 and 1972, I was conflicted. In my heart, I didn't believe that I would stay long in the Foreign Service. My dream was still to return to the study of philosophy. Hence, my social life still primarily centred around the Saturday-night dinners at the home of Colin and Barbara Davies with my old philosophy classmates and new friends. A newly arrived British diplomat,

John Gerson, joined this original circle and has remained a lifelong friend whom I have encountered in many corners of the world.

Although I had joined the government, I also mixed with "radicals" and critics who reached out to me on the basis of my reputation as a former "student radical." A group of architects who were particularly critical of the government was led by William Lim and Tay Kheng Soon, who were partners in a firm called Design Partnership (DP) Architects. They set up a nongovernmental organisation (NGO) called the Singapore Planning Urban Research (SPUR) Group. The acronym SPUR was deliberately chosen, as this group wanted to spur the government to rethink and change policies, especially in urban planning. Curiously, even though I was already a civil servant by 1971, I was appointed treasurer of this group. This would never happen today, as civil servants are not allowed to join independent critical groups.

Although SPUR has never been acknowledged as having played any significant role in Singapore's development, I believe it may have made some notable contributions. For example, I remember that in the late 1960s, long before it was fashionable, SPUR proposed that the airport be moved from Paya Lebar to Changi. Eventually, the government agreed to move the airport to Changi. Was it because SPUR had suggested the idea, or did the government arrive at the idea independently?

David Marshall, the first chief minister of Singapore, who had become one of the stoutest critics of the Singaporean government, invited me to join him for lunch. As someone from a very modest background and from a family very low on the

71

social ladder, it was quite daunting to lunch with a towering figure like David Marshall, who was a larger-than-life presence with his booming voice and confident personality. We ended up becoming lifelong friends. It was particularly strange when I ended up as his boss when he was the first Singaporean ambassador to France (from 1978 to 1993) and I was the deputy secretary of the Foreign Ministry. Life often takes interesting twists and turns.

When I joined the diplomatic service of Singapore, the MFA had no capability to train its new officers. My first encounter with diplomatic training came when I was sent to an Australian Foreign Service training course in 1972 about a year after joining the MFA. I attended three months of classes in Canberra (including an exciting visit to Papua New Guinea), followed by a five-week attachment to the Australian Embassy in Bonn. This Australian course opened my eyes in many ways. Until I set foot in Australia, I had never visited a "developed" First World country. I quickly realised that life in a developed country was far more comfortable than life in a developing country like Singapore. I understood why some of my contemporaries had decided to migrate to developed countries such as Australia, Canada, the United Kingdom, and the United States. I wasn't tempted. I don't know why not, but I may, even as a young man, have harboured great hopes for the future of Asia. Additionally, since my mother was completely dependent on me, I knew that it would be cruel to bring her to a completely new environment, especially after she had adjusted to Singapore. I felt a deep responsibility to take care of her.

In Australia, I experienced winter for the first time, since Singapore doesn't really have seasonal variation. I had a close shave with the cold weather. While in Canberra, I dated a young Australian woman, Shelley Warner, whose father, Denis Warner, had been a legendary Australian journalist in Southeast Asia. Shelley drove an old open-top sports car that had no heating. She offered to drive me to Sydney, which was three hours away. Unfortunately, as we were driving back late at night in very cold weather, her old sports car broke down. Since I had very little warm clothing, I almost froze standing out in the cold. Fortunately, we were eventually rescued. Now I always carry warm clothing whenever I go for long drives in winter.

Sydney, a dynamic and attractive city, was an eye-opener for me. I had never seen a first-rate musical performed before. Hence, I was genuinely overawed when I went to see *Jesus Christ Superstar*. The music and acting were terrific, and the flamboyant irreverence towards religion and worship resonated with my own agnostic/atheistic tendencies. I also found my Australian classmates warm, friendly, and relaxed. In Singapore, in the first six years after gaining our precarious independence, Lee Kuan Yew continually emphasised that the only way for Singapore to survive was for its people to "work, work, work." The Australian attitude seemed to be "Why work?" Indeed, one morning in Canberra, when our classes were cancelled for the whole day because a lecturer couldn't make it, the Australian students did what came naturally to them: headed to the pub. That was the first time in my life that I drank beer continuously from 10 a.m. to 10 p.m.

I experienced other luxuries in Australia. The Australian government flew me first class on Qantas Airways from Canberra to Germany, a trip that further reinforced the gap between a developing country like Singapore and a developed one. My five weeks with the Australian Embassy in Bonn left behind three indelible memories.

I arrived in Bonn just as the 1972 Olympics were opening in Munich on August 26, 1972. The Australian Embassy generously arranged a ticket for me to attend the opening ceremony and some opening events. However, I had to sleep on the floor of the Australian consulate, as no hotel rooms were available in Munich. I was expecting to experience a joyous opening ceremony. Instead, sadly, the entire opening ceremony was a sombre event as we mourned the killings of Israeli athletes just before the Games began. Over fifty years have passed since the killing of the Israeli athletes by Palestinian terrorists, yet, as the painful killings around Gaza in 2023 show, the cycle of violence between Israel and Palestine has not diminished. The world has shown little wisdom in managing the Israeli-Palestinian conflict.

My second vivid memory is also a sober one. Since I spoke some Hindi, I befriended an illegal migrant from India who was working at a gas station in Bonn. He invited me home for dinner. He lived in a small, very basic room. For dinner, he served rice and diluted milk. No curry. No spices. No vegetables. No meat. To make sure not to embarrass him, I ate the meal with great relish, telling him how much I enjoyed it. This experience opened my eyes to an undeniable reality: even in the most developed societies there lived an underclass of migrants who barely survived. However, I have no doubt that the money he earned in Germany was helping some poor village in India. As far as I could tell, the rich German society was happy to enjoy the cheap labour provided by these illegal migrants, but in German eyes, they were invisible. These migrants were both there and not there.

The third vivid memory from Bonn is not a sombre one, but the experience was shocking. Twenty-seven years after the end of World War II, West Germany had become a rich and powerful country. The prosperity was visible everywhere. Still, the greatest shock for me came from entering an entire store selling nothing but chocolates. Chocolate had been a luxury item all through my life. To have a whole store selling expensive versions of this luxury item seemed like the height of extravagance. My jaw dropped when I saw both the amounts and the variety of chocolates being offered in the store. Indeed, the opulence seemed obscene to my Third World eyes.

After leaving Bonn in September 1972, I spent less than a year with the MFA in Singapore before I was sent on my first diplomatic assignment overseas: to serve as the chargé d'affaires of the Singaporean Embassy in Phnom Penh, Cambodia, beginning in June 1973. For a junior diplomat like me who had been in service for just over two years, it was a daunting promotion to serve as head of mission (a senior position) at the age of twenty-four.

Phnom Penh was a city under siege. The Khmer Rouge forces (supported by the Soviet Union and China) had completely encircled it. The year I was there, the city was shelled virtually every day by Khmer Rouge rockets or artillery fire.

The danger was the reason why I began my diplomatic career at the top: the position had been offered first to a diplomat who was ten years older than I, but he had declined, saying that he had a wife and child to take care of. Then it had been offered to someone five years older than I. He too had declined, saying that he had a wife. Clearly, no sensible Singaporean diplomat would accept a posting to a city in the middle of a very active civil war.

When the position was offered to me, I had already been working for two years, but my family continued to live at 179 Onan Road. The one bedroom was used by my mother and my two younger sisters (my older sister had married). I slept in the other room, which was also used as a living room. I was still single. I didn't have a lot to lose, so, I foolishly accepted the job. My mother didn't object, since she had no idea how dangerous it was. She became aware of how dangerous it was only when she visited me once in Phnom Penh. Unfortunately, a rocket hit the central market just when she happened to be shopping there. Fortunately, it didn't land anywhere near her.

When I arrived in Phnom Penh in June, despite the shelling, the material quality of my life improved dramatically. I went from a one-bedroom house shared with my family to a four-bedroom bungalow. I had a resident housekeeper, a chef, a gardener, and a security guard. In addition, I was provided with a chauffeur-driven Mercedes-Benz that flew the Singaporean flag in front. Each week, flights from Singapore delivered various necessities of diplomatic hosting, including crates of champagne. My mother was very impressed with the bungalow and the household help I had. One of my guests when I hosted a dinner was the *Washington Post* correspondent in Phnom Penh, a young American woman named Elizabeth Becker. She became famous as a result of her dispatches from the front line and her subsequent books. Fortunately, she spoke some Hindi. My mother and she bonded as a result, and Elizabeth has remained a lifelong friend.

In this way, although I was living in a poor, war-torn city in a developing country, for the first time in my life, I experienced the equivalent of an upper-middle-class lifestyle. When I arrived, I didn't know the ABCs of diplomatic hosting. Indeed, when I was first invited to dinner by the German chargé d'affaires, Baron Walther von Marschall, I was amazed by the amount of cutlery placed in front of me. I didn't know what to do with all of it since I had still been eating with my fingers at home or with a spoon and fork or chopsticks at simple eateries in Singapore. I learned by observing other diplomats. Fortunately, someone told me that the rule to follow for the cutlery was to start from the outer items and work my way in.

Though I felt out of my element, I slowly gained some confidence in myself as a diplomat and political analyst. An incident one morning especially reassured me. When I arrived in the office feeling the effects of a bad hangover, my personal assistant reminded me that I needed to write my weekly report on the latest developments in Cambodia, as the weekly diplomatic bag would leave for Singapore in a few hours. Even though my brain was hazy, I managed to scribble a report. I have no idea what I said in it, but a few days later, I received a cable from the Foreign Ministry saying that they had found my report illuminating and had sent it to the Cabinet. This episode confirmed that alcohol and diplomacy go well together.

I also learned one of the most important lessons of geopolitics from my first diplomatic assignment in Cambodia: small states can suffer enormously if they fail to understand the great power contests taking place in their neighbourhood. Curiously, that lesson was expressed very clearly by the Greek historian Thucydides over 2,400 years ago. The small island of Melos tried to maintain neutrality in the conflict between the Athenian empire and the rising state of Sparta. The Athenian envoys threatened Melos with destruction if it did not submit, telling the Melians, "The strong do what they can and the weak suffer what they must."

In my fifty years of studying geopolitics, this lesson surfaced constantly. This is why the three founding leaders of Singapore, Lee Kuan Yew, Goh Keng Swee, and S. Rajaratnam, were die-hard geopolitical realists. They had no illusions about the nature of power. Great powers will always put their interests ahead of principle in dealing with small states.

This was what the United States had done with Cambodia since 1970. The United States (under the leadership of Richard Nixon and his national security adviser Henry Kissinger) was involved in a painful conflict to prevent South Vietnam from being overtaken by North Vietnamese forces. The United States sealed the border between North and South Vietnam, and North Vietnam bypassed this closure by smuggling in arms through the neighbouring countries of Laos and Cambodia. In response, the United States resorted to massive bombings of Laos and Cambodia. When this didn't work, the

Central Intelligence Agency (CIA) engineered a coup against the "neutral" ruler of Cambodia, King Sihanouk, in 1970. While he was on an overseas trip, the CIA encouraged General Lon Nol to seize power. The journalist Seymour Hersh claimed that "[Sihanouk's] immediate overthrow had been for years a high priority of the Green Berets reconnaissance units operating inside Cambodia since the late 1960s. There is also incontrovertible evidence that Lon Nol was approached by agents of American military intelligence in 1969 and asked to overthrow the Sihanouk government."

Like most military puppets installed by CIA coups, Lon Nol proved to be an incompetent ruler. In the space of three years, his government lost a massive amount of territory to the Khmer Rouge. There were many reasons for this failure. Corruption was one. Why did the shelling of Phnom Penh become more intense in the year I was there? And how did the Khmer Rouge replenish the shells they fired at the city? Each week, brave US pilots flew into the dangerous Phnom Penh airport to deliver fresh supplies of artillery shells to Lon Nol's generals. These generals would then drive truckloads of artillery shells out of the city to sell them to the Khmer Rouge for US dollars in cash. The shelling could thus take place continuously. Shockingly, these generals were prepared to take the risk of having the shells hit their own families, who were still living in Phnom Penh.

I was fortunate to meet several excellent US diplomats in Phnom Penh who were trying their best to help Lon Nol's government, as was the US government in Washington, DC. Unfortunately, given the tremendous imbalance in power between the two governments, the US government didn't just help—it took over. Soon after my arrival in Phnom Penh, I befriended a young African American female diplomat. She described her work to me. Each morning, she would receive a set of instructions from Washington, DC, where people were going to bed as we woke up in Phnom Penh. She would then drive to the Ministry of Commerce and personally hand the instructions to the minister, who would then implement them. In short, Lon Nol's government was a textbook hapless puppet government.

In personal terms, even while conditions in the city were deteriorating, I continued to have a good life as I learned more and more about the actual practice of diplomacy. Fortunately for me, Malaysia had assigned a highly sophisticated young diplomat—Renji Sathiah—to Phnom Penh. Like me, Renji was of Indian origin, but he had been educated in British schools and universities, and he had a French wife. He felt totally at ease in sophisticated diplomatic settings. I learned a lot by observing him closely. He oozed charm effortlessly. Sophisticated European diplomats hung around him to enjoy his company and to learn from him. He was the first teacher of diplomacy I encountered, and probably one of the best. He had one major flaw, which I also emulated, unfortunately. He loved to play poker, where he often lost money. When I joined him, I also lost money. Much later, we discovered that a European gentleman whom we played with was cheating and stole money from us by marking the cards.

I also experienced dangerous moments in Phnom Penh. One of my worst moments was the result of a nearby bombing, and the other was the result of inadvertently walking into a minefield. The closest I came to being bombed was not from an incoming Khmer Rouge rocket. Instead, it happened when a dissident pilot decided to bomb the palace of General Lon Nol, the CIA-installed president of Cambodia. This happened around 3 p.m. At that time, since Cambodia had been a French colony and still adhered to the office hours established in colonial times, all the offices were shut for the afternoon siesta. I was therefore at home taking my nap when the first bomb fell.

My diplomatic residence was right by the palace. Indeed, when I looked out of my dining room, I would see the tanks across the street that guarded the entrance of the president's palace. Sometimes I wondered if a tank might accidentally fire at my house. Given this proximity to the palace, the impact of the bomb was massive. The bed I was sleeping on was lifted up into the air. As I was collecting my senses, I remembered the golden rule: get under a staircase when the bombing starts. So I ran down from my second-floor bedroom to the ground floor and hid under the staircase. I got there just as the next bomb hit the palace. It landed even closer to my residence. The blast shattered all the windows and sent shards of glass flying in all directions. The staircase shielded me from the flying glass.

We learned a lesson from the bombing. After the windows were repaired, we put tape on all the glass to prevent glass shards from any future bomb blast. We also stacked sandbags up to eight feet high all around the house to absorb bomb blasts. However, the palace wasn't bombed again while I was in Phnom Penh.

This wasn't the first time the residence had felt the impact of bombing. My predecessor, Lee Chiong Giam, had been posted in Phnom Penh for three years from 1970 to 1973. He too had experienced a shelling that had damaged the residence. As soon as the MFA heard that the residence had been shelled, it asked Chiong Giam urgently whether any crockery or cutlery had been damaged by the bombing. No one asked whether he and his family were okay. Fortunately, in my case, they worried less about the china. The MFA had become more humane in the intervening years.

A few months later, in the afternoon, I heard the very loud sounds of incoming artillery fire near my home. I soon learned that the artillery shells had fallen on a market less than a kilometre from my residence. Out of curiosity and blithely indifferent to my own safety, I rushed to see the impact. When I arrived at the market, the sights were awful: mangled bodies were strewn across the streets. Artillery shells are deadly enough when they fall on muddy battlefields, where the trajectory of the shrapnel is between 45 and 75 degrees from the point of impact. However, an artillery shell is much more lethal when it lands on a concrete floor. The shrapnel flies horizontally, killing far more people. I arrived to see dozens of dead bodies. After a few minutes of horror, I abruptly realised that if the Khmer Rouge forces resumed their shelling, I would be killed instantly. I rushed back to the relative safety of the residence.

The second time I almost died was when I walked into a minefield. After living several months in a city under siege, the British chargé d'affaires, David MacKilligin; a young Cambodian teacher, Sichan Siv; and I decided to take a risk and drive out of the besieged city to see a bit of the countryside. We were bored, and the roads outside the city were deserted. The bridges were guarded to prevent sabotage by the Khmer Rouge, who were nearby. After driving for a while, we got out of the car at a bridge. Sichan asked the soldiers guarding the bridge for directions to the lake. A soldier pointed us to a sandy path. After we had walked about a hundred metres, the same soldier shouted at us. Sichan translated what he had shouted in Khmer: "I think this path is mined." The three of us froze. We looked carefully at the footprints we had made in the sand. We walked backwards slowly and made sure that we stepped only in the footprints we had previously made.

Later, Sichan suffered a great deal when Phnom Penh fell to the Khmer Rouge on April 17, 1975. Like all educated Cambodians, he was sent to a reeducation camp. Many were slaughtered or starved in these camps. Sichan lost fifteen members of his family, all except one sister, to the genocide. Sichan miraculously managed to escape, walking for many days to reach a refugee camp in Thailand. From there, he went to the United States, enrolled in the master of international affairs programme at Columbia University, and married a lovely Texan woman, Martha Pattillo. Then, even more miraculously, he got a job in the White House as deputy assistant to President George H. W. Bush.

Given Sichan's remarkable life story, *People* magazine decided to write a story about him. There was only one problem: Sichan had no pictures of his early life or family. He had left Cambodia with nothing. It happened that back in 1973, he had invited me to the wedding of one of his sisters, and I had kept photos of this wedding. These photos are the only record he has of his family. Sichan told his life story in *Golden Bones* (2009), which is well worth a read.

Sichan's life story is fascinating because it so clearly tells the hugely paradoxical story of America's impact on the world. On the one hand, few societies are as generous as the United States in welcoming foreigners. I can think of almost no other society where an adult refugee from a very foreign culture can get a job in the president's office. Sichan's story reveals the generosity of the American spirit. At the same time, Sichan's story shows the callousness and cruelty of America's impact upon the world. If the United States hadn't engineered the coup against Sihanouk in March 1970, it's conceivable that the Khmer Rouge wouldn't have taken over Cambodia. There would have been no genocide, and most members of Sichan's family would be alive today.

I had one more near-death experience in Phnom Penh. Since the elite of Cambodia spoke French, I started taking French lessons with Nicole Gillot, the wife of a military attaché in the French Embassy. As a military officer, Nicole's husband was adventurous. He organised water-skiing sessions in Tonle Sap. I had never water-skied before. The waters of the lake were calm, and it should have been safe to ski there, but as a novice, I fell off the skis often. Once, after I fell, I went underwater. As I struggled to reach the surface, I heard a huge, deafening explosion. It could have stunned me. In fact, these explosions were designed to stun. Since military equipment was cheap on the black market in war-torn Cambodia, the fishermen had discovered that the fastest way to fish was to throw hand grenades into the water. The explosions would stun the fish, which would float to the surface to be collected.

I was involved in a few other risky escapades in Cambodia. One day, the Lon Nol government decided to fly the diplomats based in Phnom Penh to another town in an effort to prove to us that it hadn't lost the whole country to the Khmer Rouge, although in fact, it had lost most of the countryside. On the appointed day, we took off from the Phnom Penh airport in the passenger plane assigned to us. We noticed that it took off steeply and flew in tight circles over the city as it gained altitude in order to avoid possible gunfire from the Khmer Rouge forces controlling the countryside. We had been in the plane for less than half an hour when we were told that we had to return to Phnom Penh, as the airport at our destination had just come under fire.

When we returned to the Phnom Penh airport, the older and wiser diplomats decided to call it a day and go home. As I was young and foolish, I decided to accept the alternative offer to go via helicopter gunship to the town whose airport had just come under fire. Since the gunship wasn't designed for passengers, I sat in the gunner's seat. To ensure that the machine gun installed on this gunship could move freely and shoot from any angle, there were no doors.

As we took off and began to fly away from the city, I admired the green countryside of Cambodia, of which I had seen little. The padi fields, which were still filled with water, were particularly beautiful. At one point, the pilot decided to bank the helicopter to make a sharp turn—and I abruptly realised that as there was no door on the helicopter, the only thing preventing me from falling out was my seatbelt.

I honestly don't remember whether we made it to the town we were supposed to see. I just remember the perilous journey.

Despite these close shaves, life in Phnom Penh wasn't unpleasant. Indeed, it still received interesting visitors, such as the famous British novelist John le Carré (David Cornwell), who was doing research for his next novel. Since Le Carré had served in MI6 in Germany, he was a good friend of the chargé d'affaires of the German Embassy, Baron Walther von Marschall. Baron Walther had become a good friend of mine, as I was one of the few diplomats willing to accompany him in one of his favourite activities: eating at open-air roadside stalls. His favourite dish was kuy teav, Cambodian rice-noodle soup. There was only one catch when it came to eating at these stalls. With one hand, we manoeuvred our chopsticks, and with the other hand, we waved away the swarms of flies trying to land in our soup.

When Le Carré came, Baron Walther invited him to join our kuy teav routine. I recall one part of our conversation well. Le Carré said that he had only two or three days in Cambodia. However, he wanted to visit several cities in this short period. I told him that this would be impossible, as the few planes flying between cities in Cambodia were always overbooked. He smiled at me and said he would simply charter an entire plane for the two or three days. I was shocked. It would cost a fortune to charter a plane. When *The Honourable Schoolboy* came out, I checked to see how many pages of the novel were set in Cambodia. Despite the high cost of the chartered plane, only three pages were devoted to Cambodia. Three expensive pages!

Since Le Carré chartered a plane, he missed one of the interesting experiences one had on a typical commercial airline flight. Immediately after we boarded, the pilot rushed the aircraft to the runway to take off. Since the plane was full, I had difficulty finding a seat, partly because some seats were occupied by animals, like goats. The plane took off while I was still walking down the aisle looking for a seat. There was a sound reason for the pilots' urgency: they knew that on the ground, the plane could be shelled by Khmer Rouge artillery. They were safer in the air, as the Khmer Rouge didn't have antiaircraft missiles.

Of course, most diplomats in Phnom Penh were worried about their personal safety. While I was there, the US Congress made the momentous decision to cut off funding for the US bombing of Khmer Rouge forces in Cambodia on August 15, 1973. Some sophisticated European diplomats believed that the weak pro-US government in Phnom Penh would collapse the next day. Hence, on the night of August 14, 1973, the British ambassador to Phnom Penh moved his bed from his residence to his office, believing that it would be a safer refuge if the city fell. Fortunately, the city didn't fall. The British ambassador sheepishly returned to his residence a few days later.

The disaster that the British ambassador feared in August 1973 came to pass in April 1975. Most Americans remember the fall of Vietnam, with the desperate and spectacular evacuation from the rooftop of the US Embassy in Saigon. Few remember the fall of Cambodia to the Khmer Rouge, which was far more disastrous.

Antony Blinken, the US secretary of state, was forced by his Republican tormentors at his Senate confirmation hearings in

January 2021 to state that China had carried out a "genocide" in Xinjiang. That statement was factually incorrect. No genocide has taken place in Xinjiang. By contrast, a "genocide" did take place in Cambodia from 1975 to 1979 as a direct result of both the CIA decision to overthrow the legitimate Sihanouk government in 1970 and the later decision of the US Congress to pull out of Cambodia. Out of the nearly seven million people living in Cambodia then, one million were killed.

One of the key Cambodian leaders used by the CIA to overthrow Sihanouk was his cousin, Prince Sisowath Sirik Matak. As Cambodia was about to fall, the US government honourably offered him safe passage out of Cambodia. Equally honourably, he refused to "leave in such a cowardly fashion," even though the Khmer Rouge had published his name on a list of traitors who were to be executed. In his refusal letter, he said, "I have only committed the mistake of believing in you, the Americans." Sirik Matak was publicly executed by the Khmer Rouge. Kissinger recounted that he was shot in the stomach and left without medical aid to die over three days.

The genocide happened after I had left Cambodia. Many of my friends died in this genocide. I recall asking a pharmacist friend if he would leave Cambodia if the Khmer Rouge took over. He said confidently that the Khmer Rouge needed pharmacists. Instead, he was killed for the sole crime of wearing glasses.

These terrible stories and personal losses made me incredibly aware of the importance of skilful diplomacy and an understanding of geopolitics in preventing the horrors of war. At the time, I wasn't fully conscious that my year in Cambodia had ignited in me a passion for geopolitics. When I left Phnom Penh in June 1974, I was still determined to abandon my diplomatic career when my five-year President's Scholarship bond came to an end in 1976 to pursue my true dream of becoming a philosopher and teaching at the university. This ambition was reinforced by another factor. In my university days, as a campus radical, I had been critical of the Singaporean government. How then could I dedicate my life to working for that government?

Yet, as a diplomat representing Singapore, I came to realise that Singapore was a small fish in the dangerous ocean of more powerful nations. In defending Singapore, I was actually defending an underdog against stronger and more dangerous forces. This may explain why I ended up spending thirty-three years in diplomacy instead of the five years imposed on me.

In my year in Cambodia, I experienced a great richness of conversation and camaraderie that developed naturally from shared experiences of the sorrow and fear of living in a benighted and shelled city. I also experienced various forms of decadence and suffering. Looking back now, I realise that it was a rich, fulfilling, and instructive year that catapulted me in the right direction: towards a lifelong study of the cruel and dangerous field of geopolitics.

CHAPTER 5

Studying Philosophy in the Cold

I F MY ONE YEAR IN PHNOM PENH IN 1973–1974 PROVED TO BE ONE of the most eventful years in my life, my one year in Halifax in 1974–1975 proved to be one of the least. I ended up in Halifax because a former philosophy professor at NUS, Roland Puccetti, had recently become the head of the Department of Philosophy at Dalhousie University. He kindly arranged for me to take up a teaching fellowship there that provided me with a stipend of C$200 a month.

I knew absolutely nothing about either Dalhousie University or Halifax. Indeed, my geographical ignorance of Halifax led to a painful journey there. The cheapest way to fly to North America from Singapore was to take the Aeroflot flight via Moscow. That was my first encounter with the gruff and unfriendly air hostesses of Aeroflot. But I enjoyed spending a few days in Moscow as the guest of the Singaporean ambassador to the Soviet Union at the time, P. S. Raman. Since I had the mistaken impression that Halifax was close to New York, I decided to take a Greyhound bus. The journey was harrowing. I had to change buses several times, and it took me over thirty-six hours to get to Halifax.

So why did I choose Halifax? The key factor was Roland Puccetti. I had developed enormous respect and admiration for him when he had been the head of the Department of Philosophy at the University of Singapore. He was a truly accomplished scholar, publishing both deep philosophical articles and novels. His classes on the pre-Socratic philosophers were dazzling. I still remember what he taught me about Heraclitus. He had a great sense of humour, and his eyes were always sparkling. As indicated earlier, he masterfully engineered my transfer to the Department of Philosophy against significant odds. I owe a great deal to this remarkable man. Given my deep admiration for him, I will digress here to tell a sad story about him.

He ended up having a tragic life. Both in Singapore and at Dalhousie, he was accompanied by his wife, a fellow American, to whom he had long been married. I don't think they had any children. Unfortunately, after I left Dalhousie, he fell in love with one of his students and left his wife. Somehow, his life went downhill from there. He couldn't get a job after leaving Dalhousie, and he lost or dissipated his savings. I later heard, with great sorrow, that he had died homeless in New York. None of us would have predicted this tragic end for the sparkling and brilliant person we had known. This news hit me and my former classmates from the Department of Philosophy hard because we had become very close to him during our university years.

My quiet year in Halifax saw three critical turning points in my life. First, it rekindled my love of philosophy, but this time in a different field: social and political philosophy. Second, I discovered that a career in academia didn't suit me after all. Academic politics proved to be as vicious as, if not more vicious than, bureaucratic politics. Third, I married for the first time.

In its own way, the year in Halifax was quite challenging. After a year of living luxuriously in a four-bedroom bungalow in Phnom Penh, with resident housekeeping staff, I ended up staying in a curtained-off end of a corridor that had been converted into a "room." When I got off my bed, my head sometimes bumped into the wall. It was the narrowest room I have ever lived in. I discovered, to my dismay, that "nice" Canadian landlords could be incredibly rapacious. As winter approached in November and December, the landlord refused to turn on the heat to save money. Temperatures reached –13°C in Halifax in December that year. By contrast, the coldest it got in tropical Singapore in 1974 was 23°C. Fortunately, my philosophy classmates saved me by lending me a sleeping bag. My hand would start to freeze if it strayed out of the sleeping bag. To this day, I have never managed to love the cold. Fortunately,

I was able to move out in January to share an apartment with a fellow philosophy graduate student, Ray Dupres.

Halifax provided other "chilly" memories. When I arrived in September 1974, some classmates told me that the ocean water around Halifax was still "warm." They invited me for a swim at Peggy's Cove. I had swum in Singapore and in the Mediterranean (in Marseille) and happily accepted. Since there was no beach in the cove, we were told to jump into the water from a jetty.

I did so. As soon as my body entered the water, I felt the coldest shock that I had ever experienced. I remember trying to jump right back up to the jetty after hitting the water.

For most of the year, I was engrossed in my studies. As a graduate student, I was assigned a carrel in the university library, and I spent hours there reading. My studies in social and political philosophy were stimulating; I discovered that Dalhousie's philosophy department had some excellent professors. I was particularly lucky that one of the leading global authorities on Marxism, David Braybrooke, was in the department. Indeed, he had penned the essay on Marxism for the *Encyclopedia of Philosophy*. The department also had a global authority on Wittgenstein's philosophy, Steven Burns, who became a lifelong friend.

Both Braybrooke and Burns supervised my thesis, which I chose to write on the topic "The Idea of Community: Rawls versus Marx." From the dawn of human civilisation, philosophers have sought to identify the key principles of how to create a good society. In the search for these principles, most political philosophers, especially in the West, have tried to understand how to achieve the key goals of freedom and equality. In my master's thesis, I decided to focus on what I could learn from two key philosophers: Karl Marx and John Rawls.

For Rawls, freedom was far more important. His first principle of justice stated that each person has the right to a set of basic liberties and that these basic liberties must be the same for all. Basic liberties can be limited only if they clash with each other—such as when criminals are imprisoned to protect society. Infringements on these basic liberties can never be justified by greater social or economic advantages. Marx had a less structured view of freedom. In his view of an ideal society, i.e., an ideal communist society in which society regulates production, people would be free to become accomplished at whatever they wanted to do and, in his words, be free to "hunt in the morning, fish in the afternoon, rear cattle in the evening, criticise after dinner, just as I have a mind, without ever becoming hunter, fisherman, shepherd or critic."

Their views on equality were even further apart. In his second principle of justice, Rawls declared that inequality—indeed, greater inequality—was justified if it resulted in an improvement in the living standards of the people at the bottom of society. He said, "All social values—liberty and opportunity, income and wealth, and the social bases of self-respect—are to be distributed equally unless an unequal distribution of any, or all, of these values is to everyone's advantage." Marx, by contrast, had a more idealistic view. He believed that resources should be divided in a society on the basis of the principle "From each according to his ability, to each according to his needs."

Before I started on my thesis, I expected to find more insights from Rawls, who was considered the greatest living American philosopher of his time. Indeed, I learned a great deal from his classic volume, *A Theory of Justice*, and I continue to cite it in my writings. Yet it became clear to me during my year of studies at Dalhousie that Marx was a much greater philosopher, delivering far greater insights into the modern human condition than any other social and political philosopher. He was also more idealistic. This comes through even from a quick read of his essays in the 1956 volume edited by Bottomore titled *Karl Marx: Selected Writings in Sociology and Social Philosophy*. In his youthful writings, Marx was truly inspiring with his idealism. Georges Clemenceau once said about his twenty-two-year-old son Michel, "If he had not become a Communist at 22, I would have disowned him. If he is *still* a Communist at 30, I will do it then." As a young man, I indeed identified more with Marx. However, as I grew older, I came to accept that Rawls's ideas are more realistic and more likely to endure.

The tragedy about Rawls is that while he is revered as America's greatest political philosopher of recent times, his ideas have been rejected by American society. I met him in person many years later when I was at Harvard in 1991. If he were alive today, he would strongly disapprove of the plutocracy that American society has evolved into. It is no secret that the American body politic is deeply troubled. Yet there is an absence of deep reflection on how and why this has occurred. One easy way to jump-start such deep reflections is by asking why and how the United States has drifted so far from the ideals that Rawls spelled out in *A Theory of Justice*. A return to Rawls would help the United States enormously.

Marx's contributions aren't fully appreciated in the world primarily because Western discourse dominates the global discourse. As Braybrooke told me, Marx is irrevocably associated with the communist regimes, especially of the Soviet Union, Eastern Europe, and China. Hence, the failure of the Soviet regime is assumed to imply a failing of Marx as a philosopher. However, the more thoughtful Western philosophers, including the legendary Isaiah Berlin, appreciated Marx's contributions. I also discovered that the later writings of Marx, such as *Das Kapital*, were written in a dense, inaccessible style, whereas his earlier writings, so well captured in Bottomore's book, were incredibly exciting and pathbreaking.

One of Marx's insights that stuck with me was the concept of "superstructure" and "substructure." We all believe that the world of "ideas" exists in a different dimension from our "material" world. Surely, the physical and mental universes are independent and separate. Yet Marx brilliantly explained how the social and political ideas that we believe in are generated by the economic conditions in which we live. Hence, when the feudal lords were economically dominant, they generated a social structure that made their serfs believe that they should be serfs and nothing else. However, when the industrial revolution happened and the economic power shifted to the industrial lords, a new belief emerged that one's station in life was determined not at birth but by one's accomplishments afterwards. Feudalism was eliminated not through ideas but through a change in material circumstances.

This powerful insight of Marx's, which he wrote about in the year 1859, remains valid almost two hundred years later. Since the Western economies are dominant in the world, they create a Weltanschauung to legitimise their power in the world. They overlook a significant contradiction: an illiberal global order, in which the 12 percent of the world's population who live in the West dominate the world order, is justified by them in the name of liberalism. One of the reasons "democratic" societies are superior to "nondemocratic" societies is that, in theory, "democratic" societies are opposed to "feudalism," where birth, not merit, determines positions in life. Yet eighty years after the creation of the International Monetary Fund and the World Bank, the West insists, for example, that a non-Western citizen cannot run either institution, thereby arrogating to itself a "feudal" right to certain offices.

I came to Dalhousie University naturally inclined towards an academic career. For me, the main attraction of academic life was that academics could lead a "pure" life, focused on intellectual pursuits and untroubled by "material" issues. It would be the exact opposite of my destiny if I followed in the footsteps of my Sindhi forefathers by becoming a merchant and a salesman.

I was naive in this belief. The academic arena is as subject to material and financial pressures as any other. Indeed, it too requires "salesmanship." I discovered this when I was first appointed as a teaching assistant. Initially, I enjoyed the assignment. The Canadian students, unlike Singaporean students, would speak out in class and engage in challenging discussions. I was happy that I didn't have to face a sea of quiet faces, as I often had in Singapore. Then I received the first batch of essays from these articulate students. The essays were atrocious and full of grammatical errors. None of them had a clear argument. It was a shock to discover that Singaporean students had a better standard of written English than their Canadian counterparts. As a result, I did what any honest academic would do: I failed them all.

That caused a bit of a fuss. The professor who taught this class invited me to his office. He completely agreed with me that the quality of the essays was poor. He fully understood why I had failed them. However, he told me that there were other, larger considerations to bear in mind. If the philosophy department were to develop a reputation of constantly failing its students, all the students would naturally flock to the Department of Religion, where no student ever failed. The Department of Philosophy would end up with few students. This would also mean less funding for the department. I got his point and passed all my students.

This wasn't the only reason why I turned away from academia. In comparing my exciting year in Phnom Penh with my unexciting year in Halifax, I realised that despite my deep love of the world of ideas, I needed to remain engaged with the "real" world. To be honest, I also didn't enjoy being "poor" again in Halifax, barely scraping by on C$200 a month. Truth be told, I became quite depressed from time to time in Halifax. Marilyn Girvin alerted me to this. She received long handwritten letters from me from Halifax that made for depressing reading. Many factors contributed to my depression. Halifax was cold. My room was cramped. The academic world was much less pure than I had hoped. My ideals had crashed into a brick wall of cold, hard realities.

There was another practical reason to return to the "real" world: I had decided to marry. Gretchen Gustafson and I had first met when she had come as an exchange student to the University of Singapore in 1971. Somehow, she ended up joining my group of friends. We dated for a while and then lost touch for several years when she returned home to Minneapolis, Minnesota. We reestablished contact when I was in Halifax. She was then studying for a master's degree at Cornell University. Somehow, I managed to visit her at Cornell. After several days together, we decided to marry. I didn't consult anybody in making this decision and only informed my mother and sisters before the marriage. I had no doubt that they would disapprove of this marriage since I was not marrying a Sindhi. Nor would my mother get a dutiful and submissive Hindu daughter-in-law. However, with my deep rebellious streak against Indian traditions, I knew that I could never be happy if I was married to a traditional Indian woman.

I had so little money that I couldn't afford to fly to Minneapolis for my own wedding, so Gretchen did the truly noble thing and drove alone from Minneapolis to Halifax, a journey of over two thousand miles, to fetch me. I found out how long the distance was when I shared the drive back to Minneapolis. In the middle of the night, I fell asleep at the wheel, and the car veered off the road. Fortunately, we rolled onto flat land instead of landing in a ditch or crashing into anything. We decided to pull over on a quiet stretch of the highway and slept for the rest of the night in the car.

We made it safely to Minneapolis, and I was housed in the basement of Gretchen's home while we waited to get married. Gretchen's parents, Arthur and Mary Jane, were among the nicest people I had ever met in my life. They weren't wealthy, as Arthur had worked in a department store all his life. But they were comfortably middle-class and lived in a detached home with a two-car garage, enjoying a standard of living far superior to mine in Singapore.

The contrast between the Third World poverty I had grown up in and the comfortable middle-class upbringing Gretchen had enjoyed could not have been greater. At that time, in the 1970s, the dreams and aspirations of many (like me) who had grown up in the Third World were to migrate and live in the much richer society of America. In the eyes of many in the Third World, I had won a lottery by marrying an American woman. I could easily have acquired an American green card, and indeed American citizenship, after marrying Gretchen. The rational economic decision would have been to stay on in the United States.

Instead, I took Gretchen back to my Third World home. In 1975, when Gretchen and I returned to Singapore, my mother had moved out of my childhood home at 179 Onan Road. She had managed to purchase a four-room Housing and Development Board (subsidised public housing) flat with the money she had saved from my salary, most of which had gone to her. When I returned to Singapore, about $1,000 of the $1,500 per month that I was earning then still went to my mother, as I was fulfilling my duty as a filial son. Gretchen and I lived on about $500 a month. Fortunately, my mother hadn't given up the house in Onan Road, which we were still renting at S$17.60 (about US$6) a month. So Gretchen and I moved in.

Even though Gretchen and I were making a huge sacrifice in giving my mother two-thirds of my salary, my mother wasn't happy. Traditional Sindhi custom dictated that after the eldest son married, he was expected to bring his mother into his marital home. Quite naturally, this could cause conflict and tensions between mother-in-law and daughter-in-law. Gretchen and I could barely afford a house of our own. My childhood home was crowded enough with the two of us staying in a one-bedroom house. Adding my mother to the mix would have severely strained our relationship. We felt that it was best for my mother to continue living in her four-room flat.

My mother was extremely disappointed as, after separating from my father, she had long dreamt of moving into the marital home of her eldest son. Even more importantly, this was what her friends in the Sindhi community expected her to do. When this didn't happen, she felt that she had lost face in their eyes. This made her very unhappy and quite naturally resulted in a tense relationship between us and her. Poor Gretchen had to deal with both emotional and financial struggles as we coped with this difficult situation.

Even though we struggled, I was fortunate to have a job in 1975, which turned out to be a recessionary year. Jobs were scarce. I owed my good fortune to the then permanent secretary of the MFA, George Bogaars. When I had finished my diplomatic assignment in Cambodia in July 1974, I had gone to see him to tell him that I was going to resign from the MFA (and pay off the remaining bond of S$4,500 with my Cambodian savings) to study philosophy at Dalhousie University. Since the Singaporean government didn't encourage the study of philosophy, I presumed that I had no choice but to resign. Wisely, Bogaars told me not to. In an exceptional act of generosity, he agreed to give me twelve months of unpaid leave. Even more generously, he gave me three months of half-pay leave since I had worked for three years at the MFA. It's unlikely that any other permanent secretary would have been as generous and brave enough to make this decision on his own without consulting the Public Service Commission (PSC), which regulated such matters. Thanks to Bogaars's split-second decision, I ended up staying thirty-three years altogether in the Singaporean Foreign Service.

Our first few months back on Onan Road were especially busy for me because I had failed to complete my master's thesis before I left Dalhousie. I had submitted the first draft to Prof Braybrooke just before Gretchen and I had driven off to Minneapolis to get married. He sent me a very nice note in response, congratulated me on my marriage, and then said that his wedding gift would be a series of "animadversions" on my thesis. I had to look up "animadversion" in the dictionary to find out that it meant criticism.

I am grateful that he was a tough taskmaster and refused to accept the first draft of my thesis, though it led to months of toil in Singapore. I worked hard all day in my office at the MFA and then until the late hours of the night to finish the thesis. Eventually, it was done, and I was proud of the result.

All the hard work on this thesis paid off in several ways. After I formally received the notification that a master's degree had been conferred on me, I received two increments of $50 each to my monthly salary. This extra $100 a month meant a great deal to Gretchen and me. More importantly, my master's thesis led Goh Keng Swee, who was then both DPM and defence minister, to invite me from my diplomatic post in KL to Singapore to deliver six lectures on Marxism to the senior officers and Singapore Armed Forces scholars in the Ministry of Defence (Mindef). I was asked to deliver this series of six lectures three times because I spoke to three different cohorts of officers who had enrolled in Mindef. However, what I remember most vividly is the first series because Dr Goh attended all the lectures, sitting in the front row of the auditorium to listen.

During the first lecture, I almost panicked. As I talked about Marx and his work, I saw Dr Goh slide down in his chair and frown. The longer I spoke, the deeper his frown became. I was seriously worried. I shared my worries after the first lecture with the then permanent secretary of the MFA, Chia Cheong Fook. He knew Dr Goh well, as he had worked with him at Mindef before joining the MFA. He told me, "Kishore, this is excellent news. If Dr Goh frowns, it means that he is listening carefully and appreciating your points." Mr Chia proved to be right, as Dr Goh invited me back to deliver two more rounds of lectures. If I am not mistaken, all the leading scholars at Mindef who went on to assume key leadership positions in government (like Lee Hsien Loong, Teo Chee Hean, Lim Hng Kiang, and George Yeo) attended these lectures.

As a result, and as a result of my friendship with Dr Goh's son, I became a good friend of Goh Keng Swee. I grew to understand what a remarkable mind he had. I enjoyed reading the lectures and essays he had written because they are truly brilliant, without a wasted word (and it's a tragedy that his books are out of print now). However, I never enjoyed attending his lectures. He would put his head down and read out his lectures from a script without making any effort to engage the audience. In this regard, he was the exact opposite of Lee Kuan Yew, who delivered sparkling lectures in a compelling manner.

In some ways, it was hugely paradoxical that my studies of Marxism led me to develop a close personal relationship with Goh Keng Swee since his political party, the PAP, had developed a deep antipathy to Marxist and communist forces after the PAP had engaged in a life-and-death struggle with the pro-communist movement in Singapore. Indeed, about ten years after I gave my Marxist lectures at Mindef, the PAP government arrested a group of alleged "Marxists" in Singapore—arrests that remain politically controversial in Singapore after several decades. I suspect that the deeper foundation of the relationship I developed with Goh Keng Swee came from his capacious mind. He was one of the most intellectually curious people I encountered in my life. He liked to ask big questions, a habit I was happy to emulate.

Goh Keng Swee was both deeply intellectual and remarkably practical, an unusual combination. It is a pity that today, few young Singaporeans are aware of the remarkable range of his contributions to almost every field of Singapore's growth and development. He made transformational contributions to defence (such as the introduction of National Service), education (the introduction of streaming[1]), the economy (the encouragement of foreign direct investment), poverty reduction (the introduction of practical social welfare measures), and finance (proposing the creation of the Monetary Authority of Singapore [MAS], Singapore's central bank, and the creation of a sovereign wealth fund, the Government of Singapore Investment Corporation [GIC]). In addition, he developed the Jurong Bird Park, the Singapore Zoo, the Singapore Symphony Orchestra, and many other public projects. He was a true Renaissance man.

He also appreciated and understood power. In the 1970s and 1980s, when I got to know him, he was clearly the second most powerful person in Singapore after Lee Kuan Yew. It undoubtedly helped my career when word got out that Dr Goh thought highly of me. I had direct confirmation of this when S. Dhanabalan, then minister of foreign affairs, called me to his office sometime in 1980 or 1981. His opening words were, "Kishore, I know you are close to Dr Goh." He then asked me to raise an issue with Dr Goh on his behalf.

Dhanabalan was one of the bravest and most independent ministers whom I worked with in the Singaporean government. The fact that he felt somewhat intimidated about raising an issue with Dr Goh confirmed what a powerful and dominating figure Dr Goh had become. This power and standing enabled Dr Goh to make powerful and radical changes when necessary. His contributions to the growth, development, and success of Singapore were as significant as those of Lee Kuan Yew. It is shocking that his contributions were so quickly forgotten after he left office.

Why did this happen? The answer is complicated. Like all societies, Singapore has politics. No society is immune from politics. However, unlike in most other societies, politics in Singapore does not take place above the surface. Above the surface, everything looks calm and stable. Beneath the surface are swirls and crosscurrents. Even though there were always differences between Lee Kuan Yew and Goh Keng Swee, probably dating from their youth, the two men respected each other a great deal and worked well together for the benefit of Singapore. Without this extraordinary partnership, Singapore couldn't have succeeded as well as it has.

Yet, though this is not publicly known or discussed, the two men drifted apart after Dr Goh left the Cabinet on December 3, 1984. Dr Goh stayed on in office as deputy chairman of MAS until 1992. In that capacity, he visited me in New York when I was ambassador to the UN. We would have private one-on-one lunches together, where he would subtly drop hints about his differences with Lee Kuan Yew and sometimes make jokes at Mr Lee's expense. For example, he once said, "Kishore, Singapore would have no problems if Lee Kuan Yew were immortal. Alas, he's mortal." The tone revealed a slight degree of scepticism. Dr Goh could sometimes be more direct. He once said, "Kishore, you know what's the problem with Lee Kuan Yew? He thinks that he is the lord of the manor."

The differences between Lee and Goh have never been fully revealed or discussed in public, and some Singaporeans may be troubled by such revelations. But Singapore should be brave and self-confident enough in its history and accomplishments to be able to admit that not everyone agreed all the time. If Singaporeans discover that their past has been sanitised of all its internal conflicts and drama, they could lose faith in their own history. This would be a tragedy because the real history of Singapore is truly unique and special. A group of remarkably strong and capable men, with different aptitudes and habits of mind, were able to work with each other for a long time. One key reason why the United States has emerged as a strong and powerful country is that most Americans, regardless of their political persuasions, feel a deep sense of pride in their founding fathers, all of whom had strong and independent personalities. The history of the United States doesn't disguise the differences among them. Americans take pride that such strong men with great differences were able to work with each other so effectively. The founding fathers of Singapore were as remarkable as, if not more remarkable than, the founding fathers of the United States. If the full and true story of their strengths and weaknesses is told, Singaporeans will feel an even greater sense of pride and commitment to their country. I hope that such an uninhibited history of Singapore will be written in my lifetime. These memoirs are intended to help the process.

Whatever the tensions at the top level of government, Dr Goh's strong signal of support for me early in my career in government certainly was a positive for me. Many people paid close attention to me, even though I was young and junior (and poor). I recall the pleasure I felt when I was invited to lunch a few times by the then minister of law, Eddie Barker, when both our offices were in City Hall. Eddie was minister of law until 1988. We would walk across the Padang and eat lunch at the Singapore Recreation Club, long known as a centre of Eurasian social life in Singapore. We would occasionally have a beer or two at lunch. Then we would play a quick game of billiards before walking back to the office.

Eddie Barker was one of the founding fathers of Singapore. He secretly drafted some of the documents that led to the separation of Singapore from Malaysia. Clearly, he was trusted and respected by Lee Kuan Yew, Goh Keng Swee, and S. Rajaratnam. Despite his huge political stature, Eddie Barker was a relaxed and easygoing person with no airs. Unlike Lee Kuan Yew and Goh Keng Swee, he didn't have an intimidating presence. Instead, he liked to joke. I always enjoyed the time I spent with him.

Looking back at this phase of my life in the 1970s, when I was in my late twenties and early thirties, it is remarkable that I had the opportunity to interact as often as I did with the country's key leaders. It was flattering. It boosted my psychological confidence. Yet, to be honest, it probably also made me somewhat cocky, leading me to develop some significant detractors among my colleagues at the MFA.

CHAPTER 6

Kuala Lumpur

I REMEMBER WELL THE MIXED FEELINGS I HAD WHEN I WAS TOLD that I would be posted to KL. I knew that I would be heading towards physical comfort and political discomfort.

The physical comfort was a result of the dramatic improvement in our financial circumstances. We moved from our one-bedroom Onan Road terrace house, rented at S$17.60 (then US$6), to a diplomatic residence in KL, which was a four-bedroom, two-storey house with a huge garden in one of the most prestigious districts. In KL, we had live-in household help and even a dog. The dog helped because he would chase the snakes that tried to enter our house from the vacant ground behind it.

I received a cost-of-living allowance in addition to my salary. Gretchen and I finally had enough to live on after sending my mother $1,000 monthly. This sense of financial security was a relief. I also had an entertainment allowance, and we often hosted dinners in our home. The most memorable dinner we hosted is one I would prefer to forget. One day, Gretchen and I decided to invite over all the graduates from the University of Singapore in KL whom I knew, along with their spouses. There must have been twenty to thirty couples. As each couple left, I suggested (foolishly) that we have one last bottoms-up drink of whiskey. I must have downed fifteen to twenty glasses of whiskey as the guests left. I remember well what happened that night. A few hours after going to bed, I woke up and retched in the toilet for several hours. My body couldn't hold down all the alcohol I had consumed. I was sick for several days afterwards. This episode taught me a valuable life lesson, and it never happened again.

The political discomfort came from the neurotic relationship between Malaysia and Singapore. Our two nations were like a couple who had married and stayed together for two years (from 1963 to 1965) until things fell apart, then had a bitter separation and divorce. But after separation, they continued living in the same home, side by side. This analogy explains the continuing ambivalent relationship between Malaysia and Singapore.

Under these circumstances, a typical hard-driving Singaporean would have been the wrong choice as the high commissioner to KL. What was needed was a man with a soft touch and, more importantly, a man who was known, liked, and respected by the leaders of Malaysia. My boss then, High

Commissioner Wee Kim Wee, filled all these requirements. It helped that he and his wife, Koh Sok Hiong, were Peranakan Chinese who spoke Malay at home. More importantly, before he came to KL, Wee Kim Wee had been a journalist all his life, not a government official. He had developed close friendships with some Malaysian leaders, which stood him in good stead when he was posted to KL. Since I attended several dinners in his home with Malaysian leaders and officials, I could see first-hand how well liked he was.

Since I had few connections with senior leaders in KL, I had the opposite experience: I encountered the continuing suspicion of and hostility towards Singapore among the Malaysian establishment. I found that Malay officials felt no need to overtly show their dislike of Singapore. By contrast, since ethnic Chinese and Indian officials wanted to demonstrate that they were loyal to Malaysia, they would take potshots at Singapore when I met them. But despite the suspicion and animus, most Malaysians treated me cordially and respectfully.

The difficulties with some Malaysian officials were mitigated by the many friends I had in KL. These were my Malaysian contemporaries from the University of Singapore, who, having mostly studied law, were practicing law in KL. This group warmly welcomed Gretchen and me to KL.

In KL, I rediscovered that (as in Phnom Penh) alcohol works wonders in diplomacy. Given Malaysians' suspicions of Singaporean diplomats, it was no surprise that they wouldn't speak openly to me about Malaysian domestic politics. But even two decades after KL had declared its independence on August 31, 1957, British diplomats were still highly regarded by the Malaysian establishment. The Malaysian elite, including the Malaysian royal family, continued to send their children to study in the United Kingdom. Hence, British diplomats were received with open arms by senior Malaysians. They picked up more political gossip than I ever could.

By a happy accident of geography, the British High Commission was located in Damansara, not far from our home. This proved to be a real blessing, as one of the British diplomats I got to know, Timothy Gee, and I discovered that we had a common love for whiskey. Once a week, he would stop by my home for a drink or two—or three—before dinner. From him, I would hear amazing stories that had been told to him by senior Malaysian figures. In this way, I managed to stay up-to-date on Malaysian politics.

The American diplomats in KL were equally open and forthcoming. Two of them, Frank Bennett and Joe Snyder, became lifelong friends, and I continued to meet up with them after I was posted to Washington, DC, some years later, in 1982 (Frank later introduced me to my wife, Anne, in Washington, DC). It helped that Singapore was basically on the side of the United States during the Cold War. And, of course, it was a real blessing that I was married to Gretchen, an American. The then US ambassador to KL, Robert Hopkins Miller, took a liking to Gretchen and me and invited us often to his house. This was a real privilege for a junior diplomat; it helped to be seen often in the home of the US ambassador.

I learned a lot about both the forms and the substance of diplomacy from American diplomats. Ambassador Miller was an exceptionally gracious host. Frank Bennett and Joe Snyder were highly effective and understood Malaysia well. Some of my best tutors in diplomacy, in both Phnom Penh and KL, were American. Yet several decades later, it's clear that the American Foreign Service has become demoralised and is much less effective. Something has clearly gone wrong. Unless some American leader intervenes forcefully, the quality of American diplomacy will continue to decline. It's truly tragic to witness the continuing deterioration in the morale and spirit of the American Foreign Service.

On May 31, 1974, Malaysia became the first Association of Southeast Asian Nations (ASEAN) country to establish diplomatic relations with China. As a result, a Chinese Embassy was established in KL in 1975.[1] While I can still vividly and powerfully recall my encounters with American diplomats in KL forty-four years after leaving the city, I have no memories of any encounters with Chinese diplomats from that era. I might have met them at diplomatic receptions, but I don't remember any such meetings. I may also have avoided them because in the 1970s, they were still carrying around Mao's Little Red Book in their front pockets and would recite from it from time to time. Times have changed: a young Singaporean diplomat arriving in KL in 2023 would encounter numerous well-trained diplomats in the Chinese Embassy. The influence of China on Malaysia has clearly become more significant.

Diplomacy is not just about personal relationships, although good personal relationships, as I had with British and American diplomats in KL, are important. Diplomacy also shows which countries are influential and which are not. When diplomats attend the national day receptions at another embassy, they look around and calculate how many senior members of the local establishment turn up. When I was in KL, the US Embassy's Fourth of July receptions would always have the glitziest turnout. Now, I'm told, the Chinese Embassy receptions often draw bigger crowds.

In addition to witnessing larger geopolitical trends, I saw a significant domestic political transition in Malaysia while I was there. In the first fifteen years of Malaysian independence, the political scene was dominated by two key politicians: Tunku Abdul Rahman (PM from 1957 to 1970) and Tun Abdul Razak (PM from 1970 to 1976). Both were powerful politicians. Unfortunately, Tun Abdul Razak died young at the age of fifty-four. He was succeeded by DPM Tun Hussein Onn, who was also his brother-in-law. Hussein Onn was a very nice man, but he was neither power hungry nor a natural politician. He took on the prime ministership mainly out of a sense of obligation. He was seen as a transitional figure.

When he took over as PM in 1976, Onn had to pick someone to replace him as DPM. Of the three eligible candidates, the one who was of greatest concern to Singapore was Mahathir Mohamed. In the years when Singapore had been part of Malaysia, from 1963 to 1965, there had been fierce arguments between Lee Kuan Yew and Mahathir in the Malaysian Parliament. Both were powerful orators who landed solid rhetorical blows on each other. It was well-known that there was strong antipathy between them. The worst choice for Singapore was Mahathir, but he was chosen by Hussein Onn. Clearly, something had to be done to repair the relationship between the two men once Mahathir succeeded Onn as PM.

Wee Kim Wee managed to stage a delicate diplomatic intervention. He persuaded Lee Kuan Yew to come to his house in KL to join a small dinner with Mahathir. I was present as a notetaker. Lee Kuan Yew was accompanied by S. Rajaratnam, Mahathir by Zain Azraai, a senior Malaysian civil servant (whom I served with later when he was the Malaysian ambassador to the UN and I was in New York from 1984 to 1989).

It could have been a fraught and tense evening. Instead, the dinner went well. Lee Kuan Yew decided to unleash his full charm and was warm and gracious to Mahathir. Mahathir responded positively to the overture. The two men didn't part as friends, but this cordial meeting laid the foundation for their good working relationship in the first decade of Mahathir's prime ministership of Malaysia, which began in 1981.

During my three years in KL, relations between Singapore and Malaysia remained challenging but stable. Nonetheless, I had to deal with surprises from time to time. One day, the then deputy secretary of the Malaysian Foreign Ministry, Tan Sri Halim Ali, invited me to his office. He handed me a diplomatic form of communication called a Third Person Note (TPN). This TPN was probably one of the most significant documents ever delivered from Malaysia to Singapore; it notified Singapore that Malaysia was about to publicly declare that Pedra Branca, an island administered by Singapore, belonged to Malaysia. No country gives up its territory voluntarily, but Singapore was being asked to do so by Malaysia. What made this move truly unfriendly was that Malaysia has a total land size of 330,803 km², whereas Singapore has only 729 km². In short, Malaysia is almost five hundred times bigger than Singapore.

Any owner of a mansion who claims land from a small adjacent hut is clearly not being generous and kindhearted.

On December 21, 1979, Malaysia further reinforced this claim by publishing a new map, "Territorial Waters and Continental Shelf Boundaries of Malaysia," which placed Pedra Branca within Malaysian territorial waters. This set off a fierce dispute over the ownership of the island. On February 14, 1980, Singapore formally protested the map by sending Malaysia a diplomatic note requesting that it be corrected. At one stage, Malaysia and Singapore almost came to blows over this issue when Royal Malaysian Marine Police (RMMP) boats entered the waters around Pedra Branca in June and July 1989, including a period from July 1 to 12 during which multiple RMMP boats took turns anchoring near or making passes close to Pedra Branca.[2] In theory, Singapore should have exercised its sovereignty and physically removed the vessels from its waters, but such an act would clearly have led to war. Instead, Singapore wisely reacted with restraint.

The dispute over Pedra Branca was finally resolved in September 1994 when Malaysia and Singapore decided to refer the case to the International Court of Justice (ICJ). The world would be a better place if other countries with territorial disputes, such as India and Pakistan, China and Japan, and Greece and Turkey, were to also refer these to the ICJ. Sadly, this rarely happens. However, Malaysia may have had an additional "secret" incentive for referring Pedra Branca to the World Court. It wanted to use the case as a precedent to persuade Indonesia to refer their territorial dispute over the islands of Sipadan and Ligatan to the ICJ. In the end, fortunately for Malaysia, Indonesia agreed to do so.

However, all these developments happened far in the future. The ICJ passed judgement on the Pedra Branca case on May 23, 2008, almost thirty years after Halim Ali had handed me the TPN. Clearly, in laying claim to an island controlled by Singapore, Malaysia was carrying out a "hostile" act against Singapore. Yet both when he handed over the TPN and in our subsequent meetings, Halim Ali was never hostile. Instead, he was always polite and friendly. We became such good friends that he invited me to a family wedding in Kedah.

Clearly, Halim Ali treated me as a close friend, as did other Malaysian diplomats over the years. In the trade of diplomacy, personal friendships among diplomats representing different countries are supposedly taboo. Since diplomats are always supposed to put their national interest ahead of all other interests (certainly the interests of friends), they are explicitly told that they should not become too friendly with diplomats from other countries.

There is a specific threat that diplomats are warned about: the danger of "localitis." A diplomat who is accused of localitis is seen as having become too friendly to the place where he or she has been posted. As a result, instead of objectively analysing the strengths and weaknesses of the host country from a detached perspective, he or she has been "seduced" by that country's perspective and therefore has become an echo chamber for the host's point of view. In the practice of diplomacy, being accused of localitis can be a serious charge.

I learned firsthand how dangerous localitis could be when I was invited to the Istana (the official residence and office of the president of Singapore) to be a notetaker for a small private session conducted in the Cabinet room. On one side of the table sat Lee Kuan Yew, then PM; S. Rajaratnam, then foreign minister; and Chia Cheong Fook, then permanent secretary (Foreign Affairs). On the other side of the table sat one of our ambassadors and me. I had, of course, heard that Lee Kuan Yew could be rough when he criticised officers for their lapses. Still, I was shocked by how brutal he was when he accused this ambassador of localitis. The man was one of our most senior ambassadors. S. Rajaratnam's fingers were trembling when Mr Lee launched his assault, and the ambassador was clearly quivering when it landed. After the session, I fully understood why Mr Lee was greatly feared. He could be merciless when he felt that he had to defend Singapore's national interests. After that session, I often wondered if I could survive a similar drubbing.

Even though personal friendships among diplomats are discouraged, they are a natural result of frequent interactions with honest, helpful, and friendly colleagues. Some of the best friends I have made in my life have been diplomats from other countries. Additionally, the personal friendships I developed over the years led to some significant diplomatic achievements for me. So, even though Malaysia and Singapore had a tense and at times even combative relationship while I was in KL, I got along well with my Malaysian counterparts.

At a personal level, Gretchen and I also enjoyed a good social life in KL. We were invited to many parties and gatherings. We also tried to start a family there but failed completely.

Indeed, we experienced a real tragedy. First, Gretchen had two miscarriages. The third pregnancy seemed to go well and went full term. Both of us became more and more excited as the delivery date drew near. We had excellent medical care in KL, and Gretchen's obstetrician and gynaecologist, Dr McCoy, was one of the best.

As the due date approached, he told us that he would fix a date for inducing the delivery. One day before this scheduled date, he called me to his office to deliver some shattering news. He said that the baby that was due the next day would not be able to live long. He had a condition called anencephaly, which meant his brain was exposed without the skull covering it. This baby would survive only a few days. However, Dr McCoy emphasised that I couldn't share this bad news with Gretchen. To ensure that she could keep her spirits up during labour and delivery, he felt that it was important for her to believe that she was giving birth to a healthy baby.

The twenty-four hours after I received this bad news from Dr McCoy were among the most difficult in my life. Supporting Gretchen through her labour and delivery was equally difficult. As I had promised Dr McCoy, I pretended to be cheerful and happy as Gretchen pushed out the baby as hard as she could. The head appeared first. I could see the exposed brain. Indeed, that was the first sight I had of the baby. Only after the delivery was complete did we share the news with Gretchen. She was shattered. So was I. Few episodes in my life have been as difficult as that one.

This episode was also difficult on another count. A couple of years after it happened, I learned that some members of the

High Commission staff had celebrated this tragedy that we had suffered. I had no clue about this when I was in KL. I was shocked by this discovery and asked myself what I could have done to have alienated my colleagues so much. Had I treated them badly? Had I been too ambitious? Had my relative success early in my career caused envy? Since I discovered this several years later, I had no opportunity to find out what had made them so unhappy.

I could think of one grievance they might have held against me. One of the perks enjoyed by all staff members in KL, including me, was that once a week, one of us would fly down to Singapore and back, carrying the diplomatic bag that contained all our sensitive documents and reports. It was a nice perk. We got to see our families in Singapore, and we were paid a small allowance for the trip. Since there were six or eight staff members, we each went home once every six or eight weeks—until Goh Keng Swee intervened.

When he invited me to deliver my lectures on Marxism to the Mindef in Singapore, he had to arrange my flights to Singapore. Mindef should have paid for these airfares. Instead, with his usual frugality, Dr Goh told the MFA to put me on the weekly courier run to save money. Since I delivered three sets of six lectures, this effectively meant that I stole eighteen courier runs from my fellow staff members. To some extent, I can understand why they were angry and resentful. Still, since I'd had no influence over this decision, I can't imagine that it was the reason they resented me so much.

Dr Goh's frugality was true to character. Even though he came from a middle-class family and made a decent salary, he was legendary for his thrift. When he travelled overseas, he never sent his underwear to be laundered but washed it himself every night in his hotel room. Even when I was very poor, I didn't do this.

Goh's frugality helps to explain one of the most extraordinary miracles that Singapore has achieved. For a country with no natural resources, and indeed with so little land, it is extraordinary that Singapore's financial reserves are among the largest in the world. The total reserves are a secret, probably because if the actual amount were known, it would stun everyone. None of our leaders have spoken about the size of our reserves except Lee Kuan Yew, who said in 2001, when he was senior minister, that we had over US$100 billion invested all over the world. He said that Singapore's huge reserves make speculators think twice about attacking the Singapore dollar.[3]

The country's financial reserves are kept in three major pools: the reserves of the MAS, Singapore's central bank; the assets of Temasek Holdings, a global investment company owned by the Singaporean government; and Singapore's sovereign wealth fund, the GIC. The reserves of MAS and Temasek are public knowledge: they were US$291 billion in January 2023 and US$299 billion in March 2022, respectively. While the GIC's reserves are never disclosed, the research firm Global SWF estimated that the GIC manages US$690 billion in assets. This would make a grand total of US$1.28 trillion. If this amount were divided among the 3.5 million citizens of Singapore, the net amount each Singapore citizen "owned" would be in the range of US$365,700. None of the rich member states of the European Union, for example, have amounts in this range.

Instead, they have large debts. Goh Keng Swee scorned debts and believed in savings. A large part of Singapore's extraordinary success is due to the values of frugality and discipline that Dr Goh injected into the financial management of its assets. Hence, while his frugality in not paying my airfares from KL to Singapore may have caused my colleagues in KL to resent me, I am nonetheless very glad that his values have made Singapore a remarkable success story.

Unfortunately, my posting in KL ended badly. At the end of a diplomatic posting, each departing Singaporean diplomat is expected to write a "valedictory report" that reflects overall on the posting, with an emphasis on the lessons learned, especially about the host country and its bilateral relations with Singapore. We were encouraged to be frank and open in these reports. I may have been a little too frank.

My valedictory report clearly and brutally stated the hard truths of our bilateral relationship: despite some surface improvements in Malaysian-Singaporean relations, the underlying hostility and suspicions between the two countries hadn't dissipated. I provided evidence and examples to back my claims. When I wrote candidly about how bad the real relationship was, I had no intention of antagonising High Commissioner Wee Kim Wee, with whom I thought I had developed a good relationship. The mistake I made could have been not to say explicitly in my valedictory report that these bad relations continued despite his good work.

In any case, he took great umbrage at my report. Without telling me, he wrote some ferocious rebuttals of my analysis. I discovered this some months later when the then permanent secretary of the MFA, S. R. Nathan, shared them with me. They contained strong criticisms of me, and they could have damaged my career. For some reason, they didn't; benign forces were protecting me. I suspect that one of them was Dr Goh, together with the two ministers of the MFA at the time, Mr Rajaratnam and Mr Dhanabalan. I ended up spending a lot of time with both of these ministers when I returned to the MFA in September 1979.

While I have emphasised in this chapter the significant political differences between KL and Singapore, it is equally important for foreign readers of this volume to understand that KL and Singapore are sister cities. In social and cultural terms, they are profoundly similar. In Singapore, I interacted freely in a society that contained Chinese, Malay, and Indian populations. In KL, I did the same.

We also share a common British colonial heritage. Even though Malaysia had switched to Malay as its national language, the elites in KL remained anglicised. Indeed, the Malay Muslim elites were often more anglicised than the rest of Malaysian society since they frequently sent their children to study at British boarding schools or universities. This is why the British diplomat Timothy Gee was so well received in KL.

Our cuisines are also similar. We are comfortable eating a combination of Chinese, Indian, and Malay food (like satay or nasi lemak) from the street stalls. When the then PM of Singapore, Goh Chok Tong (an ethnic Chinese), visited KL in the mid-1990s and stayed in the official guest house, Carcosa, he was asked by the chief butler (an ethnic Malay) what he would like for breakfast the next day. The butler was astonished when

PM Goh asked for thosai (a South Indian breakfast dish), which was popular in the Brickfields district of KL.

History also teaches us that social and cultural similarities do not prevent politically dysfunctional relationships. Indian and Pakistani societies couldn't be more similar in terms of cuisine, culture, and ethnic heritage. Like Singapore and Malaysia, they were once part of one country. The most beloved singer in India is Mohammed Rafi, whose music I am listening to even as I write these words. Yet he was brought up in Lahore, which is now in Pakistan. When Indians and Pakistanis travel overseas as individuals, they celebrate their similarities. Yet the two countries have a completely dysfunctional political and economic relationship seventy-six years after partition.

By contrast, even though Malaysia and Singapore had a bitter separation in 1965, fifty-nine years ago, they now enjoy a fundamentally functional relationship. Over the years, the leaders of both sides have made efforts to preserve a certain degree of calm and rationality in the bilateral relationship. In a small way, I hope that I contributed to improving this bilateral relationship, which is the most important bilateral relationship that Singapore has. My three years in KL, despite my personal travails, proved to be rich and productive years in terms of diplomatic dividends. The true test of friendship is the passage of time. I left KL forty-four years ago, yet many of the friendships I made there continue to endure.

CHAPTER 7

The Rome
of the
Twentieth Century

I WAS BASED IN SINGAPORE FROM AUGUST 1979 TO FEBRUARY 1982. This time, Gretchen and I were more comfortably situated, as the ministry provided us with employee housing and Gretchen became a journalist at the *Straits Times*. Without the stress and strains of poverty that Gretchen and I had experienced in Singapore from 1975 to 1976, it was truly pleasant to return home. Additionally, I began to have my first taste of multilateral diplomacy, which would eventually become a key aspect of my diplomatic career.

In September 1979, I visited Cuba to participate in the Sixth Summit of the NAM, an international organisation that represents the interests of developing countries. Personally, I was very happy to visit Cuba. Even though both Fidel Castro and Cuba were vilified by the US government, which had carried on its policy of isolating Cuba, I admired Castro's ability to stand up to the United States. Castro was personally popular in many Third World countries, even though many countries didn't completely agree with either his domestic or foreign policies, especially his close alignment with the Soviet Union. Nonetheless, his ability to resist US pressure was widely admired among the smaller postcolonial nations.

For the Singaporean delegation, Castro's closeness to Moscow was our main problem. Our main mission in Cuba was to protect the seat of the Khmer Rouge mission within NAM, even though this government had been evicted from the capital of Cambodia, Phnom Penh, by the invading Vietnamese forces on January 7, 1979. Since this Vietnamese invasion was illegal under international law, the UN continued to recognise the previous Khmer Rouge government, led by Pol Pot, as the legitimate government of Cambodia. However, the "puppet" government installed by Vietnam and led by Heng Samrin enjoyed de facto authority in Phnom Penh. The big question that we debated in Havana was which government should occupy the Cambodian seat in the NAM meeting. There is absolutely no doubt that the government of Pol Pot and the Khmer Rouge was morally abhorrent. However, the issue being debated was not a moral one; it was a legal question of who should represent Cambodia at international fora.

In theory, it should have been the Khmer Rouge government since it was still recognised by the UN as the legitimate government. It should have been an open-and-shut case. However, Cuba was prepared to go to extraordinary lengths to defend the interests of its allies, the Soviet Union and Vietnam, including by breaking procedural rules. Fidel Castro first tried to charm us. His brother Ramón invited us to visit his cattle farm, and the American-educated head of the central bank hosted a meal for us. When these efforts did not work, Castro tried to intimidate us.

His first "gangster" tactic was to house the Khmer Rouge delegation not in a hotel near the conference centre, like the rest of us, but far away. When the debate began within NAM, the members were clearly divided on who should represent Cambodia, although a clear majority favoured the Khmer Rouge government, the "de jure" authority. NAM didn't make its decision by voting. If it did, we would have won the debate. Instead, the decisions were made by "consensus." The chairman of the meeting decided what the consensus was. This gave the Cuban chairman large arbitrary powers, which Castro exploited.

Since there was no consensus among the whole group of members, Castro decided to convene a smaller group of countries, which he described as a "small, informal consultative group." Castro cleverly stacked this group with mostly pro-Soviet countries. Only two members of this group, Singapore and Sri Lanka, were non–Soviet bloc members.

Castro personally gathered this small group together in a small room for "informal consultations" just before dinner so that we had to work on empty stomachs. The Soviet bloc members were represented by their heads of state or government. Long-serving members of the Soviet-leaning bloc, like Saddam Hussein of Iraq, Hafez al-Assad of Syria, and Yasser Arafat of Palestine, were in the room, exuding power. Our delegation was led by a foreign minister, S. Rajaratnam, rather than a head of state. The whole atmosphere in the room was designed to intimidate the two non-Soviet-leaning members, Sri Lanka and Singapore.

I was in the room, and I felt intimidated. The Sri Lankan delegation was clearly terrified. Amazingly, Rajaratnam wasn't fazed. Even though the arrangement had been designed for him to be led like a lamb to the slaughter into a den of lions, Rajaratnam single-handedly fought back strongly against Castro and the other pro-Soviet thugs in the room. It was one of the most inspiring things I had ever experienced. Ambassador T. Jasudesan recalls that Rajaratnam made another stirring speech in the plenary session of the Cuba meeting, during which you could have heard a pin drop. The Cuban officials had resisted giving him an opportunity to speak and finally gave him a late-night slot in response to the Singaporean delegation's incessant badgering. This experience in Havana stood me in good stead when I faced similar circumstances in several multilateral group meetings, although none was quite as daunting.

At the end of the meeting, the chairman, Fidel Castro, had to announce the "consensus." Despite the fierce fight put up by Rajaratnam, Castro announced that there was a consensus to suspend the de jure Khmer Rouge delegation. The Cambodian seat was to be kept vacant until a decision was made. Rajaratnam again protested fiercely. After that, I understood why Rajaratnam was described as "the Lion of Singapore."

In theory, Castro had won a political victory for the Soviet bloc and Vietnam. In practice, it was a loss. Ninety-three countries took part in the 1979 NAM Summit. The NAM members made up a majority of the member states of the UN General Assembly (UNGA), which had 152 members that year. Since the NAM Summit had made a consensus decision to suspend the Khmer Rouge government from NAM, these countries should also have voted to suspend the Khmer Rouge government from the UNGA. Instead, because Castro had steamrollered the decision against the express wishes of many NAM members, most NAM members voted to retain the Khmer Rouge delegation as Cambodia's representative in the UNGA, as Vietnam had violated international law by invading Cambodia. In short, Rajaratnam's fierce resistance paid off, teaching me a valuable life lesson on the importance of fighting on, even against the odds.

Another foreign minister who inspired me at the NAM meetings in Cuba was the foreign minister of Egypt, Amr Moussa. He had an equally difficult challenge. His president, Anwar Sadat, had signed the Camp David Accords, which led to Egypt establishing diplomatic relations with Israel. This was widely viewed by the Islamic, especially the Arab, states as an act of betrayal of the Palestinians, who were suffering from Israeli occupation of their lands. Amr Moussa was completely

outgunned. To the best of my knowledge, no other delegation tried to defend him since Israel had few friends in NAM.
Despite the odds, Amr Moussa fought on, providing another
example of courage. History vindicated Sadat's decision to
normalise relations with Israel, as several Arab states that had
attacked Amr Moussa subsequently established diplomatic
relations too. Five Arab states have now normalised relations
with Israel, including Jordan, the United Arab Emirates, Bah-
rain, and Morocco. Sudan has also agreed to do so.

From Cuba, the Singaporean delegation flew to New York,
where I went on to participate in the UNGA of 1979 from September to December. This was where I first experienced the
skills in multilateral diplomacy of Tommy Koh, our ambassador to the UN. He was amazingly popular in the UN community. It was therefore not surprising that he became the
overwhelming choice to succeed Ambassador Hamilton Shir-
ley Amerasinghe as the chairman of the Law of the Sea Conference in 1980. All the Singaporean delegates to the UNGA
in 1979 were in awe of Tommy Koh. Since I had no sense that
a career in multilateral diplomacy awaited me, I must confess
that I paid little attention to the UN proceedings. I was simply
happy and excited to be in New York. Fortunately, Gretchen
was able to join me. We stayed in the apartment of one of her
friends to save money.

After New York, Gretchen and I returned to Singapore to
begin our "home posting." The MFA was still housed in City
Hall then. One of the joys of working with the MFA at the
time was that we received a weekly supply of the *NYT*. The
paper was hard to find on newsstands in Singapore, and very

expensive. Since the *NYT* was then flourishing and filled with ads, each newspaper was quite thick. A week's supply would be at least twelve inches thick, covering a lot of paper. At that time, our work week was five and a half days, including Saturday mornings. Each Saturday afternoon, I would bring home a week's supply of the *NYT*. One Saturday, I walked down to the City Hall car park, located between the City Hall and Supreme Court buildings. To free my hands so that I could unlock my Volkswagen Beetle, I put the week's *NYT* on top of the car. Preoccupied with thoughts of work, I got into the car and slowly drove to St Andrew's Road. As I turned onto St Andrew's Road, I accelerated, and in my rearview mirror, I saw a week's worth of the *NYT* flying through the air. I could have been caught and exposed as the biggest violator of Singapore's strict antilittering laws.

In February 1981, I accompanied Foreign Minister S. Dhanabalan on an official visit to India for a NAM meeting, this time in New Delhi. During the visit, Mr Dhanabalan invited me to his hotel room for a private chat after dinner that turned out to be over a very sensitive issue. He asked, "Kishore, I hear that S. R. Nathan [then permanent secretary of the MFA] throws files at the staff when he gets angry. Is that true?" I was caught completely off guard and answered spontaneously and honestly, "Yes, he does." Indeed, I vividly recall Mr Nathan throwing a file at me one Saturday afternoon when he was in a really bad mood. And it was true that many staff members were terrified of him.

When he returned to Singapore, Mr Dhanabalan must have raised the matter with Mr Nathan. I do not know what he said to

Mr Nathan, but I do know that Mr Nathan became very angry with me. I first heard of his reaction when something he had said during "morning prayers" (as the MFA daily staff meetings were affectionately nicknamed) was repeated to me. My friends who were at the meeting told me that he said, "Someone in this ministry thinks he is very smart. He will learn a lesson or two." While he never mentioned me by name, everyone knew that he was referring to me.

He must have believed that I had complained to Mr Dhanabalan about him. However, I had not backstabbed Mr Nathan or sought to criticise him behind his back. I hadn't initiated the conversation at all but had only responded honestly when asked. The one important lesson I learned from this episode is that life can be unfair. Truth doesn't always rise to the surface. I suspect that Mr Nathan held this grudge against me for the rest of his life, though of course he may have had other reasons for disliking me.

Whenever we met in person, Mr Nathan was always warm and courteous to me. Once, he and his family came to my home for dinner, and he hosted me and my wife in his home too. Indeed, I probably attended more events at the Istana when he was president from 1999 to 2011 than I did under any other president. On the surface, no one would have detected any problems between us.

Despite Mr Nathan's unhappiness with me, my career flourished after Mr Dhanabalan took over at the MFA. He introduced more modern practices of career planning and development. Under his leadership, we were promoted on the basis of our "current estimated potential" (CEP), a concept that the Singaporean government had learned from the human resources practices of Shell Oil Company. Since my CEP was deemed to be high, I was promoted rapidly.

This may have been why, to my great surprise, I was posted to Washington, DC. I was very excited when I received the news that I was going there as deputy chief of mission (DCM) to succeed Peter Chan (who went on to become the first career Foreign Service officer to serve as permanent secretary of the MFA). There was no doubt that the United States was the number-one superpower in the world, with only the Soviet Union providing any serious competition. Just as all roads led to Rome at the peak of the Roman Empire, I thought that all roads led to Washington, DC. All my experiences with my close American friends had been overwhelmingly positive, so DC felt like a dream posting.

There was one small catch. Gretchen said that she couldn't join me right away, as she had some work to complete in her job as a journalist in Singapore. So I sat alone on the plane as it descended over the Potomac to land at what was then called the Washington National Airport. Fortunately, even though it was February, a cold winter month, we landed on a bright, sunny day. I say fortunately because a few weeks earlier, on January 13, a plane had crashed into the Potomac River soon after taking off from the same airport because its wings had accumulated too much ice, preventing it from climbing after liftoff.

The Singaporean ambassador to Washington, DC, was Punch Coomaraswamy, a famous lawyer. He was close to the founding leaders of Singapore, especially Lee Kuan Yew. Punch (as he was known then) had helped PM Lee with a court case.

He was extremely warm and generous to me. However, he had a violent temper, which he would take out on his personal assistant. Since our embassy was housed in two small townhouses at 1824 R Street (close to Dupont Circle), the whole building could hear him when he bellowed at his PA.

I received a warm reception from the US State Department and the cluster of think tanks that combine to produce Washington's foreign policy elite. It was a sharp contrast to the cold, sometimes hostile reception I had received from some Malaysian officials when I had served in KL. The staffers on Capitol Hill were equally welcoming.

All went swimmingly in my first year in Washington, DC, until two good friends of mine, Goh Kian Chee and Tan Siok Sun, who had married each other, visited me. During their stay, we took a walk in the woods in Rock Creek Park. Our conversation was meandering and felt slightly awkward until the moment when Kian Chee pulled me aside and whispered to me, "Kishore, I think you ought to know this. Gretchen has found somebody else." I was completely blindsided. Soon after that, Gretchen came to visit me in Washington, DC, and confirmed the news. I made every effort to save the marriage, but I failed. At the time, it was a huge personal blow, but after much agonised discussion, we were able to part amicably. We have remained good friends ever since. Indeed, after marrying Liu Thai Ker, the famous Singaporean architect and urban planner, Gretchen made me the godfather of their first child.

Quite naturally, I became very depressed immediately after Gretchen left. I knew that I could hit the bottle (as my father had) or hit the road. Fortunately, my home in Washington,

DC, was on Unicorn Lane, close to Rock Creek Park, a beautiful natural setting with excellent jogging paths. I decided to participate in the Washington, DC, marathon, which was scheduled to be held in April 1983. As part of my training, I would run six miles (ten kilometres) to my office downtown in the morning and then run home again at the end of the day. All this training paid off, and I completed my first and only marathon. The sheer physical exhaustion from the training drove away the depression.

PM Lee Kuan Yew came to visit Washington, DC, from July 18 to 22, 1982. President Ronald Reagan hosted him to lunch at the White House on July 21. As a result, I visited the White House for the first time and met Ronald Reagan for the first time. As the most junior member of the Singaporean delegation, I was the official notetaker.

PM Lee began the meeting by giving a broad geopolitical review of the world. He pointed out that the global situation remained grim, as the Soviet Union continued to be expansionist, supporting the illegal occupation of Cambodia and Afghanistan. What he said must have been music to the ears of President Reagan and his delegation (which included senior figures like Secretary of State George Shultz and Defense Secretary Caspar Weinberger) because the Reagan administration was known for its strong opposition to the Soviet Union. Indeed, Shultz and Weinberger nodded in agreement several times.

As the notetaker, I kept waiting for President Reagan to respond so that I could record his words (since he was, without doubt, the most powerful man in the world at the time).

Finally, he spoke. After PM Lee had referred to the British, President Reagan cleared his throat and said something along the lines of, "Yes, the British. I just met the queen, and she was complaining about her horses." As I noted his remarks, I found myself thinking, "What is he talking about? Horses? There must be some deep message here." After Reagan's brief interjection, PM Lee continued his discourse, providing further insights into the state of our world. Once he had decided to make a thoughtful presentation, few in the world could have matched it. It clearly impressed Reagan and his delegation. Later, when PM Lee again referred to the British, Reagan interjected again with something like, "Yes, I spoke to the queen, and she was complaining to me about her children."

The queen? Horses? Children? What message was Reagan trying to send? There were probably no deep meanings behind his musings. Instead, Reagan, who felt uncomfortable in intellectual conversations, was trying to participate in the conversation in the way he knew best: by engaging in small talk. In terms of character and personality, Reagan and Lee Kuan Yew could not have been more different. Reagan had clear views on what was right and wrong, especially in geopolitics. He understood the threat that the Soviet Union posed to the world as well as anybody else, but he wouldn't try to present his views in a highly intellectual framework. Instead, he would use clever anecdotes and witty one-liners. (His most famous one-liner was what he told his wife, Nancy, after he was shot: "Honey, I forgot to duck.") Even though Lee Kuan Yew was a powerful intellectual and Reagan was not, the two men saw eye to eye, and the overall chemistry between them was good.

I must confess here that my first face-to-face encounter with Reagan matched the negative view I had developed of the president from reading the *NYT* every day while I was in Washington, DC. The *NYT* was condescending towards Reagan. Anyone who read the *NYT* regularly would have received the impression that Ronald Reagan (whom the *NYT* constantly described as a B-grade actor in Hollywood) was a dim-witted, intellectually challenged person who didn't have the intellect needed for the job of president. Unfortunately, my first face-to-face meeting with Reagan only served to confirm that impression.

None of this *NYT* reporting would have prepared the American public for the fact that Reagan turned out to be one of the most consequential presidents in US history. His achievements in foreign affairs were enormous! Ronald Reagan spoke of "morning in America"; he exuded confidence and good cheer. He made Americans laugh with his many jokes, especially about the Soviet Union. He told these jokes like a music-hall old-timer, and his folksy delivery worked very well. His favourite joke was about the ten-year delay in the delivery of automobiles in the Soviet Union: a man pays for his car, and the person in charge tells him, "Okay, come back in ten years to get your car." The buyer asks, "Morning or afternoon?" The fellow behind the counter says, "Ten years from now, what difference does it make?" The buyer replies, "Well, the plumber is coming in the morning."

In political terms, the right-wing Republican Reagan couldn't have been more different than his left-wing Democratic Speaker of the House, Tip O'Neill. They had fierce political differences, yet they developed a healthy respect for each other. As Reagan wrote in his diary, "Tip is a true pol. He can really like you personally & be a friend while politically trying to beat your head in."[1] Reagan's White House chief of staff, James A. Baker III, said that despite their strong philosophical disagreements, "there's a real affinity between them. There's real good chemistry as long as they're swapping Irish jokes and not talking policy. I think they really enjoy each other's company."[2] Former Reagan aide Max Friedersdorf's account of the time O'Neill visited Reagan in hospital after the president had been shot is particularly moving:

> When the Speaker came in, he nodded my way and walked over to the bed and grasped both the president's hands, and said "God bless you, Mr. President." The president still seemed groggy . . . with lots of tubes and needles running in and out of his body. But when he saw Tip, he lit up and gave the Speaker a big smile. "Thanks for coming, Tip," he said. Then, still holding one of the president's hands, the Speaker got down on his knees and said he would like to offer a prayer for the president, choosing the Twenty-third Psalm. . . . Once they'd finished, the Speaker let go of the president's hand, stood up, and bent to kiss him on the forehead.[3]

Reagan's greatest achievement was to bring an end to the Cold War against the Soviet Union. Reagan was fiercely anti-communist. He called the Soviet Union an "evil empire." He ferociously outspent the Soviet Union with a massive military buildup. The Strategic Defense Initiative (SDI), known as the

"Star Wars" programme, was a significant component of this buildup. It was an anti–ballistic missile programme that aimed to develop the technology necessary to guard against attack by nuclear weapons. Although this idea appears to have stemmed from Reagan's sincere desire to improve national security, it was received as a dangerous escalation of the arms race, as it threatened to undermine the deterrence policy of mutually assured destruction. George Shultz recalled that it "in fact proved to be the ultimate bargaining chip. And we played it for all it was worth."[4]

Reagan's Soviet counterparts should have considered Reagan the devil incarnate. Yet when Mikhail Gorbachev emerged and assumed office as the general secretary of the Communist Party of the Soviet Union on March 11, 1985, and initiated a U-turn in Soviet policies, he needed to find an American president who would compromise and meet him halfway. Despite his fierce anticommunist beliefs, Reagan proved to be the right man for the job. Recognising that Gorbachev's intended domestic reforms would serve US interests, Reagan "set about trying, through intense, sustained personal engagement, to convince Gorbachev that the United States would not make him sorry for the course he had chosen," as Strobe Talbott put it in a Brookings article.[5] Before his first meeting with Gorbachev—which he took seriously, going so far as to rehearse for it in a mock summit—Reagan wrote in a memo, "Whatever we achieve, we must not call it victory," as that would only make the next achievement more difficult. He also made a note to avoid making any demands for "regime change" and to look instead for areas of common interest. After meeting

Gorbachev, Reagan said, "There's a chemistry between the two of us, we listen to one another, we don't agree but maybe there's a way to continue. We've got a long way to go here and hopefully we can find some kind of a common ground."[6] The two leaders attended multiple summits together and exchanged dozens of letters. Reagan gave Gorbachev most of the credit for the cooling of tensions between the two countries and wrote in his memoirs that the last time he met Gorbachev as president, "We parted as partners to make a better world."[7]

Indeed, Reagan came close to saving humanity from the greatest scourge it faces: the threat of extinction from nuclear war. In January 1984, before Gorbachev came to power, Reagan said in a speech, "In our approach to negotiations, reducing the risk of war, and especially nuclear war, is priority number one. A nuclear conflict could well be mankind's last. . . . I support a zero option for all nuclear arms. As I've said before, my dream is to see the day when nuclear weapons will be banished from the face of the Earth."[8] Unfortunately, when Reagan spoke of zero nuclear weapons, he frightened the US military-industrial establishment, which worked hard behind the scenes to undermine him as he tried to implement this policy. He received backlash from fellow conservatives for the Intermediate-Range Nuclear Forces (INF) Treaty he and Gorbachev had signed on December 8, 1987—Howard Phillips, chairman of the Conservative Caucus, even accused him of "fronting as a useful idiot for Soviet propaganda."[9] Still, Reagan and Gorbachev both managed to get the treaty ratified, successfully eliminating an entire class of nuclear weapons.

Reagan turned out to be one of the most consequential American presidents, but I feel ashamed to admit that I didn't realise any of this when I spent two and a half years in Washington, DC, monitoring him and his presidency.

While I was very busy on the work front, the years 1983 and 1984 also proved to be happy ones on the personal front after Gretchen left me. For a newly single man, there was no shortage of young women to date in Washington, DC. However, one young woman stood out to me very clearly. Her name was Anne King Markey. She was introduced to me by Frank Bennett, the American diplomat I had first met in KL. Anne was working as a lawyer at the Commodity Futures Trading Commission (CFTC). In early 1983, she and Frank attended a senior executive training programme in Charlottesville, Virginia, where they bonded. At the end of the course, Frank apparently said to Anne, "Let me introduce you to the best single young man I know in Washington, DC." Frank proposed that he and his wife invite Anne and me to dinner. Anne later told me that she viewed the prospect of a blind double date with dread. Hence, she suggested that Frank get me to call her at her office so that she and I could arrange to have lunch together.

After Frank briefed me on his meeting with Anne, I dutifully called Anne's office and left a message. I then waited and waited and waited for her to return my call. Finally, after eight weeks, she did. Anne later told me that she called me back only because she saw in her diary that Frank was returning from a two-month overseas trip that week, and since she knew that Frank would immediately call to ask her opinion of me, she felt that she had no choice.

We had lunch, probably in late 1983, at a Sichuan Chinese restaurant conveniently located halfway between her office on K Street and my office on Dupont Circle. There was no great spark at that first meeting, but we agreed to see each other again. And we did. I fell in love with Anne before she did with me. According to Anne, I never really proposed to her. Instead, I just began arguing my case on why we should get married. However, she acknowledges that I sent a bouquet of roses to her office every week. She once heard one of her colleagues saying in the corridor, "Not again! She has got flowers again this week!" One reason why I kept sending flowers to her weekly was that we had become geographically separated. In August 1984, I was sent to New York to succeed Tommy Koh as Singapore's ambassador to the UN.

My persistence paid off. In December 1984, about a year after we met, I attended the annual Christmas Day reception hosted by the Canadian PM in Ottawa, Ontario. I did so because in addition to being ambassador to the UN, I was also the nonresident Singapore high commissioner to Canada. Just before I was about to leave my hotel to walk in cold, blustery weather to the Canadian Parliament building to attend the reception, the phone rang. It was Anne calling to say that she had finally decided to marry me. It was an unforgettable moment, even though we were miles apart and the frigid temperatures and howling Canadian wind were not my kind of weather. But I was warm inside from euphoria.

Before I moved to New York, Anne and I had spent a lot of time together. I was able to entertain regularly at my Unicorn Lane house because I had recruited Prema, a good cook from

Malaysia, before we arrived in Washington, DC. Another good friend of mine in Washington, Elizabeth Becker, helped to make Prema known there. Elizabeth and I had become good friends when she had served as the *Washington Post* reporter in Phnom Penh, Cambodia, during the war in 1973–1974. Reporting from war-torn zones is considered a "man's job." When this young, single, and extraordinarily attractive woman began filing stories from the front lines, she became well-known in Washington. "Beth," as we called her, ended up marrying Jim Hoagland, one of the most famous columnists in Washington.

The *Washington Post* reigned supreme in Washington in those days, especially after its spectacular exposure of Watergate a decade earlier. The publisher of the *Post*, Katharine Graham, and the executive editor, Ben Bradlee, were legendary in Washington circles. I met many members of the *Washington Post* family, including Karen DeYoung and John Burgess (whom I had met earlier in Cambodia). Most importantly, Beth connected me with the social editor of the *Washington Post*, who decided to write an article about how special Prema's cooking was. After that, I had no difficulty inviting people to come to my home for dinner.

I made a wide circle of friends in Washington. One of them was Strobe Talbott, then a correspondent for *Time* magazine. We played squash together. When I visited Washington after he became deputy secretary of the State Department from 1994 to 2001, he often made time to see me (and S. R. Nathan, who was Singapore's ambassador to Washington, DC, at the time), even though I represented a small country. This relationship confirmed once again that in diplomacy, personal relationships matter greatly.

Even though I was busy in my work in 1983, I believed that my career in the Singaporean Foreign Service had stalled. In the early 1980s, the Singaporean government was still very strict and conservative. It would never have selected any candidate to serve as a minister or member of Parliament if he or she had been divorced. I therefore presumed that as a divorced man, I wouldn't receive my next promotion to ambassador. (Tommy Koh later told me that Lee Kuan Yew was upset when he heard about my divorce and criticised me for it. Tommy defended me, explaining that it was Gretchen who had wanted the divorce and that we remained on friendly terms. Lee Kuan Yew accepted this eventually, and I am eternally grateful that Tommy was in my corner.) I had always been ambitious, so the realisation that my career may have encountered an insuperable obstacle might have added to the misery of the divorce itself.

Instead, an old survival mechanism kicked in. Instead of agonising about the tomorrows of my career, I put all my ambitions on hold and focused on enjoying my todays in Washington. I had an active social life, and I was dating Anne; thus, 1983 was a happy year.

I also decided to write to the editor of the influential international affairs journal *Foreign Affairs* to propose an article on Cambodia. That was a rather audacious move. I was a young and junior diplomat from a small, insignificant country. I hadn't published anything of any significance. Until then, my most widely read article was probably "A Question of Decorum," published in the NUS student newspaper.

Foreign Affairs was clearly the Mount Everest of international affairs journals. It was held in extremely high regard, both in the foreign policy circles of the United States and in leading capitals of the world. It had a famously rigorous editorial process, and its cast of contributing writers was stellar. The *Foreign Affairs* authors of the early 1980s included major politicians such as Shimon Peres of Israel; foreign policy elites such as former US secretary of defense and president of the World Bank Robert S. McNamara; influential academics such as the highly acclaimed scientist and author Carl Sagan; and well-known journalists such as André Fontaine, the editor-in-chief of *Le Monde*. No Singaporean had published there before. Indeed, very few Asians had done so. I still don't know what possessed me to write to Bill Bundy, the editor of *Foreign Affairs*, to propose the article—it was such a long shot, taken on impulse, that I did it without first seeking the permission of the MFA.

Bill Bundy was of patrician stock. Both he and his brother, McGeorge Bundy, the national security adviser under Kennedy, were colossal figures in the political and intellectual establishments of the United States. I might have expected to find an arrogant and condescending man when I walked into his office (and indeed, I have met many arrogant people in imposing offices). Instead, Bill couldn't have been warmer or more gracious when he received me. We sat side by side and went through the article, page by page. It was like a great college tutorial—indeed, Bill was a professor at Princeton as well as editor of *Foreign Affairs*—and reminded me of some of the moments I had most enjoyed as a student at NUS.

I was more surprised when Mr Dhanabalan, our minister of foreign affairs, almost immediately responded positively when I finally got around to sending my draft article for his approval. I was lucky that Ambassador Punch Coomaraswamy, who could have been upset that his deputy (who was twenty-three years younger than he) was upstaging him by publishing an article in *Foreign Affairs*, was also entirely supportive.

At that time, getting any article published in *Foreign Affairs* was a big deal. The main thrust of my essay was that the international community should come together to persuade Vietnam to leave Cambodia. It explained how this could be done. The country that felt the most threatened by the Vietnamese invasion of Cambodia was Thailand, since the formidable Vietnamese army sat close to its eastern border. Any pressure on Vietnam to leave would be welcomed by Thailand. Perhaps that was why the most enthusiastic reaction to my article came from Air Chief Marshal Siddhi Savetsila, the foreign minister of Thailand, who wrote and told me so. It was unusual for a foreign minister of another country to write a personal letter of appreciation to a junior diplomat.

By the end of 1983, by letting go of some of my ambition for promotion and focusing on developing the parts of my life and career that I could, I had regained my self-confidence, and my prospects even seemed a little brighter. It helped that the staff of the Singaporean Embassy were a close, supportive community and the economic counsellor, Jack Choo, was a great colleague. The Singaporean community used to meet regularly for meals at the large suburban house of a Singaporean businessman, Raymond Teng.

Several senior Singaporean leaders visited us in Washington, DC. When DPM Goh Keng Swee came, I accompanied him to his call on Paul Volcker, the chairman of the Federal Reserve. Volcker was a literally towering figure in Washington—he stood six feet seven inches tall—having successfully killed the dragon of inflation by allowing interest rates to reach nearly 15 percent in March 1980. I had no idea how powerful Volcker was until Dr Goh educated me. He told me that a small frown or a slight smile on Paul Volcker's face could move markets. Despite his enormous power and influence, Volcker received Dr Goh and his delegation very graciously. The delegates included Koh Beng Seng, then managing director of MAS at the age of thirty-two. At one point in the conversation, Volcker asked Dr Goh who was the Paul Volcker of Singapore (i.e., the governor of the Central Bank). When Dr Goh pointed to Koh Beng Seng, who then looked like a schoolboy, Volcker looked astonished.

As I had believed that my career had been derailed as a result of my divorce from Gretchen, it came as a total shock when I was told, probably in early 1984, that I was going to receive a big promotion. Ambassador Punch Coomaraswamy had been appointed to the Supreme Court, and Tommy Koh was succeeding him as ambassador to the United States.[10] At the tender age of thirty-five, I was assigned to fill Tommy Koh's shoes as the Singaporean ambassador to the UN. I was overwhelmed by the news. The first person I told was Anne. We hadn't yet decided then to either get married or become a couple. So I broke the news to her as I tried to make sense of this enormous responsibility that had been thrust upon my shoulders. Anne was very supportive, and I felt that I could take on this daunting challenge with her support.

Tommy Koh (who was then forty-six years old) was already a legend both in Singapore and in the UN. He had made history as a very young man when in 1961, he had become the first Singaporean to graduate with first-class honours in law from the University of Malaya (as NUS was known at the time). He followed this achievement with higher degrees from both Harvard and Cambridge Universities. He was first appointed as the Singaporean ambassador to the UN on July 24, 1968, when he was just thirty years old. He served a second term as Singaporean ambassador to the UN for ten more years from 1974 to 1984. When I was assigned to succeed him, he had already been the Singaporean ambassador to the UN for over thirteen years. Currently, Tommy Koh and I are the only two Singaporean diplomats who have served twice as ambassador to the UN.

Tommy Koh had become a legend at the UN because of his formidable negotiating skills. Most UN diplomats acknowledged that if he hadn't been the chairman of the UN Conference on the Law of the Sea, the world wouldn't have succeeded in concluding the UN Convention on the Law of the Sea (UNCLOS) in 1982. Tommy Koh had made a significant contribution to world history by finalising UNCLOS and making the world a safer place.

Tommy Koh succeeded because he could work out brilliant compromises between the many contending factions and interest groups at the conference. He was particularly good at working with the US ambassador to the conference, Elliot Richardson, who managed to secure significant concessions to benefit US interests (like extending the Exclusive Economic Zones [EEZs] to two hundred nautical miles offshore). Given his close relationship with Ambassador Richardson and the US delegation, Tommy Koh was unprepared for what must have been the greatest diplomatic betrayal he would experience in his life: the United States refused to ratify UNCLOS after "pocketing" a lot of concessions. This came as a great shock. As usual, this decision to *not* ratify UNCLOS was made not by the thoughtful US policymakers who supported ratification but by corporate interests that wanted freedom to mine deep seabed resources with American technology without UN restrictions. This will go down as one of the most selfish acts in human history.

Tommy Koh had also done a masterful job of marshalling strong international support for the UN resolution condemning the Vietnamese invasion of Cambodia. In 1983, the year before I arrived, 105 of 158 member states of the UN had voted in favour of this resolution.[11] It turned out that my main responsibility as Singaporean ambassador was to ensure that this number never went down. Fortunately, during my term, Singapore succeeded in adding to the number of countries in favour of the resolution, increasing it to 122 votes in 1988.

I felt that massive responsibilities were thrust onto my shoulders when I was asked to succeed Tommy Koh. Fortunately, the physical move to New York was easy. Tommy called me to suggest that we do a two-way transfer with the two cars of the New York mission. He and his wife, Siew Aing, and their two sons, Wei and Aun, would drive down from New York to Washington with some of their belongings in the two cars of the New York mission. Then I would drive up to New York with my belongings in the same cars and move into his spacious apartment in New York City.

Since Tommy was a celebrity, our appointments were widely reported in the Singaporean media, and I have no doubt that all the coverage must have boosted the morale of my parents. For my mother, the increased respect with which she was received in the Sindhi community meant a lot. She had been somewhat shunned after my father had gone to jail and she had separated from him (since separation and divorce were frowned on in conservative Asian communities). After my appointment, she could go to Sindhu House on Mountbatten Road, where she regularly attended prayer (Satsang) sessions, with her head held high. And I saw how proud my father was when I came home for a visit: he took out his wallet and showed me all the press clippings about my posting that he had neatly cut and saved. The increase in the prestige and standing that both he and my mother felt was as important to them as the new financial security we enjoyed.

It was all heady for me too. Before I heard the news of my posting, I had been convinced that my career was becalmed after Gretchen had divorced me. Instead, I had been catapulted upwards. This posting at the age of thirty-five proved to be one of the greatest blessings of my life.

CHAPTER 8

New York,
New York

I TOOK TO THE UN LIKE A FISH TO WATER. AND I FELL IN LOVE WITH
New York City, especially Manhattan. I arrived in New York
in August 1984 as a single man, and I left New York in 1989
happily married with two children. Clearly, my first New York
posting was one of the happiest periods of my life, although it
had one or two dark patches that would haunt me later in life.

Walking into the UN headquarters building and experiencing a real global village of representatives from 159 countries
was always a thrill for me. In theory, this diverse community
of representatives from Asia and Africa, Latin America and
Europe, North America and the Middle East should have

experienced, on a daily basis, many clashes of civilisations, as they came from strikingly different cultures and traditions. Yet what I experienced was the common humanity of these people from different regions. Indeed, I forged many close friendships with my fellow UN ambassadors.

When I joined the UN, some of my Arabian colleagues declared that I belonged to their tribe because my surname, Mahbubani, comes from an Arabic/Persian word, "mahbub," which means "beloved." Sind, which is located in the north-western corner of the Indian subcontinent, was conquered as early as 712 CE by invading Muslim armies from the Umayyad Caliphate. As a result, most Sindhis are Muslims. When I learned to read and write Sindhi as a child, I learned to read and write in the Perso-Arabic script, not the Devanagari script used in Hindi. Due to my Sindhi roots, I felt some degree of cultural affinity with both the Arab countries and Iran. And since I sported a beard then, I was occasionally mistaken for an Iranian diplomat when I was seen without a tie.

The community of ambassadors that I naturally stepped into was that of ASEAN. We were from the five founding member states of ASEAN—Indonesia, Malaysia, the Philippines, Singapore, and Thailand—and since we had a common mission of increasing votes in the UNGA for the ASEAN resolution condemning the Vietnamese occupation of Cambodia, we came together like comrades in arms. The ASEAN countries, like most member states, sent very effective ambassadors to the UN: Ali Alatas from Indonesia, Zain Azraai from Malaysia, M. L. Birabhongse Kasemsri from Thailand, and Luis Moreno Salcedo from the Philippines. Apart from Ambassador Salcedo, who was much older, these ambassadors went on to have distinguished careers after their stints at the UN. Ali Alatas served as the foreign minister of Indonesia from 1988 to 1999; Zain Azraai served as Malaysia's secretary general to the treasury and chairman of the Malaysian Industrial Development Finance Berhad (MIDF) before sadly dying of lung cancer at the relatively young age of sixty; and Bira went on to become the head of the royal household in the Thai Palace, one of the most prestigious posts in Thailand.

Dealing with first-rate ambassadors from all over the world was one of the great joys of serving in the UN "global village." Even the United States, the most powerful country in the world, made a point of sending outstanding people as ambassadors. The two US ambassadors I served with from 1984 to 1989 were Jeane Kirkpatrick and Lt. Gen. Vernon Walters. Although they both represented the same country, they could not have been more different. Vernon (or Dick, as he was called affectionately by his friends) saw it as his mission to work in the UN and win friends for the United States. Kirkpatrick showed total disdain for the UN and saw the UN posting only as a stepping stone to higher office in Washington, DC. Sadly, many US ambassadors to the UN have shared her view.

When I arrived in August 1984, I requested a visit with Kirkpatrick. Since she wasn't often in New York, it took months to obtain an appointment. She clearly felt that she was doing me a favour by allowing me to call on her. The meeting went badly because she wasn't a good listener. After she misheard something I said, she gave me a stern professional lecture and threw me out of her office. Fortunately, her deputy was in the meeting. He saw the mistake she had made and arranged a lunch so that we could patch things up. He did this only because the United States and Singapore were working closely together in the UN against the Vietnamese invasion of Cambodia.

By contrast, Walters was truly an old-school gentleman. When I first met him in 1985, he was sixty-eight years old and I was thirty-six. He was senior to me in every way. Once, Walters asked to meet me. Since he was much older, I offered to walk to his office, which was two blocks away. He absolutely refused. He was a diplomat of vast experience, having served as a military attaché in Italy, Brazil, and France in the 1960s; acted as an interpreter, negotiator, and troubleshooter for five presidents; and visited more than a hundred countries as ambassador-at-large from 1981 to 1985. He therefore insisted on normal diplomatic protocol and, because he had requested the meeting, walked to my office instead. Walters won my heart with his generosity.

Reflecting on these contrasting experiences in later years made me aware of what has gone wrong with US diplomacy in recent decades. Walters saw it as his mission to use his UN posting to win friends for the United States, and he did so brilliantly with his charm, graciousness, and sense of humour. He was one of the best-loved ambassadors to the UN. By contrast, Kirkpatrick gave harsh lectures and speeches scolding the UN community so that she could look tough and strong in the eyes of the right-wing politicians who dominated domestic policy in the Reagan administration. She was sacrificing the national interests of the United States to serve her narrow ideological agenda and her personal ambitions to rise further in

Washington, DC. If there was justice, she should have been demoted for this approach. Instead, she was rewarded, as she became a media star in the United States, even while alienating her fellow UN ambassadors.

Walters spoke many languages, including Dutch, French, German, Italian, Portuguese, Russian, and Spanish. His command of foreign languages, including difficult languages like Japanese, was amazing. When President Nixon (whom Walters knew well) went to Japan, Walters was able to translate from English to saikou keigo, the highest level of honorific speech in Japanese, which is used to address the emperor.

Yet Walters was always self-deprecating. When I once asked him how many languages he spoke, he replied, "Kishore, my friends say that I speak thirteen languages and think in none." He was also an admirer of Singapore. Somewhat unusually, he was an aficionado of underground subway systems and had visited most of them around the world. He told me admiringly that the Singapore Mass Rapid Transit (MRT) system was the only such system to have been built ahead of schedule and below cost.

He was also a devoted admirer of Lee Kuan Yew. He told me that he had once told Richard Nixon that it was fortunate that Lee Kuan Yew was the leader of only a small country like Singapore. If he had instead been the leader of a large country like China, the United States and the Soviet Union would have hugged each other for comfort instead of being Cold War rivals. Walters understood better than most ambassadors I met in my life that the personal touch matters. Each year, I received a handwritten Christmas card with a generous personal message from him. I asked him how he found the time to send handwritten notes. He told me that he took the Christmas cards on long flights. He would then write an individual note to each UN ambassador.

Did US influence in the UN diminish when the charming Walters left? Absolutely not. Here, I learned that for great powers, such as the United States, their influence doesn't depend on the quality and ability of their ambassadors. Power speaks more eloquently than personality in generating influence. The ambassadors of small states understood well what would happen to them if they ran afoul of the US ambassador to the UN: they would lose their jobs. I wasn't surprised when this happened to ambassadors of small countries, but I was shocked when US Secretary of State Madeleine Albright (who had served as the US ambassador to the UN from 1993 to 1997) managed to get the Brazilian ambassador to the UN, Celso Amorim, transferred because he wasn't falling in line with the US agenda against Saddam Hussein of Iraq.

By contrast, since ambassadors from small states don't have national power to fall back on, they have to use other weapons. As ambassador to the UN, I would tell my staff in the UN mission that we, the Singaporean diplomats, had only three resources on which to draw: reason, logic, and charm. Charm is an elusive trait and difficult to describe. Yet, when it's used correctly, it can have a magical effect. The other important lesson I learned in my first posting as ambassador to the UN is that people appreciate authenticity. It's important to be oneself and not pretend to be someone else.

One of the major decisions I made after arriving at the UN was that I shouldn't try to be Tommy Koh. He had been enormously successful as ambassador to the UN with his unique style and charm. I decided that I couldn't replicate it. Instead, I had to be myself. That worked well enough. Tommy Koh was also a good public speaker. Here too, I decided not to emulate his style. Instead, I developed my own voice. I made sure that I learned lessons from the best public speakers I heard, especially from Lee Kuan Yew. The most important lesson I learned from him was that a good speech shouldn't contain fluff but should always have substantive and meaningful content. The public speaking skills that I developed as an ambassador have stood me in good stead ever since.

I also learned to filibuster. Each year, ASEAN's main goal was to increase the votes for the UNGA resolution condemning the Vietnamese occupation of Cambodia. To obtain the votes, we had to ensure that all the ambassadors from the countries supporting us were in the UNGA Hall when voting began. Some of the small countries had only one or two diplomats. Once, when it was almost time for voting, we ASEAN representatives noticed that the seats of several small states weren't occupied. If the voting proceeded without them, it would appear as if support for the resolution were declining, which would have been a political defeat for us. To buy time, the other ASEAN diplomats told me to go to the podium and continue speaking until the seats of all our supporters had been filled. I must have spoken for an hour or so without any notes. I'm not entirely sure what I filled the time with. But fill it I did. I stopped only when the Thai ambassador, Bira, gave me the thumbs-up to signal that we were ready for the vote.

I also learned how power dynamics distorted the decisions of the UN. I got to know this well because of all the communities in the UN; the one I became closest to (after the Asian community) was the community of African ambassadors. I found them to be the most reliable and trustworthy ambassadors. If you became friends with them, they would remain steadfast and stick with you through thick and thin. I guess my close friendship with many African ambassadors was obvious. Hence, when the UN launched a new programme called the UN Programme of Action for African Economic Recovery and Development (UNPAAERD) in 1986, Singapore was asked to chair the oversight committee. Most of the negotiations in this committee took place between the ambassadors for the rich Western donors (and Japan) and the community of African ambassadors. The Western donors were happy to have Singapore as a neutral chair, as we were known to be conservative and prudent on financial matters. And the African ambassadors had taken a liking to me because I treated them with great respect.

Accordingly, I took on the chairmanship of this committee with great enthusiasm, convinced that I could play a helpful role for both the wealthy Western countries and the poor African countries. But I was in for a rude shock. Since the Western countries had given passionate speeches in the UNGA announcing their commitment to improving the lives of Africans, I expected them to shower the poor Africans with resources as a concrete demonstration of their commitment to help. Instead, the opposite happened. Every time an African ambassador tried to add a paragraph soliciting a concrete, firm, and binding commitment from the Western ambassadors, the skilful Western diplomats would artfully tweak the document so that the firm commitment became more like a conditional intention. The simple addition of three words such as "if circumstances permit" would provide an escape for the Western countries that wished to avoid following through on their commitments. Other examples included "whenever possible" and "as appropriate." Another tactic was to commit to "making every effort" to provide resources.[1] I had no idea that the English language had so many qualifying phrases until I began chairing the UNPAAERD committee. The skill of the Western diplomats in these negotiations was amazing. By contrast, the African diplomats had less experience in such things. As I had to be a neutral chairman, I sometimes felt that the poor African diplomats were being led like lambs to the slaughter. They were defenceless.

There was one occasion when I had to intervene. On the final days of the negotiations, after several weeks of discussions, when we had a document that had been more or less accepted by everyone, the US delegation walked in and said that the US Treasury had studied the final draft and wanted to introduce further amendments to the painstakingly negotiated document. I decided to lose my temper, both sincerely and tactically, and gave the US delegation a public scolding. Most of the delegates present, especially the African representatives, were shocked. Since the United States was the number-one superpower in the world, few dared to scold its representatives

161

publicly in UN fora. I was taking a great risk in doing so. Fortunately, my bluff worked. The US delegation withdrew its last-minute amendments, and we proceeded to adopt the UNPAAERD document.

When word about this episode got around the UN community, my stature in the UN went up. Episodes like this, and my speaking abilities, helped to ensure that the status and position of the Singaporean ambassador to the UN—which Tommy Koh had raised to a high level—remained high. The Canadian ambassador to the UN then was Stephen Lewis. Somewhat unusually, even though the PM of Canada at the time was Brian Mulroney, from the right-wing Progressive Conservative Party, he had appointed the left-wing Stephen Lewis from the New Democratic Party as ambassador to the UN. Some Canadian officials later explained to me that this was a Machiavellian move by PM Mulroney, as it gave him political cover to grant patronage appointments to his right-wing friends. At the same time, Canada's standing in the UN went up because Stephen Lewis showed genuine empathy and concern for the delegates from Third World countries. Stephen also had a very open mind. He was very impressed when I quoted lines from *A Man for All Seasons* in a speech at the UN.

The strongest criticism of the UN, which has even now taken hold in many Western minds, is that the UN, especially the UNGA, is a mere "talk-shop." But that's the whole point of the UNGA. We live in a remarkably diverse world, with many radically different civilisations and cultures, histories, and traditions. There's both a moral and a political imperative to create a functioning global assembly where all of humanity can speak to one another. Indeed, if the UNGA didn't exist, we would probably have to invent such a meeting place. Since the world has shrunk and become a small and interdependent global village, especially over the last thirty years as globalisation has accelerated, the need for a global village council like the UN has never been greater.

This is why it has been a strategic mistake for the US government (with the silent complicity of its wealthy European and Japanese partners) to weaken the UN. This complicated subject is the core theme of my book *The Great Convergence*. I found it equally shocking that rational American voices didn't point out this mistake. The *NYT* was particularly disappointing. Instead of seeing it as its responsibility to both explain and defend the utility of the UN to the long-term interests of the United States, the *NYT* actively joined in the process of denigrating the UN, pointing out its shortcomings (which were many) without emphasising that it was an indispensable global assembly that was vital for the long-term interests of humanity. Sadly, the *NYT* just couldn't see the big picture. In his article of December 6, 1988, the *NYT*'s UN bureau chief Paul Lewis painted a rather comical picture of the way "the General Assembly ritually curses Vietnam for invading Cambodia, South Africa for apartheid and Israel for its treatment of Palestinians." He described the UNGA process as a series of "word wars" waged by hundreds of diplomats "shut away in subterranean committee rooms," "shifting a comma here, changing an adjective there." He also pointed out that "when resolutions were contested last year, the majority sided with the United

States only 18.5 percent of the time" and that even when Western resolutions were passed, they were first watered down by Third World representatives. "But," he concluded wryly, "the human race will be expressing a new collective wish, although a bit ambiguously. That is how the United Nations makes progress."[2]

One particular issue may explain why the *NYT* had developed an animus towards the UN. In the 1980s, when the Cold War was still ongoing, the Arab states, with the support of the Soviet Union, passed a series of resolutions against Israel. Some were fair and balanced, calling on Israel to withdraw from the Palestinian territories it had occupied illegally. These resolutions were in conformity with international law. Others were unfair and unbalanced. A famous resolution tabled by the Arab states declared that "Zionism is a form of racism and racial discrimination." It was adopted by the UNGA in 1975 with a vote of 72 in favour and 35 opposed.

This resolution provoked huge outrage (and justifiably so) among the American Jewish community. Hence, the *NYT* coverage of the UN also became very critical. Singapore had to walk a fine line in its voting on resolutions on the Middle East. On the one hand, as a small state, we had to defend the principles of international law. Therefore, we couldn't condone the illegal occupation of Palestinian territory. On the other hand, since Israel had generously helped Singapore to build its armed forces, we couldn't support any resolutions that questioned the right of Israel to exist. To maintain this balance, I developed close personal relations with both the Palestinian ambassador to the UN, Zuhdi Labib Terzi, and the Israeli ambassador to the UN, Benjamin (Bibi) Netanyahu, who went on to serve several terms as the PM of Israel after he left New York.

In November 1986, Singapore took the bold step of inviting the Israeli president at the time, Chaim Herzog, to visit Singapore. Since none of our three Muslim-dominated neighbours had established diplomatic relations with or recognised the state of Israel, this visit by Herzog led to demonstrations in Malaysia and Indonesia. (Brunei also lodged a diplomatic protest.) Given the fierce anti-Israel public opinion in these capitals, especially in KL, one Palestinian ambassador in our region, Ahmad Al-Farra, who was based in KL, publicly criticised Singapore for hosting President Herzog and made disparaging remarks about President Wee Kim Wee.

The Singapore Foreign Ministry told me to raise Ambassador Al-Farra's criticisms with the Palestinian ambassador to the UN, Terzi. Since Terzi was a friend of mine, he listened sympathetically to me. He agreed with my legal point that Singapore had a sovereign right to host the head of state of a country it was friendly with. Terzi told me that he would persuade his leader, Chairman Yasser Arafat, to rectify the situation. To my absolute astonishment, Arafat did so. He said, "We do not approve, in any way, any disparaging reference to the President of Singapore whatever his position on political issues. We respect the sovereignty of Singapore and its right to receive or reject any message from any source including a message from the Palestine Liberation Organisation. We do not permit any one of our representatives to make slighting comments about the President of Singapore." The Singaporean government was equally astonished. I learned that PM Lee Kuan Yew was particularly impressed. We, of course, publicised this statement by Arafat. Undoubtedly, it embarrassed the Malaysian government that while it had protested the visit of the Israeli president to Singapore, the leader of the Palestinian people, Chairman Arafat, had reaffirmed the sovereign right of Singapore to receive anyone.

Lee Kuan Yew was equally impressed by what Bibi Netanyahu, the Israeli ambassador to the UN, once told me in private. Since the Israeli government was not recognised by many Third World governments in the 1980s, their ambassadors would not attend a dinner with Bibi. Anne and I decided to invite just Bibi Netanyahu and his wife, Fleur, to dinner at our residence in New York. We had a good dinner as a foursome. After dinner, we opened all the windows of our apartment so that Bibi could enjoy his cigar and liqueur. He was quite relaxed by then. This gave me the courage to pose an uncomfortable question. I shared with him one undeniable demographic statistic: the population of Israel was 4.2 million, while the total population of the Arab countries was just under 200 million. I asked Bibi how long 4 million people could fight 200 million people. He paused, took a few puffs of his cigar, and then replied, "This is why we have a stranglehold on the US Congress." This fact was, of course, well known. Any reasonable observer knew this. Still, Lee Kuan Yew was impressed by Bibi's candour.

Diplomatic moments like this enhanced my career in the 1980s. These successes must have gone to my head because they didn't prepare me for one of the biggest bumps in the road that I would experience in my career. Since I was doing well in my work, Minister Dhanabalan approached me and asked if I would consider a career in politics. Without making any promises, he said that I would be given a senior position in government if I accepted the invitation. After discussing the invitation with Anne, I decided to accept it.

Even though it seemed to be a done deal, I had to go through the bureaucratic procedures. I dutifully filled out the application to become a member of the PAP. Then I was asked to fly to Singapore to attend a series of interviews. Since I was based in New York, all my interviews were crammed into a few days. The initial interviews went well. The first formal interview with the committee chaired by Lim Kim San went well. He was very friendly. Similarly, my meeting with Goh Chok Tong, who was then the first DPM and minister of defence, went well. However, my meeting with Brig Gen Lee Hsien Loong, who was then the minister of trade and industry, went less well. Unfortunately, my meeting with him was scheduled just before I was supposed to attend a lecture by DPM Goh Chok Tong. Since I did not want to be late for the talk, I may have inadvertently given Minister Lee the impression that I was in a hurry to leave. This was possibly a serious mistake.

Since most of my one-on-one meetings had gone well, none of them prepared me for the shelling I received when I went into the final interview, chaired by PM Lee Kuan Yew and held in the Cabinet room of the Istana. Since I had been asked to apply, I naturally expected a friendly welcome by this committee. In the hour I must have spent in this interview, only one man spoke: Lee. All his questions were hostile. Although I can't remember most of them, I remember one vividly: "Why don't you have any friends?" This question puzzled me. I rattled off a long list of friends. This didn't impress him, and the hostile questioning continued. Since PM Lee could be remarkably fierce when he chose to take a hostile attitude, I was clearly rattled. I may not have given the most coherent answers. I may also have been unwise in reacting angrily to some of his hostile questions. This episode reminded me of the shelling he had given a Singaporean ambassador whom he accused of localitis, when I was the notetaker. This time, I was the target of the bruising encounter.

At the end of the interview, it was clear that I had been rejected for a job that I had been asked to apply for. I never formally received any letter from the PAP that my application for party membership had been rejected, nor did anyone formally tell me that I had failed the interview process. But I would have to have been a fool not to realise that the whole process of joining politics had been killed at the final interview. Mr Dhanabalan did informally indicate to me that no career in politics awaited me. As far as I know, only one other person went through this same experience: Ho Kwon Ping, who served as chairman of the board of the Singapore Management University from 1997 to 2023.

The kind interpretation of my rejection was that I was too independent a soul to accept the tight party discipline of the PAP, one of the most disciplined political parties in the world. The less generous interpretation was that I was too self-centred and not a "team player." Some years after my failure to be accepted into the party, I asked Goh Keng Swee whether I had failed because I wasn't perceived as a "team player."

New York, New York

Surprisingly, he was very critical of the party he had formed and disparaged the emphasis on "team playing." I still remember his exact words to me: "Team playing means you scratch my back and I will scratch your back." Dr Goh's son, Goh Kian Chee, had been asked to provide a letter of recommendation for me. In the letter, he may have indirectly confirmed that I wasn't a team player when he said, "Unlike most Ministers in the Cabinet, Kishore will speak his mind and tell the truth." It's probably accurate to say that at that time, the PAP valued conformity and loyalty very highly. Its leaders had fought real political struggles to get into office: from the Japanese occupation to the communists, from the merger with Malaysia to independence, it had all required great discipline and considerable courage. The stakes were high, so that generation was very strict in what it demanded from its party members.

The transition between the political generations had begun while I was away from Singapore, and as a result, I wasn't fully aware of it. Gradually, the first generation of political leaders had been stepping down from their ministerial positions in the 1980s: Lim Kim San and Toh Chin Chye in 1981, Eddie Barker in 1983, Goh Keng Swee and Howe Yoon Chong in 1984, and S. Rajaratnam in 1988. Anyone who knows anything about them knows that they were very tough individuals who would not be intimidated by a major political fight. These strong street-fighting skills were exactly what Singapore needed, as it had to deal with major external and internal political challenges.

By the 1980s, all the major political struggles around independence had been won. Since the Barisan Sosialis[3] had walked out of the Parliament in 1966, there were no longer any major internal political schisms. Instead, the focus was on economic growth and development, combined with a focus on improving social living standards. The skill sets needed for fighting for political independence were different from those needed for nation building. This was why many first-generation leaders in the Third World failed. Leaders like Sukarno, Sirimavo Bandaranaike, Kenneth Kaunda, and Kwame Nkrumah were great freedom fighters. However, most of them were not good nation builders. This is one of the reasons why Lee Kuan Yew was such an unusual leader for his time. He was a great freedom fighter, and few could match his political and oratorical skills. Yet he was also a good nation builder. And he carefully chose nation builders as members of the second-generation team.

So my nonselection for the PAP may have indicated that my skill set was not appropriate for the times. But at the time when I was rejected, I couldn't really fathom it, and I simply saw the entire episode as a great personal failure.

I did not dwell on my humiliation. I remembered my mother's resilience. None of my troubles could match those that she had experienced. I did not allow my spirits to sag. It helped that in a very short time, Anne became convinced, as she is to this day, that one of the best things to happen in my life was that I never went into politics. She's convinced that I would have quickly become miserable.

There was another wonderful event to distract me from any rueful looking back. On August 15, 1986, our eldest son, Kishore Richard Mahbubani, was born in Mt Sinai Hospital in New York. The only other time I had experienced a childbirth was when I had cheered on Gretchen to deliver a baby, knowing full well that the baby wouldn't survive. In August 1986, I experienced the birth of an entirely healthy baby, with ten fingers and ten toes. His birthday turned out to be an auspicious day, as it coincided with a number of religious festivals: a Muslim holy day (the Day of 'Arafah) and a Roman Catholic holy day (the feast of the Assumption of the Blessed Virgin Mary). Coincidentally, August 15 is also India's Independence Day. Hence, my mother wanted us to name our son "Bharat," a synonym for India in Hindi. Metaphorically, Bharat also means "motherland." (Incidentally, PM Narendra Modi is trying to change the name of India to Bharat. If my mother were alive, she would have approved of this.) Fortunately, Anne and I had already decided in advance that if we had a boy, he would be named Kishore Richard.

A month later, the UNGA opened. As usual, Mr Rajaratnam, who was then senior minister, came to the UNGA with his wife, Piroska Rajaratnam (who was of Hungarian origin). As usual, Anne and I hosted them to dinner at our home. Since I was still ecstatic about the birth of our baby, I had the baby on my shoulder throughout the dinner. Piroska frowned in disapproval and said babies shouldn't be present at formal dinners. Fortunately, the minister of finance, Richard Hu, was also at the dinner. Like me, he had become a father at a late age. He fully understood my attachment to the baby and encouraged me to hold him.

The seven years I spent in the United States (from 1982 to 1989) proved to be an intense learning experience for me and contained many lessons that would stay with me for the rest of my life. One big lesson was, of course, the ambivalent relationship between the US government (especially the Reagan administration) and the UN. In theory, the US government was committed to stronger multilateral institutions. In practice, it was always trying to weaken them, especially by starving them of funding. A constant complaint of the United States was that the UN had a fat, inefficient, and bloated bureaucracy. This was exactly what George Shultz (a good friend of Lee Kuan Yew) said to Foreign Minister Dhanabalan when the US and Singaporean delegations had their regular pre-UNGA consultations in New York. Yet Shultz, an honest and decent man, blushed when Dhanabalan, with his usual directness, asked him why, if the United States wanted a strong bureaucracy, it always selected weak individuals to serve as UN secretary-generals. This was an undeniable truth. It was also an undeniable truth that the two great superpowers of the day at that time, the United States and Soviet Union, disagreed on almost everything but agreed that the UN should always have a weak secretary-general. Yet another valuable lesson I learned was that some undeniable truths are also unmentionable in public. While everyone in the UN knew that the two superpowers agreed that only spineless individuals should be selected for secretary-general, no one could state this truth publicly.

The opposing views of Singapore and the United States on the UN aren't surprising. As a small state, Singapore is protected by multilateral rules and institutions. As a great power, the United States is constrained by them. Hence, while Singapore wants to strengthen the UN, the United States wants to weaken it. This clearly means that the United States and Singapore start from opposing positions. Yet despite these opposing positions, Lee Kuan Yew always found ways and means to win political dividends from the United States, as he believed strongly that Singapore should have stronger ties with the United States than its neighbours, especially Malaysia and Indonesia, did.

The first time Lee leaned towards the United States was in our response to the decision of the Reagan administration to invade Grenada on October 25, 1983. The UN Security Council (UNSC) was convened on November 2, 1983. Though I was based in Washington, DC, I was sent to New York to join Tommy Koh's delegation. I sat behind Tommy Koh when he delivered his usual eloquent but black-and-white speech declaring (correctly) that the US invasion of Grenada was a violation of the principles of the UN Charter and of international law. He said,

> Barbados, Jamaica, the United States and the Member States of the Organisation of East Caribbean States are friends of my country. It is extremely convenient for me to acquiesce in what they have done or to remain silent. To do so will, in the long run, undermine the moral and legal significance of the principles which my country regard as a shield. This is why we must put our adherence to principle above friendship. This is why we cannot condone the action of our friends in Grenada.[4]

Yet, as I was to learn from American officials later, when Lee Kuan Yew subsequently met with US leaders, he said that he would personally have taken a more nuanced position on the Grenada invasion. Clearly, the priority of Lee Kuan Yew was to keep his special ties with the Reagan administration intact.

The second time was when the Reagan administration decided to leave the UN Educational, Scientific and Cultural Organization (UNESCO). The United States declared that it was quitting UNESCO because of the agency's "repeated management failures" and "misguided policies and programs."[5] However, as the *Washington Post* reported at the time, this departure was seen as being "motivated more by the Reagan administration's conservative ideology than by UNESCO management problems." The United States had accused UNESCO of "[promoting] 'Soviet-inspired' world disarmament in some of its education programs, boosting the needs of states over the rights of individuals and demanding a 'new international economic order' critical of free-market capitalism." In addition, "Poor, Third World nations [had] used UNESCO forums to vote sanctions against Israel, praise revolutionary organizations and to denounce and routinely outvote the United States."[6] At the time, Singapore's voting positions on the Israel-Palestine issue—and, indeed, on most UN issues—were more in line with those of other members of the NAM than with those of the Reagan administration. Nonetheless, after the Reagan administration left UNESCO, only two other countries, Singapore and Britain, followed suit. Since I was the ambassador to the UN, I was asked to help draft the Singaporean statement explaining our departure. The public statement, delivered by David Marshall, who was then our permanent representative to UNESCO, was that we were leaving the organisation because of "the high level of its annual membership assessment." He offered the explanation that as a small country, "Singapore must practice economy in its international activities."[7] I contributed to this statement with little enthusiasm since I knew this wasn't the real reason we were leaving. Our departure together with that of the United States won us some useful political dividends from the Reagan administration. These were far more useful for Singapore than any loss we suffered from leaving UNESCO (in any case, we rejoined UNESCO in 2007, as did Britain in 1997).

The close ties that Lee Kuan Yew developed with the Reagan administration proved to be useful for both the external and internal interests of Singapore. Abroad, they expanded the geopolitical space of Singapore vis-à-vis our neighbours. We had more influence and room to manoeuvre on the international stage than our geographical size should have allowed. At home, it gave Lee Kuan Yew a free hand to manage the political transition of Singapore to a new PM without too much interference from external sources—especially the United States, which was promoting the export of democracy, even under the conservative right-wing Republican administration of Reagan. Traditionally, it was the Democratic administrations that promoted democracy and human rights, as exemplified by the Carter administration, which had preceded Reagan. It's well-known that Lee Kuan Yew had little respect for Jimmy Carter as president, as Carter was a human rights evangelist rather than a geopolitical realist. Lee Kuan Yew viewed Carter as a naive do-gooder. He was astounded on reading Carter's book *Why Not the Best?*, in which Carter recounted having been punished for taking a penny out of the collection box as a boy. "I said, why does the man do that? Having done it, how does telling the world that he was a petty thief help?" He told American journalist Tom Plate that Carter was the worst American president he had met. "There's something not quite right about him," he said. Commenting on Carter's malaise speech of 1979, he added, "Your job as a leader is to inspire and to galvanize, not to share your distraught thoughts. You make your people dispirited."

By contrast, Lee Kuan Yew always praised the contributions of Ronald Reagan. He told the president, "The Reagan years will surely be a noticeable landmark in American history. You have restored American leadership in the maintenance of a just and equitable world order."[8] He also told *Fortune* magazine, "I like him. . . . He is just a great President. He feels good about America, and he is able to transmit his feelings to the American people and make them feel good, make them feel upbeat and make them achieve."[9]

Internationally, two events caused friction between the Reagan administration and Singapore. The first was the arrests of the alleged "Marxists" in 1987, known as Operation Spectrum. Many of the people arrested were not the Chinese-speaking members of the Communist Party of Malaya. Instead, most of them were English-educated and members of the relatively affluent middle classes of Singapore. Many of them were professionals in areas like law and academia. The arrest of the "Marxists" was one of the most controversial chapters in Singapore's history, as some government ministers have admitted. For example, Tharman Shanmugaratnam has said publicly, "Although I had no access to state intelligence, from what I knew of them, most were social activists but were not out to subvert the system." It is widely believed that S. Dhanabalan left the Cabinet because of his discomfort with the way the PAP dealt with the incident. I was not involved in any way (unlike the time my good friend, Jeffery Sng, was arrested on February 17, 1977, and I wrote a letter in his defence). The episode led to criticisms by members of the US Congress, who wrote a letter to S. Jayakumar (who was then the minister of home affairs) urging "that those arrested be either charged promptly or released, and that any trials that do take place be held publicly and in conformity with international standards."[10]

The second major event that affected ties between Singapore and the Reagan administration was the request by the Singaporean government to the US government to withdraw a US diplomat, Mason Hendrickson, in May 1988. The government explained that it was seeking Hendrickson's withdrawal because he "had involved himself in Singapore's domestic politics" by "[arranging] meetings with disaffected lawyers in order to attack the Singapore government, and [instigating] them to stand for elections against the government." He had also implied during one such meeting that he would be able to secure funding for their election campaigns.[11] By any standard, this request was a serious matter. Indeed, Singapore had rarely made such a request.

This call for the removal of a US diplomat caused a crisis in US-Singaporean relations. The United States insisted that Hendrickson had done nothing wrong and requested the withdrawal of Robert Chua, a diplomat of Hendrickson's rank, from the Singaporean Embassy in Washington, DC. Then DPM Ong Teng Cheong, who was also the secretary-general of the National Trades Union Congress (NTUC), led a four-thousand-strong union rally protesting foreign interference in Singapore.[12] At the rally, he said that "the Hendrickson affair confirms our assessment of U.S. bureaucracy—sneaky, arrogant, confused and untrustworthy," and called Chua's tit-for-tat removal "childish and unbecoming of a superpower." After the rally, union members chanted protest slogans from buses as they were driven past the US Embassy.[13]

Both Tommy Koh, who was the Singaporean ambassador to Washington, DC, and I (as the then Singaporean ambassador to the UN) were recalled to Singapore to help the country manage the crisis. When Lee Kuan Yew addressed the Singaporean Parliament on June 1, 1988, after four days of heated parliamentary debate on the Hendrickson affair, he said that he had decided to recall Tommy Koh and me "to explain and help [him] understand why they thought American officials have acted in this way," as he was perplexed, bewildered, and nonplussed by their interference.[14] In his address, he proposed that a neutral committee of international law experts be appointed to determine whether Hendrickson had indeed interfered in Singapore's internal affairs and said that he would apologise to the US State Department if such a committee decided in Hendrickson's favour. However, the United States did not take him up on this suggestion.

I spent more time with Lee Kuan Yew over this episode than any other period of conversation I had with him. In 1988, he was sixty-five years old. He had been in office as PM since

1959, almost thirty years. He was probably at his peak as a politician. His power in Singapore was unchallenged, as all his peers had left office. Additionally, his international status had never been higher. Watching him play politics at that time was like watching Tiger Woods or Roger Federer when they were unbeatable.

One of the great gaps in Singapore's history is that the extraordinary skills of Lee Kuan Yew, both as a domestic politician and as an international statesman, have not been properly studied. It was impossible during his lifetime since he was an overwhelming and intimidating presence. Since he left the political scene, and since his passing in 2015, a proper political history of Singapore has not been written. As a result, many young Singaporeans have no idea quite how remarkable a leader Lee Kuan Yew was.

One practical way of remedying this deficiency would be to adopt an American form of learning about leadership: the case study. The Harvard Business School and the Harvard Kennedy School (HKS), for example, have brilliant case studies that document how extraordinary leadership was displayed from time to time in US institutions. Singapore should prepare a similar case study on the Mason Hendrickson affair.

One of the lessons I learned from this episode (especially since I participated in it) was that Lee Kuan Yew always had multiple objectives when he launched a political initiative. I could see that he was a political juggler of the greatest skill. This is why I believe that Lee Kuan Yew is, by far, the greatest politician I have dealt with. He could well go down as one of the greatest politicians of all time if and when a comprehensive political history of Singapore is written. As I will be discussing his multiple agendas in the Hendrickson episode, I must emphasise that he never shared these agendas with me directly. Instead, I worked them out personally, sometimes years later, after carefully analysing and reflecting on his actions.

Lee Kuan Yew managed complexity well. On the surface, he had only two obvious goals. The first was to defend Singapore's sovereignty in accordance with international law. According to Article 41 of the Vienna Convention on Diplomatic Relations, which both the United States and Singapore have ratified, diplomatic agents "have a duty not to interfere in the internal affairs of that State."[15] The second was to show that Singapore, as a small state, wasn't afraid to stand up to a great power like the United States. Tommy Koh confirmed to me that "Lee Kuan Yew took advantage of the Hendrickson case to demonstrate to the world that Singapore is not an ally or stooge of the US. The week-long debate in Parliament, and Ong Teng Cheong's protest march to the US Embassy, were unprecedented." Both these dimensions of the Hendrickson episode were real.

However, beneath the surface, many other dimensions of this episode were equally important. When a leader of a small state takes on a great power, it's seen as a David-versus-Goliath fight. All the admiration goes to David, not Goliath. Hence, Lee Kuan Yew's political standing in Singapore, which was already high, increased and became even more unchallengeable. Why was this important? The year was 1988. The political succession of Singapore was approaching: in two years, Goh Chok Tong would be made PM and Lee Hsien Loong (Lee

Kuan Yew's son) DPM. (In Singapore, the president appoints the leader of the political party holding the majority of the seats in Parliament to be the PM. Functionally, this means that the PM is selected by his or her peers.) Political successions are inherently tricky. To ensure that everything went well, everyone had to understand that the will of Lee Kuan Yew couldn't be thwarted. The Hendrickson episode reinforced this point.

Equally importantly, Singapore was a small state sandwiched between two large neighbours: Indonesia and Malaysia. Since the dawn of human history, larger neighbours have tried to impose their will on their smaller neighbours. According to the realist school of international relations, it would have been perfectly reasonable for both Malaysia and Indonesia to try to impose their will on Singapore. However, the success of Lee Kuan Yew and Singapore in standing up to the most powerful lion in the jungle, that is, an even greater power like the United States, significantly reduced the temptation for other predators to bully Singapore. In short, Lee Kuan Yew significantly increased the geopolitical space of Singapore vis-à-vis its neighbours by standing up to the United States. Of course, none of this was expressed publicly, but I'm sure it was part of the strategy behind this event.

However, even while both the Singaporean public and Singapore's neighbours watched a brave David stand up to Goliath, they were not aware that Goliath (the United States) had no vested interest in squashing David (Singapore). Instead, the United States wanted Singapore to remain strong. Why? The larger geopolitical context was the Cold War. The United States was still preoccupied with the Soviet Union, and Singapore had been very useful in this fight. Hence, while Lee Kuan Yew was taking a risk in standing up to the United States, he calculated privately that it would be a small risk.

Lee Kuan Yew's strong network of close friends in Washington, DC, including (as documented earlier) Ronald Reagan, George Shultz, and Henry Kissinger (who remained influential behind the scenes), was able to reassure the US government that Lee Kuan Yew was in no way inherently anti-American. US leaders were shrewd enough to realise that Lee Kuan Yew was expelling Hendrickson for domestic political reasons. Hence, as Lee Kuan Yew predicted, the Reagan administration didn't respond strongly to Singapore's move, even though it was an insult to the United States. The requested withdrawal of Robert Chua was a token retaliation.

Lee Kuan Yew told Tommy and me that he had called us back to Singapore to help him understand why the United States believed that it should try to improve the political system of Singapore. The answer we gave him was an obvious one: Americans believe that they have a moral responsibility to spread the values of democracy. They also believe that democracies create better societies. When the United States tried to improve Singapore's democratic structures by having Hendrickson encourage dissatisfied lawyers to stand for election, it was doing to Singapore what it had done to many other countries. This type of action was clearly not unique to Singapore.

It was a real privilege to spend many hours conversing with Lee Kuan Yew on American politics and the state of our world. Lee Kuan Yew was warm and genial as he listened to us. I retain powerful visual memories of Tommy Koh and me sitting in front of Lee Kuan Yew's desk in his Istana office. At one stage, we discussed why the United States supported press freedom. During this discussion, I remember taking a small risk when I suggested that the Americans were justified in thinking that the Singaporean *Straits Times* was more like the *Pravda* and *Izvestia* of the Soviet Union than the *NYT* or *Washington Post* of the United States. He could have reacted angrily; instead, he listened and smiled.

This was one of the important secrets I learned about Lee Kuan Yew. While he didn't react well to public criticisms (and often refuted them strongly), he was a very good listener in private. Hence, while he wouldn't have liked to hear the suggestion that the *Straits Times* was perceived to be a government-run newspaper, he was keen to find out how Singapore was perceived. He never wanted us to sugarcoat negative feedback in private. He was strong and confident enough to hear it all.

What made these conversations with Lee Kuan Yew even more remarkable is that they were taking place less than a year after I had been excoriated by him during my interview in the PAP selection process. As these two encounters took place not far apart, I was able to see both sides of him. He could be a fierce and intimidating presence, and he could also be a warm and genial person. These experiences reminded me of a story once told to me in private by Yeoh Ghim Seng, who was the speaker of the Singaporean Parliament from 1970 to 1988.

In his later years, Prof Yeoh suffered from cancer. One of his wishes was to see New York. His daughter, Ng Saw Kheng, granted his wish and brought him to New York, where I met him, in the 1980s. There, Prof Yeoh described the Lee Kuan

Yew he had known in his younger days, probably in the early 1960s. He said that Lee Kuan Yew was a great party animal. He loved to drink and socialise with his political colleagues in the evenings. However, he was also a strict disciplinarian. Prof Yeoh said that if he met Lee Kuan Yew the morning after a party, it was taboo to mention the party. Anyone who tried to recall the merry evening of the night before would receive murderous looks from Lee Kuan Yew. Play was play. Work was work.

When I got to know Lee Kuan Yew well in the 1980s, I never saw him at play. He had given up golf by then (even though he was a very competitive golfer in his younger days). Instead, when I travelled with him, I only ever saw him at work (although he exercised a great deal). Even though he was obsessed with his work, there's no doubt that he enjoyed it. He loved the game of geopolitics and spent all day and night constantly absorbing information so that he could stay on top of it.

I shouldn't give the impression that I spent a lot of time with Lee Kuan Yew. I am speaking about him at length in this chapter only to explain that I learned a lot from him, directly and indirectly. At the same time, sadly, little has yet been written about Lee Kuan Yew that captures his immense political genius. Hence, I hope that my few observations will spark greater interest in learning more about this remarkable man who did so much to shape the future of Singapore. It was a real privilege to spend time with him, even when I was verbally battered by him, as I was from time to time.

He was always a tough taskmaster. Former civil servants (and some politicians as well) sometimes traded stories about how we had been figuratively "beaten up" by Lee Kuan Yew in the course of our work. Among those of my generation, it has even become a badge of honour to say, "I was beaten up by Lee Kuan Yew for . . ." There's no doubt that Lee Kuan Yew could be truly brutal when he put someone down, as I experienced a few times. But he was not petty or vindictive. When the job was done and the scolding was over, life would go back to normal.

As I got to know him better, I began to realise that I had a small competitive advantage in dealing with him. Most Singaporeans were reluctant to speak out in front of him. For unknowable reasons, I never hesitated to do so. I recall attending some dinners at the Istana where I would be seated at the end of the table, as I was the most junior person in the room. When the conversations began, the foreign guests would join in enthusiastically. Most of the Singaporeans at the table would wisely and prudently remain silent. Foolishly, I would join the conversation.

Looking back now, I am still not sure what gave me the confidence to do so. Was it my training in philosophy, which had taught me to raise questions on any subject that was being discussed? Was it my training in diplomacy, which had taught me to have conversations with anyone under any circumstances? Given my childhood background, and the poverty and dysfunctional family I had experienced, confidence in myself was the last thing that I should have developed. Yet even by the time I went to university at the age of eighteen, I had developed the confidence to speak out. Was it nature or nurture? The simple answer is that I don't know. I only know that I have been lucky in developing this confidence.

One other reason for my psychological confidence was that I had developed a close relationship with the other two key founding fathers of Singapore, Goh Keng Swee and S. Rajaratnam. I had many intense conversations with them over the years, and they always seemed interested in my views, which made me feel that I had something meaningful to say. The two of them couldn't have been more different. Dr Goh was, like Lee Kuan Yew, a formidable and overwhelming presence. He could be gruff, stern, and intimidating. By contrast, S. Rajaratnam was a "soft" presence with a constant smile on his lips and, more importantly, in his eyes. We rarely felt intimidated by him.

Even though Dr Goh could be gruff and intimidating, I was able to see the "softer" side of him, as I often attended dinners or social events with him; his son, Goh Kian Chee; and his daughter-in-law, Tan Siok Sun. I got to know Dr Goh well enough to invite him to attend my wedding with Anne in New Jersey in March 1985. He was the only former government minister to attend my wedding. Dr Goh and I also had good one-on-one lunches when he visited New York in the mid-1980s.

I had many more conversations with S. Rajaratnam in New York from 1984 to 1988, as he came to New York for the opening of the UNGA every September. We candidly discussed many subjects, including his fellow Cabinet members. Since he was an inveterate book lover and bought many books each time he came to New York, I once asked him what books Lee Kuan Yew read. He guffawed and said, "Harry doesn't read any books, he only reads magazines." Indeed, Lee Kuan Yew read many contemporary journals and newspapers and was always up-to-date on the state of the world.

The only other minister who candidly discussed Lee Kuan Yew with me was S. Dhanabalan. He too would come to New York for the UNGA sessions. During one of these visits, we drove up to Connecticut to visit Yale University. As we were walking around the hallowed grounds of Yale, he asked me if we could arrange a fellowship for Lee Kuan Yew at Yale for a few months or years. I asked him why. He replied that the second generation of leaders would never know whether they were capable of running Singapore without Lee Kuan Yew as long as he was around and participating actively in the political scene of Singapore. That was a brave and insightful comment.

Clearly, my elevation to the post of Singaporean ambassador to the UN in August 1984 had raised my social and intellectual standing in the eyes of these Singaporean leaders. They felt comfortable discussing even sensitive subjects about Singaporean politics with me. To be fair, Dr Goh had shown this kind of candour much earlier. I remember having dinner with him not long after J. B. Jeyaretnam had a shock win over the PAP candidate in the Anson by-election on October 31, 1981. He asked me how the government would handle Mr Jeyaretnam in Parliament. I replied that my mother had told me that Lee Kuan Yew would go all out to "crush" Mr Jeyaretnam. Dr Goh guffawed when he heard this and said, "Your mother is politically brilliant. That's exactly what Harry will do." Indeed, this was exactly what happened.

Dr Goh also didn't hesitate to disparage ministers he didn't respect. Once, referring to a minister who had spent decades in the Cabinet, Dr Goh said to me, "Do you know what his job is?" I said that I didn't know. He told me, in his usual earthy fashion, "If we tell him to pull his pants down and sit on a hot stove, he will do so." That was his way of signalling to me that this minister wasn't a heavyweight in the Cabinet but was politically useful.

Some Singaporeans may be upset with these candid revelations about people who have, in one way or another, served Singapore honourably. Yet it's critical for Singaporeans to know that Singapore's exceptional success was due to the fact that its founding fathers were remarkably tough-minded—indeed, even brutal—in their analysis of people and situations. They were not softhearted in any way and would view with total scorn the culture of political correctness that has swept the world of Western politicians today. They belonged to the group who insisted on calling a spade "a bloody shovel." They didn't mince their words, and they believed that Singapore would suffer if its leaders engaged in self-deception. They were interested only in hard truths.

During the ten years when I went from being thirty-two to forty-two, my many close encounters with these three founding fathers, Lee Kuan Yew, Goh Keng Swee, and S. Rajaratnam, transformed my life. They fundamentally overturned my worldview. I went from being a "pacifist" (who was thrown out of the office of Goh Keng Swee) to a "hard-nosed realist" who saw that the world of international affairs was a jungle. Indulging in idealist fantasies could prove to be fatal for a small state like Singapore.

Two or three decades later, when I started to write books, many of the ideas they contained depended on what I had learned, consciously or unconsciously, from these three founding fathers. From them, I learned that geopolitics is an art, not a science. Yet they also followed some key principles. Their key goal for Singapore, as a small state, was always to create more geopolitical space between it and its two large neighbours, Malaysia and Indonesia. This would help to ensure that we were not bullied by them and that we could take independent foreign policy positions that differed from theirs, such as inviting the president of Israel to visit Singapore. To do so, we had to deliver exceptionally good domestic governance, which we did. In addition, we had to have closer ties with the great powers that mattered to our region. In the 1980s, US power was clearly the dominant force in our neighbourhood. Hence, despite the ups and downs in our relationship with the United States, we always remained closer to the United States than to any of our neighbours.

In theory, as a small state, Singapore should have stoutly defended the principle, firmly embedded in the UN Charter, that small states should not be invaded or occupied by their larger neighbours. Indeed, that is exactly what I did as ambassador to the UN. However, Dr Goh had little faith in these principles of international law. He believed that power was more important than principle. Indeed, one of Dr Goh's greatest achievements was to build up the Singapore Armed Forces into one of the strongest military forces in Southeast Asia.

The 1980s were a critical growth decade for Singapore. Our GDP went from US$11.9 billion in 1980 to US$36.14 billion in 1990.[16] Since I was posted to Washington, DC, from 1982 to 1984 and to New York from 1984 to 1989, I didn't experience this decade of growth personally. However, Anne and I were acutely aware that given Singapore's rapid growth, we had to rush if we were ever to buy a home there. When we came back to Singapore for five weeks in January 1987 for official consultations and a personal vacation with our six-month-old son, we went on a frantic house-hunting spree. Fortunately, I ran into one of my childhood Sindhi friends, Ramesh (Pancho) Kirpalani, whose father had been one of my father's bosses in High Street in the 1950s. Pancho was living in Frankel Estate. He told us that his neighbour, Gurcharan Singh, was keen to sell his house. As his asking price was exactly the same as our maximum budget, we wanted to purchase it immediately. Pancho, however, insisted on negotiating the price down, and with his help, we ended up paying 10 percent less than we had budgeted for. It proved to be our best investment ever. In 2022, this house is worth far more than we paid for it in 1987.

The climb up the property ladder in Singapore that we experienced with our purchase was also experienced by many other Singaporeans of my generation. Indeed, some of my friends and classmates were able to purchase several properties in the 1980s and 1990s. We were all fortunate that we could purchase our property at the right time.

As the 1980s drew to a close, I should have felt happy and satisfied with my life. The decade that had begun with a painful divorce ended with me happily married and with two wonderful children, as our daughter, Shelagh, was born in New York in 1988. My career had prospered, and I had been promoted several times up the Civil Service ladder.

On the surface, all looked serene. Yet once more, I began to feel that my career might have peaked. Many of my fellow ASEAN ambassadors had gone on to assume bigger jobs after their postings to New York. By contrast, when I left New York in January 1989 and was appointed deputy secretary (DS) at the MFA, it was clearly not a promotion. My boss, Permanent Secretary Peter Chan, was exactly the same age as me. Indeed, we had both received the President's Scholarship in the same year and had both graduated with first-class honours from NUS. Even though we were the same age, he had already served (with distinction) as permanent secretary from 1983. By contrast, when I returned home in early 1989, six years later, there was no sign that I would be appointed as permanent secretary anytime soon.

The physical move back from New York to Singapore proved to be a painful experience. The MFA had still not become very good at facilitating family moves. Anne and I returned home with an eighteen-month-old son and a six-month-old daughter. We weren't sensible enough to move into a hotel for a few days to make the transition easier. Instead, we moved straight into our home in Frankel Estate, which supposedly had basic furniture and had been cleaned after the departure of the previous tenants. However, when we arrived, it didn't even have a refrigerator, and cockroaches were skittering around the dirty dustcloths left on the floor. Although it was a busy time for me, three decades later, one of my strongest memories was of my painful experience of trying to buy a secondhand refrigerator for same-day delivery from a dingy shop on East Coast Road. It took us several months to make the house liveable.

At the beginning of my posting to New York in 1984, I had felt elated at the extraordinary promotion I had received. By contrast, I remember feeling somewhat depressed on returning home in early 1989. Things didn't look promising for me. Fortunately, my fears proved to be ill-founded.

CHAPTER 9

The Sweet Life of a CEO

On September 13, 1988, Wong Kan Seng was appointed minister of foreign affairs to succeed S. Dhanabalan. Although Dhanabalan had been very supportive of me throughout his stint as minister of foreign affairs from 1980 to 1988, I knew Kan Seng much better from the time we were both poor undergraduates who took the bus regularly to study at the Bukit Timah campus of NUS. We used to debate and discuss in the crowded bus while holding on to the ceiling straps. We studied different subjects—he did English literature—but we connected.

I also got to know George Yeo when he served as minister of state for foreign affairs from September 1988 to November 1990. He was six years younger than I and was widely perceived as a rising star. When I went on a trip with George to attend the NAM Summit in Belgrade in September 1989 (i.e., when Yugoslavia was still intact), I realised why he was so special.

During the visit to Belgrade, we were given a guided tour of tourist sites. A local guide took us to see some ramparts and explained how the medieval kingdom of Hungary had fought off the Ottoman Empire in the fifteenth century. The guide was very proud of this history. Yet, immediately after the guide had completed his historical account, George picked up the story and proceeded to give more details of what happened during this period. I still recall the expression on the local guide's face. His jaw dropped on seeing a foreigner display so much knowledge of his country's history. I marvelled that George, who was an engineer by training, had such a deep understanding of history. This first encounter was the start of a lifelong friendship, as our paths crossed several times in subsequent decades. He was also later responsible for appointing me as the founding director of the Civil Service College (CSC).

The year 1990 was also critical for Singapore, as it witnessed the transition from one PM, Lee Kuan Yew, to another, Goh Chok Tong, on November 28. It was the first handover of the PM's office since Singapore's independence in 1965, as Lee had been continuously reelected ever since. His departure from office marked the passing of the baton by Singapore's founding generation of leaders: it was time for a new era. Remarkably, the political mood was absolutely calm; there was a widely shared sense that Singapore would continue to prioritise political stability. Thus, very little changed.

Perhaps because the political situation was so calm, with Singapore set on a path of steady economic growth at home and the end of the Cold War tensions abroad, I managed (somewhat unusually) to secure a "sabbatical" from the Singaporean Civil Service in 1991–1992. After doing some research, I discovered a programme run by the Center for International Affairs (CFIA) at Harvard University. The CFIA encouraged midcareer diplomats to come spend a year at Harvard. The fees were high, as were the living costs, and the CFIA provided no financial support. Since Anne and our three children accompanied me to Harvard, it proved to be an expensive year overseas for us, although I continued to draw a salary. The program served as a "cash cow" for Harvard. During their one year at Harvard, CFIA fellows had the opportunity to enrol in any course if the professor admitted them. Apart from an occasional seminar among CFIA fellows, the CFIA essentially left the fellows alone, although it did organise two overseas trips: one to Canada and the other to Brussels to meet EU officials.

Thirty years later, I am still conflicted about the experience of my one year at Harvard. On the one hand, I was repelled by the enormous arrogance of the Harvard community. Even though the CFIA programme promised to facilitate encounters with Harvard professors, it provided little assistance to this end. Since I had decided to write a monograph on Japan, I requested an appointment with a leading professor on Japan, Susan J. Pharr. I made the request in September. I got an appointment two months later, in November. On the appointed date,

I arrived at her office at 3:45 p.m., fifteen minutes before the scheduled time of 4 p.m. I was kept waiting. If my memory is correct, I was admitted to her office at 4:20 p.m. I began to explain my project on Japan to her. Before I could finish my explanation, she looked at her watch at 4:30 p.m. sharp and said that she had another appointment. After waiting two months, I got nothing from her.

I discovered that I was not the only one to experience this dismissive attitude. A young American journalist, Marcus Brauchli, had come to spend a year as a Nieman Fellow on a sabbatical from the *Wall Street Journal*. He asked to see Robert Reich, who later became Bill Clinton's secretary of labour. When he spoke to Reich's secretary, Marcus initially got the same response I did: he would have to wait two months to see Reich. However, Marcus thought faster than I did. He immediately told the secretary that once he completed his Nieman Fellowship, he would go on to become the *Wall Street Journal*'s Asia correspondent in Hong Kong. The secretary dutifully conveyed this information, and Marcus got an appointment to see Reich the very next day. And he got to spend an entire hour with Reich.

The contrast in our experiences was telling. It demonstrated the power that journalists, even junior journalists, had within the American system. In theory, a former ambassador to the UN should have enjoyed a certain prestige, and my experience should have been of interest. Yet this meant nothing to Harvard professors, who realised that getting their ideas across to the American media was more important. Second, I discovered that fellows were neither man nor beast within the Harvard community. Students interacted regularly with their professors, and the professors, of course, fraternised with each other as members of a community. Meanwhile, the fellows fell between the cracks and were essentially regarded as a nuisance.

After I completed my Harvard tour in June 1992, I wrote a brutally honest report that declared that even though CFIA Fellows paid the same fees as students (or perhaps more), they were given no privileged access to the faculty or the Harvard community. I also hinted that many CFIA fellows were acutely aware that this one-year "fellowship" was essentially a boondoggle in which they were given one year off for rest and relaxation. In theory, the fellows were expected to submit a paper at the end of their fellowship. However, as far as I could tell, no one read these papers or paid any attention to them. My frankness proved to be a great mistake, as the PSC took the CFIA programme off the list of offerings for midcareer civil servants. Some of my contemporaries complained to me that I had destroyed the possibility of other Singaporean civil servants taking advantage of this programme.

In retrospect, it was a tactical error to write such a negative report. It was written in the immediate aftermath of the course, when my sense of missed opportunities was probably at its highest. Later, I came to realise that the year at Harvard had generated many long-term dividends. Unlike most of that year's CFIA fellows, I tried to publish as many articles as possible, and I turned my year-end essay for the CFIA into a paper for publication in *Foreign Policy* magazine. It was published with the title "Japan Adrift" in the autumn 1992 issue. In addition, I published two other essays, "The West and the Rest" in the summer 1992 issue of the *National Interest* and "Pol Pot: The Paradox of Moral Correctness" in *Studies in Conflict & Terrorism* in 1993. Looking back, it seems clear that my writing career probably received a significant jump-start from the year of relaxed reading and reflection at Harvard. Equally importantly, I happened to be at Harvard during a critical turning point in Western history when the Soviet Union spectacularly collapsed on December 25, 1991. Quite naturally, it led to a surge of triumphalist spirit, best expressed in Fukuyama's essay "The End of History?" two years earlier.

Many leading Harvard minds were convinced that with the collapse of the Soviet Union, Western dominance would remain unchallenged. They couldn't consider alternative possibilities. One of the leading minds at Harvard then was Stanley Hoffmann, a renowned scholar of European studies. Even though he was a nice man, he became apoplectic when I suggested that the twenty-first century (nine years away at the time) would be the Asian century. I deeply appreciated his strong negative reaction, as it reinforced my determination to continue writing about the resurgence of Asia. Perhaps the first seeds for this memoir were sown at Harvard.

At the personal level, despite my negative experience with Susan Pharr, I developed close friendships with some truly distinguished Harvard professors, including Samuel Huntington, Roderick MacFarquhar, Joseph Nye, and Ezra Vogel, all of whom visited me in Singapore in subsequent years. I also met Fareed Zakaria when he was a young PhD student at Harvard, long before he became famous as the host of the *Fareed Zakaria GPS* show on CNN. In short, I made some lifelong friends and contacts during my year at Harvard. All the knowledge and connections I had developed there were to prove useful twelve years later when I became the founding dean of the Lee Kuan Yew School of Public Policy in 2004. By then, I knew for sure that the sabbatical had turned out to be a valuable year for me.

Still, when I returned home from Harvard, I did so with great foreboding. I knew that I was going to return and serve as the DS of the MFA at the age of forty-two, at a time when many of my contemporaries had become permanent secretaries. Clearly, I was the laggard in this group. As far as I could tell, there were no clear prospects of promotion.

At the same time, I received many other signals that my personal contributions, especially my intellectual contributions, were considered valuable. The new government of Goh Chok Tong wanted to show that it was not completely reliant on the first generation of leaders in international affairs. Quite understandably, it wanted to develop its own expertise and understanding. Hence, I was invited by the PM to set up a brainstorming group, including bright young civil servants and academics, to examine the prospects for the world in the post–Cold War era. I chaired a lively group that included up-and-coming civil servants like Tharman Shanmugaratnam, Teo Chee Hean, and Lim Hng Kiang and bright academics like Tan Kong Yam.

The discussions were fascinating. If anyone had secretly taped or recorded our conversations, they would have been impressed by the quality of the deliberations. Indeed, at the end of the discussions, we submitted a report or two to PM Goh through the Institute of Policy Studies, the official convenor of the group. This report contained no confidential information but offered an assessment of the future based on the best available public knowledge. However, given the culture of secrecy that has become deeply embedded in Singapore, such reports have never been published, even two or three decades later. It may be appropriate for Singapore to consider whether the time has come to release them now. They would provide young Singaporeans with an inkling of how carefully the previous generation had prepared for the future—one reason why the young generation has inherited a stable and secure country. The 2020s could well prove to be as uncertain as the 1990s, as we are entering the end of the unipolar era, so the lessons of how previous generations of Singaporeans prepared to manage such an abrupt transformation in the past may be newly, and perhaps urgently, relevant.

Through the chairmanship of this sparkling group, I also came into direct contact with another key trait of Singapore's governance culture. At the end of the exercise, when we had submitted our report, I thought that my work was over. Instead, I discovered that something far more important was to follow. The head of the Civil Service called me to his office for a private discussion. He told me that the government would like me to rank all the individuals who had participated in this brainstorming exercise on the basis of their "potential." I dutifully did so, although it was a difficult exercise, as the group contained many brilliant individuals. I ranked Tharman Shanmugaratnam first in this group. I am glad that my assessment has been validated over time.

Partly as a result of my active involvement in think tanks like the Institute of Policy Studies (IPS), my constant writings, and my year at Harvard, I began to develop a reputation as a more "academic" civil servant. Then I was invited by George Yeo to become the founding director of the CSC in 1992. Initially, I was flummoxed by the offer of this appointment. Since I had joined the Civil Service in April 1971, I had served only in the Foreign Service. I had had no experience in the domestic Civil Service. Hence, I initially demurred. However, George insisted that I could do a good job.

What happened next was a complete shock to me. I was caught in some political cross fire. Since one of the ministers I knew best from the first generation was Goh Keng Swee, and as he had made major contributions to the governance of Singapore, I went to consult with him about this appointment. By 1992, Dr Goh had retired from all of his official appointments and was serving only as head of the Institute of East Asian Political Economy (now known as the East Asian Institute [EAI]). Yet, he remained politically influential. In May 2023, when I was visiting Hong Kong, I learned from Daniel Bell, who had been affiliated with the EAI in the early 1990s, that Dr Goh had had regular weekly lunches with Lee Kuan Yew in the 1990s. Dr Goh always described Lee Kuan Yew as brilliant. Hence, the falling-out between Lee Kuan Yew and Dr Goh that was to come later had not yet happened. The two men were still on good terms.

I was surprised when Dr Goh firmly advised me to turn down the appointment as director of the CSC. One of his key arguments was that the Civil Service would only carry out instructions from political leaders; it couldn't develop an independent political identity and purpose. Since Dr Goh was regarded as one of the political giants of Singapore, I had no choice but to report his views to George Yeo. I believe that this was then reported to the Cabinet in Singapore.

In response, I was called to another meeting with George Yeo. He told me that the government had decided that I should accept the appointment as director of the CSC despite Dr Goh's opposition. He added that then DPM Lee Hsien Loong, who was in charge of Civil Service matters, would call me in for a meeting. At this meeting, which took place a few weeks later, DPM Lee told me that in view of Dr Goh's opposition, it was important for all civil servants in Singapore to know that my appointment as head of the CSC had the full support and blessing of the Singaporean government. DPM Lee told me that he would be sending out an "epistolary letter" to all civil servants. Since I had had little acquaintance with Christianity (even though my wife, Anne, is a Catholic), I was puzzled by the phrase "epistolary letter." DPM Lee patiently explained it to me. Undoubtedly, being the subject of an "epistolary letter" from him boosted my standing. Fortunately, Dr Goh didn't seem too upset with my decision to take on the CSC appointment. We continued to see each other regularly in the 1990s, and I continued learning from him.

Indeed, Anne and I may have almost killed Dr Goh when we hosted him to dinner at our house in 1991. Anne was still breastfeeding our youngest son, Jhamat. Dr Goh and Phua Swee Liang, his wife, arrived at 7 p.m. The food was mostly prepared. However, as Anne had to breastfeed Jhamat around 7 p.m., we served drinks and delayed the service of the meal. We didn't know then that Dr Goh was suffering from diabetes.

He had taken his insulin injection just before coming to dinner. It was a medical requirement that he had to eat some food almost immediately afterwards. We had no idea. Since the food was delayed, Dr Goh began to have a diabetic seizure. Fortunately, Dr Phua knew exactly what to do. She rushed to our refrigerator to see what food was available. We had some Kit Kat bars. She grabbed them and put them into his mouth, and Dr Goh recovered quickly. Both Anne and I were traumatised by this incident. Fortunately, the dinner proceeded without any further drama.

All the good work that I had done for the Singaporean government eventually resulted in my appointment as permanent secretary of the MFA on October 15, 1993. Yet, looking back now, it's clear that it wasn't a straightforward process. It may not have happened if I hadn't nudged my then boss, Wong Kan Seng. Fortunately, he was a good friend. I don't know how, but he overcame the resistance to my appointment. Without his decisive intervention, I probably would not have been made a permanent secretary.

After my appointment, I also came to learn where all the resistance had come from. DPM Lee was then in charge of Civil Service matters. He instructed the Public Services Division, which ran the administration of Civil Service human resource matters, to share with me all the negative reports that had been written about me by some of my previous bosses. There were pages and pages of negative comments. The reason I was shocked was that there was a rule that senior officers were obliged to share any negative comments in the annual confidential reports with the civil servant they were reporting on. This point was explicitly made clear. I always abided by it and told my junior officers about any negative comments that I made. Yet, in my case, none of my senior officers had shared any negative comments with me.

DPM Lee made sure that the comments had been anonymised. I could make educated guesses as to where they had come from, but I couldn't be absolutely sure. The only boss of mine who had shared his criticism with me was Peter Chan, who had called me a deeply insecure person when I was his deputy secretary. Of course, I resented this description, but after I reflected on it, I realised that there was some truth to it. Given all the poverty, uncertainty, and insecurity that I had experienced in my childhood, and since I hadn't had a privileged background, my insecurity was probably a normal reaction. This experience confirmed what I had learned in a course on the philosophy of the mind in university: self-knowledge is inherently difficult.

Those insecurities had been concealed behind my very self-confident—at times excessively self-confident—outward personality. It was my mother who had taught me how to hide my insecurities. When I was a child, she had told me and my sisters that even though we were poor, we must not reveal it or complain about it. In her words, "Even if you are feeling hungry, don't show it. Put butter on your lips and smile." Implicitly, she was also saying, "Never be a beggar." For a large part of my life, I walked around with deep insecurities while smiling with metaphorical butter on my lips to give the impression that all was well.

Another feature that was confirmed in several of the reports about me was my ambition. I had never sought to hide it, so this was hardly a revelation. But next to the other criticisms, I found myself wondering whether my ambition too was a defence mechanism against the poverty of my upbringing. I was a striver; I had had to be in order to provide for my mother since I was a boy. I had never lost the reflex because I had no wish to slide back towards the poverty of my youth. From the negative reports I read, it was clear that my ambition had turned off many of my superiors. Yet without it, I never would have climbed the ladder of life.

Having grown up poor, I also felt a deep moral obligation to take care of the people at the very bottom of society, as that was where I had come from. On the first day that I became permanent secretary, I took a lift down from my office on the thirty-eighth floor of the building in Raffles City to the lower levels (probably six to ten stories) where most of the officers were. I decided that I should meet everyone in the office, from the senior officers to the cleaners; from the heads of departments to the clerks. Whenever I could, I thanked them for being part of the team. I may have been the first permanent secretary who had done so. I was committed to improving the morale of all the staff who reported to me.

At the same time, I knew that I was inheriting a healthy organisation, which allowed me the freedom to think about what difference I could make as permanent secretary. The job proved to be among the most satisfying I'd ever had. I know that I made a significant difference in some critical areas. Some of the more delicate negotiations I was involved in, like the water talks with Malaysia, are still too sensitive to publish.

One of the boldest decisions I made as permanent secretary was to push for a significant expansion of the Foreign Service. The size of the ministry had remained stable for many years. Yet I could feel in my guts that as Singapore continued to succeed as an economy and society, the foreign demands on interactions with Singapore would increase. It was also clear that it took years, probably a decade or more, to train a good diplomat. Little of this education could take place in a classroom. Instead, young officers had to be pushed off the deep end and sent to overseas postings. I had learned a lot from being posted to KL and Phnom Penh. Indeed, I was amazed that quite often, a shy and withdrawn young officer sent overseas would return home as a self-confident and articulate diplomat. The transformations could be dramatic.

I made the decision to quadruple the annual recruitment. I did this for several years running, leading to a significant expansion of the Singaporean Foreign Service. The rewards of this effort came ten or fifteen years later (after I had stepped down as permanent secretary), but they clearly helped the MFA to take on the more significant responsibilities that came its way. Of course, I received criticism that the ministry could not absorb so many new officers so quickly and even that I was behaving like a megalomaniac in expanding the organisation. Fortunately, the passage of time vindicated my decision.

Apart from building up the MFA as a stronger institution, the other part of my job that I enjoyed was participating in the ASEAN Senior Officials Meetings (SOMs) as the leader of the Singaporean delegation. Although the formal ASEAN decisions were made at the annual Ministerial Meetings, there was no doubt that most of the hard negotiations of the texts took place at the SOM level.

Anyone who thinks of hard negotiations among diplomats probably has a vision of officials spending hours huddled over texts in formal meeting rooms. This did happen. But the real genius of ASEAN was that some of the trickier issues weren't dealt with across conference room tables; they were resolved on the golf course.

One of the major diplomatic initiatives launched by PM Goh Chok Tong was the proposal for an Asia-Europe Meeting (ASEM). Transatlantic ties between the United States and Europe were kept intact by institutional mechanisms like the North Atlantic Treaty Organization (NATO). Ties between the United States and Asia had been formalised by the Asia-Pacific Economic Cooperation (APEC) process. The missing link was between Asia and Europe. Hence, the proposal by PM Goh made eminent sense. Unfortunately, given the antagonistic relationship between Singapore and Malaysia, since PM Goh proposed it, PM Mahathir opposed it. PM Goh asked me if I could solve this problem by speaking to my Malaysian counterpart, Tan Sri Kamil Jaafar. Fortunately, I had gotten to know him well because we played golf together and drank beer together after a game. I told Tan Sri Kamil, using the Malay word "tolong," which means "help," "Help me! I can't get promoted until Malaysia agrees to this Asia-Europe meeting." Tan Sri Kamil answered, "Kishore, for you I'll do it." He went to see PM Mahathir and persuaded him to withdraw his opposition to the

Asia-Europe meeting. The ASEM meeting was finally held in Thailand in 1996.

The game of golf helps diplomatic interactions in other ways too. Often, I find that the best way to assess people's character and integrity is to watch their performance on the golf course. If they kick the ball out of the rough or fail to make the final putt even when required to do so, I immediately begin to question their integrity. Over the years, I have found that the judgments I have made on the golf course have often proven to be correct assessments of a person's character.

Some difficult political issues could be resolved at the SOM-level meetings that I participated in. Others could be resolved only at summit-level meetings. One such issue was the effort by Singapore to bring in India as an ASEAN dialogue partner. Indonesia and Malaysia were happy to admit India, but they also insisted on parity for Pakistan, India's traditional rival, and insisted that both countries should be admitted at the same time. Singapore was naturally concerned that the admission of both could lead to the ASEAN meetings being paralysed by their traditional disputes.

Since this matter could not be resolved at the SOM level, it was eventually raised to the summit level. These summit-level discussions took place at the ASEAN summit meeting that was held in December 1995 in Bangkok. I was part of the delegation that accompanied PM Goh to this meeting. We briefed him on the issue just before he went into the closed-door leaders-only retreat. I remember standing outside the door waiting for him to come out. As soon as the doors opened and PM Goh came out, he spotted me from a distance. He raised his hand and gave a thumbs-up signal. It was a clear sign that he had succeeded in getting India admitted as a dialogue partner by itself.

On the issue of the ASEM, after Malaysia finally agreed to proceed with it as an ASEAN initiative, we still had to persuade the Europeans to participate. In theory, the country in the EU with which Singapore had the closest relationship was the United Kingdom, which was then led by PM John Major. However, we sensed that the British were not enthusiastic. We decided to work with France instead. French president Jacques Chirac was enthusiastic about developing links with Asia. "Among tomorrow's centres of power those that are emerging in Asia are surely visible to all," he said in a 1996 speech in Singapore, identifying Japan, China, India, and ASEAN as particularly likely to play a pivotal role in the twenty-first century. He argued that Europe needed to assert itself as a major partner of Asia: "The time has come for us to rediscover one another. We must realise what we have become, and all that we can achieve together."[1] Even with the support of France, we still had to go door-to-door selling the ASEM to all the key European capitals. This task was assigned to me, and I marched from Dublin to Berlin, from Madrid to Rome. This door-to-door salesmanship worked. Eventually, all the European countries agreed to join the ASEM.

PM Goh wisely decided that even though the ASEM was a Singaporean initiative, the first summit shouldn't be held in Singapore. We offered it to Thailand. A shrewd Thai journalist, Kavi Chongkittavorn (who later became special assistant to the secretary general of ASEAN), once insightfully observed that whenever Singapore came up with a good idea, Thailand became "pregnant" with that idea. It was clearly a good partnership. Hence, the first ASEM summit was held in Bangkok in March 1996, with a major turnout of Asian and European leaders. Sadly, after the East Asian countries experienced the Asian financial crisis in 1997–1998, the European countries became much less confident in the region and lost interest in the ASEM; they proved to be fair-weather friends of ASEAN.

In addition to the ASEM, one other high-level partnership that I worked on was the strategic partnership between Singapore and Australia. The Australian PM then was the visionary Paul Keating, who understood well that Australia's long-term destiny lay in closer relations with Asia. He also had a strong and dynamic secretary of the Department of Foreign Affairs and Trade, Mike Costello. Mike and I had become friends since we had attended many ASEAN-related meetings (like the ASEAN Regional Forum) together. Our good personal chemistry helped our negotiations. Hence, I was happy to join the delegation of PM Goh Chok Tong when he went to Canberra for an official visit on September 12–15, 1994. PM Goh and PM Keating launched the Singapore-Australia New Partnership two years later, in January 1996, when Keating came to Singapore.

The one big lesson from all these efforts to sell diplomatic initiatives to other countries (on behalf of Singapore) was that while the quality and substance of the initiative was important, it was equally important to have good personal relationships in order to market initiatives. Just as my personal relationship with Tan Sri Ahmad Kamil Jaafar had helped to overcome the initial Malaysian opposition to the ASEM, my good personal relationship with Mike Costello helped to move along the strategic partnership with Australia. In theory, personal friendships shouldn't count in international relations. Lord Palmerston famously said, "We have no eternal allies, and we have no perpetual enemies. Our interests are eternal and perpetual, and those interests it is our duty to follow." Yet my long experience with diplomacy proves that personal friendships make huge differences. Human beings are human beings: trust develops with good person-to-person interactions.

While it was important to get along with other diplomats, it was sometimes equally important to stand up to them. In theory, both US and European diplomats were part of the same "Western" camp. However, while Americans could be very direct and candid in their comments, they rarely engaged in cultural condescension. By contrast, I experienced this condescension from European diplomats when we discussed "human rights" issues at ASEM SOMs. The European desire to preach about these issues was irrepressible. This was where my philosophical training helped. It was easy to expose the hypocrisy and double standards in the sanctimonious statements made by European diplomats. After a few bruising encounters, the Europeans learned to hold back their preachiness in dealing with us. Here too I had learned much from Lee Kuan Yew, who never hesitated to confront his detractors directly.

In the early 1990s, the main debate that Singapore was having on human rights issues was with the Americans, not the Europeans. By now, it's well known that two major events triggered a new wave of evangelism by the United States on human rights in the 1990s. The first was the end of the Cold War (which made unsavoury allies, like Zaire and Pakistan, dispensable) and the consequent triumphant spirit, best expressed by the Project for the New American Century, which declared that the United States was a preeminent power that could and should expect to shape the world for the foreseeable future. The second was the election of Bill Clinton in November 1992 after the collapse of the Soviet Union in December 1991.

Looking back now, it's clear that the election of Bill Clinton in 1992 must have been excruciating for Lee Kuan Yew. For over a decade, since the election of Ronald Reagan in November 1980, Mr Lee had secured privileged access to the White House through his close friendship with many Republican Party "grandees" such as Henry Kissinger and George Shultz. Indeed, whenever he travelled to the United States and met US luminaries, he was treated with reverence and respect as the "great sage from Asia." At the end of the 1990s, I discovered how much respect President George H. W. Bush had for Lee Kuan Yew when I was invited by the then CEO of PepsiCo, Indra Nooyi, to attend a conference organised by PepsiCo in St Petersburg, Russia. Many American luminaries, including George H. W. Bush, Henry Kissinger, Zbigniew Brzezinski, and Samuel Huntington, were there. Former president George H. W. Bush was interviewed by David Frost, the legendary British broadcaster. Frost asked Bush who was the single most impressive leader he had met in his life. Bush replied, "Lee Kuan Yew"—who couldn't have been more delighted when I reported this to him.

To go from a situation where he had special and unique access to the most powerful leader of the world to one where he had no access (and, indeed, was even snubbed) by the most powerful leader in the world must have been painful. Yet if it bothered him, he never showed it. He was very philosophical about it. I can say this with great confidence, as he decided, in the early 1990s (after he had stepped down as PM), to invite Tommy Koh, Chan Heng Chee, and me to regular lunches at the Istana.

All three of us had served as ambassadors to the UN in New York (and Tommy Koh had also served as ambassador to the United States from 1984 to 1990). Lee appreciated these lunches because he could receive candid and unvarnished feedback from us. Each of us, in our own different ways, had been viewed as a "dissenting voice" within Singapore.

By the early 1990s, Lee Kuan Yew had become a formidable and intimidating presence. Most Singaporeans, including many senior members of the establishment, were intimidated by him. This was understandable. He suffered no fools. Anyone who made a silly comment would receive a swift and cutting put-down. Hence, many decided to keep their mouths shut when he was around. But this deprived him of the feedback and intellectual input he needed and liked. So he invited us for these intimate lunches in a small, circular room on the second floor of the Istana. The round table could comfortably seat four to six people. The menus were never exciting. The cuisine was almost always Western, as Lee Kuan Yew avoided rich Asian food. His wife always tried to keep him healthy. The lunches would conclude around 2:30 or 3 p.m.

Lee was immensely curious. He would ask questions over a wide range of issues. He wouldn't chew our heads off if we said something he disagreed with. He was shrewd enough to realise that he would never get candid feedback if he reacted angrily to views he disagreed with. Hence, he almost always bent over backwards to encourage us to speak freely, and especially about the United States—about which he knew less than the three of us did.

His behaviour at these informal lunches was therefore quite different from his behaviour at official meetings, especially with Singaporean civil servants. At official meetings, if he had a clear point of view to express, he would do so clearly and forcefully. As permanent secretary of the MFA, I recall attending a meeting where he explained at great length why Singapore had decided to help China build an industrial park in Suzhou, a traditionally beautiful Chinese city west of Shanghai. Through the grapevine, we had heard that Goh Keng Swee disagreed with this decision. Philip Yeo, who was then chairman of the Singapore Economic Development Board, has spoken about it publicly. He said, "When Lee Kuan Yew announced they were going to Suzhou, Dr Goh (Keng Swee) called me up. He said: 'This project will fail and they will call for you.' He was against the concept from the beginning."[2] At such formal meetings, held when big decisions had already been made, Lee Kuan Yew wasn't looking for dissenting views.

By contrast, at informal lunches with the three of us, Lee Kuan Yew was relaxed and open to alternative views. Both Tommy Koh and Chan Heng Chee have shared with me their memories of these lunches. Tommy Koh wrote, "I remember with great pleasure the lunches we used to have with Senior Minister Lee Kuan Yew. Contrary to his public image, he was actually very consultative and willing to listen to the views of others. I think he enjoyed the robust but cordial exchanges of views among us. He was also very courteous, insisting that we be served first." This is how Chan Heng Chee recalled these lunches:

We were ushered into a small room. I can't remember which part of the Istana it was located at! We were not exactly sure what the lunch was about. It was Lee Kuan Yew who initiated the conversation with a question. Subsequently, at other lunches, we were more relaxed. I think occasionally Tommy and Kishore would start the conversation. I was the rookie. I always waited for both these two seasoned diplomats to speak first. We talked about the US a great deal. The Soviet Union had just imploded. Lee Kuan Yew was trying to think through "What now?" He did most of the talking. We ate spartanly, all of us with our best table manners. I never saw such a huge basket of fruits—or was it a plate? Lee Kuan Yew would put on his surgeon's gloves. There was an air of deliberateness about it. All three of us watched this little act with fascination. He explained that his fingers were allergic to fruit skin. We were all intrigued how much fruit Lee Kuan Yew could eat! Bill Clinton had become President of the US. He was interested to know more about Clinton. He was trying to get a sense of the man. I remember Lee Kuan Yew's stent operation put a stop to the lunches.

The informality of these regular lunches contrasted sharply with the formality in official meetings. In 1994, we met to discuss how Singapore should respond to an appeal from President Bill Clinton to President Ong Teng Cheong that the American teenager Michael Fay not be caned for the crimes of vandalism that he had committed. He had been sentenced to six strokes of the cane and four months in jail. The American liberal media was horrified at the prospect of an American citizen being caned. The case of Michael Fay became a cause célèbre. According to S. R. Nathan, who was then Singapore's ambassador to Washington, Clinton stressed in his letter his "respect for the competence of the Singapore judiciary and his belief that Americans overseas must respect the laws of foreign countries. However, he appealed for Fay's sentence of caning to be commuted in view of his youth, his status as a first offender, and his personal circumstances."[3]

The meeting was conducted in Lee Kuan Yew's office, with several ministers and civil servants present. Lee's office was always intimidating. When the doors opened, the first thing that struck me as I walked into his room was the great aura of power he emanated as we entered his presence. It's significant that his office has remained unoccupied since his death in March 2015. I have heard that Lee Kuan Yew offered his office to his successor, Goh Chok Tong, when he stepped down as PM in 1990. But Mr Goh wisely declined to use it.

At the meeting on Michael Fay, we freely discussed the pros and cons of accepting or rejecting the appeal from President Bill Clinton. After the debate, Lee Kuan Yew summarised all the points made and then said that since Singapore couldn't totally rebuff the president of a friendly country, we should agree to reduce the strokes from six to four. I reacted impulsively with the first thing that came to my mind. I said, "Cutting the strokes from six to four would be seen as an insult since it would show that Clinton's appeal was only worth two strokes." In response, Lee Kuan Yew glared at me. Everyone knew then that the decision had been made.

This decision to preserve the caning despite Clinton's appeal proved to be a wise one. On the surface, it appeared as though Singapore had made a concession. Yet it was also clear that everyone read the decision as a rebuff to the United States. In 1996, when Clinton ran for reelection against former senator Bob Dole, Dole made clear the nature of the insult by saying, "We know how much Clinton is worth: two strokes of the cane." This line won Dole a lot of laughs, but it didn't derail Clinton's reelection. On our side, by rebuffing and standing up to the United States, Singapore's stature rose all around the world. Indeed, the then Indian high commissioner to Singapore, Ambassador Prem Singh, told me that even a large country like India wouldn't have rebuffed a US president. It would have quietly allowed the United States to smuggle Michael Fay out of the country. By standing firm, Singapore gained the respect of the world. I also know that our neighbours, Indonesia and Malaysia, were impressed by Singapore's decision. While Singapore paid a short-term price in terms of being denied official visits to Washington, DC, for a couple of months, its standing in the rest of the world rose significantly. Singapore was seen as a brave small state that had stood up to the big US bully.

Michael Fay was caned on May 5, 1994. He was subsequently sent back to the United States after completing his jail term on June 21 (having been released early for good behaviour). All this should have left the Clinton administration embittered about Singapore. However, Washington, DC, is a capital where memories don't last long. Three years and five months after Fay's departure, an APEC Summit meeting took place in Vancouver in November 1997. Following the usual practice, we requested a thirty-minute courtesy call by PM Goh Chok Tong of President Clinton in Vancouver. Chan Heng Chee, our new ambassador to the United States, called me when she got the response to the request: "Kishore, they're insulting us. We requested an official meeting. They are offering a golf game instead." I immediately replied to her without consulting anybody, "Heng Chee, please accept the golf game immediately." She asked why. I replied that in an official meeting, PM Goh and President Clinton would spend only thirty minutes together. In a golf game, they would spend four hours together. PM Goh and President Clinton bonded over the golf game, which led to a subsequent golf game and another APEC meeting in Brunei in November 2000, which paved the way for the US-Singapore Free Trade Agreement (FTA) in January 2004. Sometimes, split-second decisions, like accepting a golf game, can make a huge difference.

As an aside, I must mention that the first improvement in relations between the Singaporean government and the Clinton administration took place at the first-ever APEC Summit, hosted by the United States on Blake Island, off Seattle, in November 1993. Bill Clinton was completely unknown to the leaders of Singapore, as he hadn't held national office before becoming president. I was present when the first handshake took place between President Bill Clinton and PM Goh Chok Tong at the end of a ramp onto a boat. Since Blake Island was an island, the only way to get there was by boat, and President Clinton stood patiently at the end of the ramp to greet each leader.

This was how I discovered what a great politician Bill Clinton was. He made sure that he had a good conversation with each leader as he shook their hands. When PM Goh went up the ramp, I stood back to allow the two men to have an unhurried conversation. When they finished, I followed PM Goh up the ramp, as that was the only way to get on the boat. I expected Bill Clinton to cursorily shake my hand, as most leaders would, and then move on to the next leader. Instead, he looked squarely into my eyes. He had noticed that I was wearing New Balance running shoes, and he engaged me in a conversation about the wonderful qualities of New Balance. He had improvised quickly, found a connection, and boosted an American sportswear brand, all in the space of a few seconds. The only other leader I know who is as engaging as Bill Clinton in one-to-one conversation—where he makes you feel that you are the most important person he has met—is Tony Blair. Both leaders had learned the art of looking into the eyes of the person they were talking to and making them feel that they have his complete attention.

Bill Clinton unleashed his political skills even more when we arrived at Blake Island. The entire meeting was conducted in a massive tent, as the island had no major conference facility. The lasting significance of this APEC Summit meeting was that this was the first time that the leaders of the United States and China were meeting after the 1992 presidential elections.

Most people were expecting tension between Bill Clinton and President Jiang Zemin, as Clinton had famously said in his 1992 electoral campaign that, unlike President George H. W. Bush, he wouldn't "coddle the Butcher of Beijing" (referring to the Tiananmen Square events of June 4, 1989). Indeed, President Jiang must have been expecting trouble, as he had read off his speech quickly and nervously when each leader made his opening statements.

But during the coffee break, I noticed that Clinton made a point of approaching Jiang. He then unleashed his full charm, having clearly moved on from his campaign rhetoric. The moment also proved the importance of multilateral meetings. After the harsh statements made by Bill Clinton against China in the 1992 campaign, it would have been difficult to organise a "bilateral" meeting between Clinton and Jiang. One side or the other would have lost face. The multilateral APEC Summit provided a way for the two sides to meet. Historians may well record that this Blake Island meeting changed the course of history in two ways: it was a step on the road towards China becoming a member of the World Trade Organization (WTO), a development that would transform the global economy over the next quarter century, and it may have helped to prevent an immediate crisis over Taiwan.

A former US ambassador to Thailand, Ralph "Skip" Boyce, revealed to me that he had attended a heads of mission meeting of US ambassadors in Hawaii in that period that was entirely focused on the possibility of a war between the United States and China, as President Clinton had decided to send two aircraft carriers to the Taiwan Strait in March 1996 after China had fired some missiles that had landed off Keelung and Kaohsiung. Fortunately, in this case, war was avoided, partly because Clinton and Jiang had established a relationship on Blake Island in November 1993.

Similarly, a good relationship was established between President Clinton and PM Goh on Blake Island. This may explain why Clinton invited Goh to a golf game at the APEC leaders' meeting in Vancouver in November 1997. This invitation must have been satisfying to PM Goh, as there was a real concern that Singapore had lost its privileged access to the White House after Lee Kuan Yew had stepped down as PM in November 1990. But the invitation to a golf game showed that both Singapore and PM Goh were still held in high regard in Washington, DC.

With hindsight, it's clear to me that I was somewhat politically naive in my understanding of Singaporean politics then. Fortunately, my bosses in the foreign ministry were much more politically shrewd than I was. They understood well that there were three key decision-makers on foreign policy in Singapore: PM Goh Chok Tong, DPM Lee Hsien Loong, and Senior Minister (SM) Lee Kuan Yew. Once, after we had submitted a request for a decision on a foreign policy issue to the three of them, we received the agreement and approval of DPM Lee and PM Goh almost immediately. With this agreement, I asked my bosses whether we should proceed to implement the decision. They wisely decided to wait to hear from SM Lee, whose approval eventually also came in.

George Yeo better understood the complex political dynamics of Singapore at the time. In his memoirs, *Musings*, he wrote candidly,

> By the time I entered politics [1988], Lee Kuan Yew's political dominance in Singapore was complete. This freed him to concentrate on Singapore's long-term development. Ministers and civil servants were highly responsive to his views and some became intellectually and psychologically dependent on him. This was a strength and weakness: a strength because it enabled the job to be done quickly and efficiently; but also a weakness because it also bred a dependent mentality in Singapore.[4]

Since I was not fully aware of the political dynamics between PM Goh Chok Tong and SM Lee Kuan Yew, I was inadvertently caught in some cross fire.

As I had clearly developed a close relationship with my Malaysian counterpart Tan Sri Kamil Jaafar, I received a request from PM Goh to go and see Tan Sri Kamil in KL to sound out the possibilities of improving bilateral relations between KL and Singapore. Overall, relations between Singapore and Malaysia remained troubled, and ironically, they remained troubled because of the underlying reasons I had spelled out in my valedictory report of 1979 (for which I had been severely criticised by the then high commissioner Wee Kim Wee). Additionally, it was clear that the chemistry between PM Mahathir and PM Goh wasn't great because PM Mahathir, for historical reasons going back to the painful separation of Singapore and Malaysia, had a negative view of Singapore. So PM Goh asked me to explore whether we could work with Tan Sri Kamil Jaafar to improve relations with Malaysia.

I was happy to do this, as I knew how important our relationship with Malaysia was. I dutifully flew to KL and spent a few pleasant days with Kamil. We played golf a couple of times, had a meal or two, and engaged in some bilateral talks where notetakers were present. I told Kamil that my mission was to explore possibilities for improving relations. I emphasised to him that as permanent secretary, I had no authority to make decisions. However, I added that I would try to use "my persuasive powers" to convince the Singaporean government to agree to any proposals.

These notes were circulated to the Cabinet, and then the fireworks began. Lee Kuan Yew took strong exception to my remark that I had "persuasive powers." I don't know why he objected to the phrase, but he was very upset. Lee Kuan Yew could become brutal when he was angry. Hence, he wrote some blistering criticisms of me and my claim to have "persuasive powers." I felt as though several rockets had been fired at me. And when the rockets came at me, I soon found that I was alone. There was no protection from this incoming fire. It was a painful experience, and I felt seared by it. Some years later, I shared my experience with fellow public servants who had had their own encounters with Lee. It became a badge of honour among civil servants to tell stories of how they had received a shellacking from Lee Kuan Yew.

PM Goh continued to have confidence in me despite the small furore over KL. From time to time, he would meet the permanent secretaries over informal lunches or dinners. I recall one evening when all the permanent secretaries (there were about twenty of us) were invited to an informal dinner conversation with Goh at the Istana. During the dinner, Goh spoke candidly about his term as PM. He told us that one of his serious concerns had been whether Singapore's international influence would decline after he took over from Lee Kuan Yew as PM. However, after several years as PM, he realised that he needn't have worried, as we had developed a very competent Foreign Ministry. This was clearly understood by other permanent secretaries as a compliment to me. Indeed, Peter Ho (who later became head of the Civil Service) whispered to me as we were walking out, "Congratulations, Kishore; you have done well."

As permanent secretary, I accompanied PM Goh when he went on overseas trips. I went on several with him, but I mainly remember two. The first was to Europe in the mid-1990s, and the second was to China in the same period. On the visit to Europe, I remember that we took a boat trip somewhere in Germany. As the boat was cruising down the river, we were chatting away, and Goh asked me, "Why are there only three well-known Singapore diplomats overseas, namely, Tommy Koh, Chan Heng Chee, and you?" This question revealed Goh's deep concern about how to develop and nurture a new generation of leaders and officials who could carry on the success story of Singapore. This is a pleasant memory. The memory from China is an unpleasant one. During the visit to Beijing, Eddie Teo (who was then permanent secretary of Mindef) and I were busy one day in our hotel rooms trying to transcribe the notes of a meeting. As we were occupied with these notes, we failed to come down on time to join the motorcade that took PM Goh to a meeting with President Jiang Zemin within the hallowed grounds of the compound, called the Zhongnanhai, that housed the leaders of China. When Eddie and I turned up late, we were denied entry at the gate. As a result, I have never seen the inside of the Zhongnanhai. This is one of the eternal regrets of my life.

During my term as permanent secretary, I learned firsthand how competent Singapore had become in formulating and executing world-class public policies. One of my great privileges as permanent secretary was to drive into the Istana every Saturday morning to read the Cabinet papers that had been tabled for the week. There was a good reason for sharing the Cabinet papers with the permanent secretaries: it made them aware that they should take an "all of government" approach to solving problems. They could only do this if they knew what other branches of the government were doing.

My mind was truly blown by the brilliance of some of these Cabinet papers. The quality was amazing. The years of hard work put in by the first generation of political leaders, especially Lee Kuan Yew and Goh Keng Swee, in emphasising the importance of good writing had paid off. As a young civil servant, I remember Lee Kuan Yew convening a meeting of civil servants and sharing with them a book called *The Complete Plain Words* by Ernest Gowers. This book emphasised the effectiveness of short, sharp sentences and the importance of brevity.

Lee Kuan Yew always insisted on short and precise Cabinet memos. He wanted civil servants to cut to the chase and present the key considerations for any major public policy decision clearly and crisply. The details could go into the annexes, if necessary. The main goal of the paper was to weigh the pros and cons of each potential approach to solving a problem. All pages had to end with a clear and strong recommendation. We were never allowed to be two-handed economists, saying "on the one hand" and "on the other hand."

The values of the first generation of leaders also shone through in these papers, many of which emphasised the need for policies that promoted the public good, not private interests. This was not inevitable; the most powerful and admired country in the world in the 1970s was the United States. Howe Yoon Chong, a brilliant first-generation leader, complained to me that it was absurd that it took Singapore so long to build highways, as the United States had effortlessly built thousands of miles of roads. I wasn't sharp enough to respond that the rapid building of thousands of miles of highways had been driven by private interests: the automobile and oil companies. Indeed, the Americans even came out with a saying that "what's good for GM is good for the country." The dominance of automobile manufacturers and oil corporations meant that the United States has not built good passenger railway systems to complement its highways. By contrast, Singapore put the public interest first and built good highways and good railway systems.

This emphasis on the public good did not mean that there were no fierce debates within the government. For example, one of Singapore's biggest national assets is its port, which contributes significantly to its prosperity. However, the land it occupied in places like Tanjong Pagar and Pasir Panjang was close to the city centre. The Port of Singapore Authority (PSA) naturally wanted to retain this land, as it had occupied it for a century or more. However, the Urban Redevelopment Authority (URA), which carried out urban planning, saw better use for this prime land. Naturally, this led to fierce debates between organisations like the PSA and URA. Contrary to the popular perception of Singapore in the Anglo-Saxon media, such important decisions were not made unilaterally by a dictator. Instead, they were a result of robust debates and careful public policy deliberations. This aspect of Singapore's decision-making is not widely known in the world.

Throughout the Cabinet papers, the long-term public good of Singapore always trumped short-term political considerations. Since all the Cabinet papers were marked "confidential" or "secret," I cannot disclose their contents even though twenty-five years have passed since I read them. But details of two major public projects have since been publicly revealed. The first was the deep tunnel sewerage system (DTSS). In the mid-1990s, the government decided to spend approximately S$10 billion building a 146-kilometre-long "superhighway" for used water that would benefit Singapore over the next one hundred years. The first phase was completed in 2008, and the second is expected to be completed in 2026.[5] As Prime Minister Lee Hsien Loong explained,[6] the easier and cheaper option in the short term would have been to expand the existing system of pumping stations and reclamation plants to meet the needs of Singapore's growing population. However, this would have taken up too much valuable land. The government came up with the creative solution of channelling used water through deep tunnels to two large water reclamation plants, one at each end of the island. This would free up the nearly one thousand hectares of land occupied by the existing sewerage system for development. In addition, the DTSS allows all the used water to be collected, treated, and reused. This is of strategic importance, as Singapore seeks to be water independent. Unlike some Western governments, which were hesitant to persuade their voters to pay a short-term economic price for long-term good, the Singaporean government never hesitated to invest in the long-term future. Another bold decision was to divert thousands of hectares of expensively acquired reclaimed land to a national park—Gardens by the Bay—rather than sell it all to developers of office towers and condominiums and generate a lot of revenue. The commitment of the government to preserve and expand the tree cover in Singapore has led to the city having vastly more greenery than most cities. The decision was based on the Cabinet papers that carefully argued the case for the long-term benefits.

It's a real pity that none of these papers have been declassified and shared, especially with young Singaporeans, who are unaware of the depth of consideration that the first generation of Singapore's political leaders gave to both the issues of their day and to planning for a future that would outlast them. It's good that some of these Cabinet papers have been shared with foreign leaders who have visited Singapore. I recall that when the then PM of Papua New Guinea, Michael Somare, visited Singapore in the 1990s (I believe), the government allowed him to attend a Cabinet meeting and even to read some of the Cabinet papers. He and his colleagues must have been impressed by the brilliance of these documents. It's time now to share this brilliance with young Singaporeans.

There's no doubt that the five years I spent as permanent secretary were among the most satisfying in my life. I enjoyed all dimensions of my job, from the administrative tasks of growing and expanding the Foreign Service to the political tasks of providing good advice in Cabinet memos and marketing Singaporean initiatives such as ASEAN and the Singapore-Australia Strategic Partnership. I also truly enjoyed working with my ASEAN colleagues in the ASEAN SOM circuit. I would have been happy to spend many more years as permanent secretary of the MFA.

However, the inevitable happened. I began to make mistakes. Unwittingly, I stepped on the toes of some important people. These episodes are too delicate to be mentioned here. As a result, the government decided that my term as permanent secretary should come to an end. This ending was executed in two steps. First, a more senior permanent secretary, Brig Gen Tan Chin Tiong, was appointed to a senior position over me at MFA. Although my new title was permanent secretary (Policy) of the MFA, everyone knew that I was now outranked. The usual thing then happened: I found that I had fewer friends than I had thought. I also found out who my true friends were. Second, I was told that I would be sent back to be the Singaporean ambassador to the UN so that I could campaign for the election of Singapore to the UNSC for the years 2001–2002. While I loved the UN, it was clear that returning to a job I had held previously was not exactly a promotion. I felt a great sense of injustice. Overall, as the record showed, I had done a good job as permanent secretary. My reward was to be publicly demoted. I felt angry and depressed.

Many years later, as dean of the Lee Kuan Yew School of Public Policy, I would tell each graduating class of the school that they should always prepare for ups and downs in their career. I illustrated this with my own experience. When I was first appointed as Singaporean ambassador to the UN at the tender age of thirty-five in 1984, I viewed it as the single biggest promotion of my life. Yet when I was reappointed Singaporean ambassador to the UN at the age of forty-nine in 1998, I viewed it as the single biggest demotion of my life. Essentially, I had gone from being the CEO of an organisation—the MFA—with an annual budget of S$100 million to becoming a brand manager of a unit with an annual budget of S$1 million. Moreover, as UN ambassador, I would be reporting to officers who had been my erstwhile juniors for most of my career. It hurt.

S. Jayakumar, who was then the minister of foreign affairs, tried to soften the blow by saying that the move would be good for my family. He was right. Anne would once again be close to her parents in New Jersey, who were ageing. Equally important, our three children, who were then twelve, ten, and eight, would have access to some of the best schools in New York. So my career failure could also be viewed as a family success. I had spent less time with my children in the 1990s due to my overwhelming responsibilities as permanent secretary, but I would be able to spend more time with them in New York.

Although I could grasp these advantages rationally, they didn't diminish the emotional blow. I went through a rough patch until the natural emotional resilience that my mother had nurtured in me kicked in. I reminded myself that none of my travails could ever compare to hers. I had no excuse to either feel or act depressed. I put butter on my lips and smiled at the world.

CHAPTER 10

The UN Security Council

W HEN I HAD FIRST ARRIVED IN NEW YORK IN AUGUST 1984 AS Singapore's permanent representative to the UN, I had been a single young man. Fourteen years later, in 1998, I was married and had three children, aged twelve, ten, and eight, in tow. So the first priority for Anne and me was to find good schools in Manhattan for our children.

Manhattan had many excellent private schools, but gaining admission into them was almost as tough as getting into the best Ivy League universities (and almost as expensive). We didn't consider public schools, as many Manhattan public schools had a poor track record and we heard stories of violence in these schools. We could have stayed in suburbs where good public schools were available, but the commute would have meant that I'd hardly see our children. So we returned to the official residence, the same apartment in St James Tower where we had lived before, and embarked on some expensive education, which was fortunately paid for by the government.

My predecessor as permanent representative, Bilahari Kausikan, had spotted an apartment for sale adjacent to our old one, also a duplex. He persuaded the Singaporean government to purchase it just before we arrived. Anne and I had to undertake the disruptive construction work of merging the two apartments, but we were grateful to have the additional space for the six years we would spend in New York. Indeed, for the first UNGA that we experienced on our return, in September 1998, the children of S. Jayakumar (who had come to New York for the UNGA) were able to stay in this new adjoining apartment, still separate from ours.

Our search for good private schools led us to Collegiate School for the boys, KR and Jay, and Convent of the Sacred Heart for our daughter, Shelagh. Anne took the children to New York in November 1997 for the required testing and interviews. The big challenge of getting them admitted then began. We soon learned that these very different schools required very different approaches. We heard that Collegiate School had people from the New York financial sector on its board, so I approached the big boss of the GIC, Ng Kok Song, for help. Kok Song dutifully wrote letters to a few friends in the New York financial sector. A few weeks later, one of them responded, "I have a very good feeling about their admission prospects into Collegiate. Please don't do anything else." We didn't. Sure enough, KR and Jay were admitted into Collegiate, which provided them with an excellent education during the six years they were in Manhattan.

Convent of the Sacred Heart, fortunately or unfortunately, had no connections we knew of with the financial sector. No external recommendations could help Shelagh. After making several inquiries, I was advised to write a heartfelt letter to the school principal, who was a nun. One night, sitting in our bedroom in Singapore, I wrote in longhand to the principal. I sent the letter by regular mail. A few weeks later, we received the good news that Shelagh had been admitted.

The admissions director later told Anne that when the principal had received my handwritten letter, she had immediately marched over to the admissions office of the school and asked, "Why are we torturing this young girl, Shelagh, from Singapore? Why don't we admit her?" And all I had done was tell the principal the truth: each night, Shelagh went to bed hoping and praying that she would be admitted to Sacred Heart. This episode with both Collegiate and Sacred Heart taught me a valuable life lesson: sometimes in life, the mind and material considerations can win the battle. In other cases, the heart and the tug of emotions are more effective. We were truly blessed that our three children received six good years of education in New York.

With the children safely ensconced in school, I could focus on my main mission in New York: to get Singapore elected to the UNSC for the first time in the country's history. Since Singapore had been endorsed by the Asian Group, we didn't face a competitor. We could have relaxed. Instead, we did the opposite. The

Singaporean government culture of competitive paranoia kicked in, and we were determined to try to get the maximum number of votes for our election. PM Goh Chok Tong asked me what would constitute a good result. I told him that we should aim to get all votes from all members, barring two or three (since rarely did states get *all* the votes). He asked me what would happen if we lost more than five votes. I said, only partly in jest, that I would commit suicide. Fortunately, the end result was that we lost only five votes.

I was disappointed since every member state of the UN had promised us its vote in writing or verbally. Clearly, Singapore had been betrayed by five of its friends. We could not tell who they were since voting was secret.

The loss of five votes was galling, as I had spent two entire years cultivating all the permanent representatives to the UN by calling on them in their offices, hosting them to lunches and dinners, and attending all their National Day receptions. I wasn't joking when I said that I had to sacrifice my body for this job: it was tough work eating and drinking all the time to win votes! Fortunately, I exercised a great deal too. And I took particular pleasure in my weekend runs around Central Park.

Life as the UN representative wasn't all wining and dining. There were many UN agenda items that kept us busy, one of which led to a particularly bruising fight between the Singapore and US delegations: the question of how much Singapore should pay the UN for its regular assessed dues. This rather technical matter blew up into a god-almighty row.

It all began when one of my "best friends," Ambassador Richard Holbrooke, was appointed as the permanent representative of the United States to the UN. "Best friends" was how Ambassador Holbrooke (or "Dick," as I called him) described our relationship when he arrived in New York sometime in late 1999 and discovered that I was one of the more popular ambassadors. He seemed to think that he could leverage his "best friendship" with me in the UN community.

We were not "best friends." We were, at best, close acquaintances, although I had met him several times over the years, stretching from the time when he had served as the assistant secretary of state for Asia and the Pacific during the Carter administration. In this role, he had played an important role for both Singapore and ASEAN. In January 1977, when Jimmy Carter became president, the ASEAN countries were still traumatised by the fall of Indochina to the communists. In short, the potential "dominoes" of Southeast Asia were nervous. To make matters worse, Jimmy Carter, in contrast to Richard Nixon, was perceived as a weak president. Holbrooke could have made matters worse if he had been weak too.

Fortunately, he wasn't. In the 1980s, when the Republican Reagan was president and Holbrooke, a Democrat, was out of government office, he had an office in Manhattan, where he worked as a senior adviser to Lehman Brothers. As the then Singaporean ambassador to the UN, I had visited him in this office. Right behind his desk, prominently displayed on his office wall, was a framed letter of appreciation from PM Lee Kuan Yew praising him for the strength and resolve he had shown in shoring up the confidence of the nervous ASEAN countries. Lee Kuan Yew was known to be very sparing in his praise. Hence, the compliment was a sincere one. Holbrooke deserved it.

Holbrooke returned to office when Democrat Bill Clinton took office in January 1993. He was hoping to become secretary of state after Warren Christopher stepped down on January 17, 1997. However, Hillary Clinton insisted that the job should go to a woman, Madeleine Albright. The consolation prize given to Holbrooke was the appointment as special envoy to the Balkans from 1997 to 1999, when conflict was rife in the region. The second "reward" was his appointment as the PR of the United States to the UN, a Cabinet-level appointment, on August 5, 1999.[1] That was how our paths crossed again.

Holbrooke's great strength (and perhaps weakness) was that he was always a man on a mission. He had enormous energy, indomitable will, and a huge ego. The most memorable headline I ever saw about him was along the lines of "The real truth about Dick Holbrooke is that he is a dick, but he's our dick." After he sadly passed away on December 13, 2010, Hillary Clinton paid him a memorable tribute by saying at his funeral, "Few people have ever left a larger mark on the State Department or our country. From Southeast Asia to post–Cold War Europe and around the globe, people have a better chance of a peaceful future because of Richard's lifetime of service."[2]

Unfortunately for me, the big mission that Holbrooke decided (in consultation with the Clinton administration) to undertake as permanent representative of the United States to the UN was to reduce the amount of US dues paid to the UN. One of the major problems that the United States faced at the UN was that several senators had been passing resolutions cutting off US funding to the UN. This was a problem because if the United States withheld more than two years of its UN dues, it would lose its vote in the UN. Consequently, it would also lose its veto in the UNSC, which would have been a disaster.

To solve the problem of unpaid dues, Holbrooke reached a private deal with the chairman of the Senate Foreign Relations Committee, Senator Jesse Helms of North Carolina: Helms would allow Holbrooke to repay the unpaid past dues to the UN. In return, Holbrooke would obtain a reduction of the annual US assessed dues to the UN.

However, there was one serious problem with this deal. A country's share of assessed UN dues is based on its share of global GDP. In the year 2000, the US share of the global GDP was around 30 percent, yet it was paying only 25 percent of the UN budget. In short, the United States was already receiving a discount—and Holbrooke wanted an even bigger one. Moreover, if the United States paid less, other countries had to pay more, and Holbrooke decided that Singapore was rich enough to increase its contribution.

Holbrooke was trying to fix a problem caused by the governance system of the United States (where a powerful senior senator could withhold legally required payments) by passing the burden on to other countries, especially (in his own eyes) the "richer" states like the Arab Gulf states and Singapore. To those countries, Holbrooke's move was manifestly unfair, and I was told to resist it. As a result, I went from being Holbrooke's "best friend" to being public enemy number one in his eyes.

In the process, I came to discover why Holbrooke had been so successful in his career. He was totally ruthless. At many informal gatherings with other diplomats, he would single out

Singapore (and me personally) for special mention as being unreasonable. He happened to do so at one gathering where our deputy permanent representative, Tan Yee Woan, was present. She stood up to him and refused to cave in, showing the reputation for toughness that Singapore's founding fathers had created.

Holbrooke also hoped that the "poor" African states would join him in putting pressure on "rich" Singapore. But the African diplomats tended to be loyal to their friends. Since I had developed a close relationship with many of the African ambassadors, almost none of them sided with him publicly. Indeed, the then Namibian ambassador to the UN, Martin Andjaba, told Holbrooke publicly at a meeting of the African Group that he couldn't support his campaign against Singapore. When Holbrooke asked, "Why not?," Andjaba replied, "Because Kishore is a friend of mine."

This bruising battle lasted many months. It proved to be a major distraction for the Singaporean Mission to the UN, as it was taking place in the year when our main priority was to get Singapore elected to the UNSC. This issue was finally resolved just before Christmas 2000, when the UNGA had to end its deliberations. The Europeans and others made a special appeal to Singapore to agree to pay a little more to close a compromise deal. In a gesture of goodwill, the Singaporean government agreed to pay around US$1 million more to the UN annually.

By Christmas 2000, it had also become evident that the Democratic Clinton administration would be replaced by a Republican one (after George W. Bush got the Supreme Court on his side in his contest against Al Gore). Hence, Holbrooke was right in trying to resolve this painful issue before the Republicans came in, as the Republicans were clearly much less sympathetic to multilateral organisations than the Democrats.

December 2000 proved to be a special month for the Singapore Mission to the UN. After we were elected to the UNSC on October 10, 2000, we discovered that we would hold the presidency on the very first day of our membership. The presidency of the UNSC rotated alphabetically. As the president of the UNSC in December 2000 was Russia, Singapore would succeed Russia in the presidency in January 2001. Since it would have been difficult for Singapore to preside over a council in which it had no experience (since we had never been a member before), we made a special appeal to the UNSC to allow us to sit in on its deliberations in November and December 2000. Surprisingly, the other members agreed. It was surprising because nonmembers are almost never allowed to sit in on UNSC deliberations, especially closed-door informal sessions.

The most important deliberations don't take place in the open chamber, which is regularly shown on TV. Instead, they take place in a small conference room with a small U-shaped table that can barely accommodate the fifteen permanent representatives, a few UN officials, and the two additional diplomats per delegation. Two empty seats were found for the Singaporean delegation. As a result, unlike most other nonpermanent members, we took part in the UNSC for twenty-six rather than twenty-four months. This was a great privilege.

I believe that I learned more about the state of affairs of our world, and the conduct of diplomacy, from these twenty-six months on the council than I had from my previous twenty-nine years in the Singaporean Foreign Service. I had nurtured many illusions about our world. The UNSC firmly scrubbed them out. Before we joined the council, I believed that in the contest between ethical principles and brute power, ethical principles would have some sway. After twenty-six months on the council, I came to the conclusion that power always trumped principles.

I was truly fortunate that the Foreign Ministry assigned an A-team of Singaporean diplomats, including Ms Christine Lee, deputy permanent representative; Brig Gen Yap Ong Heng, military adviser; Foo Chi Hsia and Umej Singh Bhatia, first secretaries; and Zainal Arif Mantaha, counsellor. This UNSC team was sent in addition to another A-team assigned to UNGA activities, which included Tan Yee Woan, deputy permanent representative, and Juniper Lim, Lynette Long, Vanessa Chan, and Gerard Ho, first secretaries. Hence, the team of diplomats assigned to assist me was more than double the size of the team assigned to me in my first term as PR to the UN.

With such strong teams in place, our presidency of the UNSC went well. Like most other presidents, Singapore decided to propose a special initiative on peacekeeping operations. As a result, on January 31, 2001, I made a statement on behalf of the council establishing a working group that was to "undertake an in-depth consideration of, inter alia, . . . ways to improve the three-way relationship between the Council, the troop-contributing countries and the Secretariat."[3]

The two years of working in the UNSC were among the most intense of my life, as we had to undertake a great learning journey to master a diverse range of subjects. The UNSC dealt only with problematic subjects, especially in conflict zones. It would be hard to summarise in any meaningful fashion all the issues we covered. This is why I tried to capture all my learning about global governance in the book *The Great Convergence*.[4]

An overview of the two years would show that we served on what were effectively two different versions of the UNSC: first, the one before 9/11 and second, the one after. Like many other institutions, the UNSC was transformed after the 9/11 attack on the World Trade Center towers on September 11, 2001. The world was not the same.

One constant was the US domination of the UNSC. As the only true superpower in a unipolar world, the United States was by far the most influential member. We discovered this in the very first month after we joined the UNSC in January 2001. One routine task that the UNSC had to complete was to appoint the various chairpersons of the Sanctions Committees. Since Singapore was the president of the UNSC, in theory, we could have played an influential role in appointing the chairpersons. In practice, we had no power. Even though Holbrooke was a lame-duck ambassador to the UN (since he would have to relinquish his appointment on January 20, 2001, when the Bush administration replaced the Clinton administration), he had all the power. We discovered this firsthand. Since Singapore is an Asian country, we wanted to chair the Sanctions Committee on Afghanistan. Instead, Holbrooke "assigned" the Liberian Sanctions Committee to Singapore. I asked the Foreign Ministry whether we should fight Holbrooke on this arbitrary assignment, and the Foreign Ministry decided not to. Most times, what the United States wants in the UNSC is what the United States gets.

I discovered other expressions of US dominance. Before any issue is discussed in the UNSC, the UN Secretariat issues a report on the state of the issue. In theory, the UN Secretariat is supposed to make an independent assessment of the subject. However, I happened to give a US diplomat a ride home on a rainy day after a diplomatic reception. His phone rang while we were in the car together. I could hear the entire conversation clearly, and I heard the US diplomat give precise instructions to the UN Secretariat official on which paragraphs had to be removed from a report that we were going to discuss in the UNSC on the following day.

Curiously, the United States has always made a point of complaining about the "weakness" of the UN. Yet one of the key reasons why the UN is "weak" is that it's the deliberate policy of the United States to keep the UN weak. It's shocking how few Americans know this important fact about the UN.

After Holbrooke left the UN on January 20, 2001, the US delegation (under the new Bush administration) showed little interest in the UN or the UNSC. This was clearly signalled by the fact that the Bush administration failed to send an ambassador to the UN until September 2001. In the interim, the US Mission to the UN was run by Acting Representative James B. Cunningham. James was an accomplished and seasoned professional diplomat. Hence, things ran smoothly.

One of the US officials, Cameron Hume, once paid a compliment to the Singaporean delegation after Foo Chi Hsia had delivered a statement on Afghanistan in which she raised an obvious question: What was the purpose of the UNSC sanctions on the Taliban regime? Would they transform the regime or improve the condition of the Afghan people? The answer was clearly no. Cameron told Chi Hsia that he thought that Singapore had raised a valid question. However, since the United States was a great power prone to imposing sanctions whenever a problem appeared, there was no question of changing US policy.

However, everything changed after 9/11. The US delegation went from being one of the most detached to being frantically active. This was signalled by the decision of the Bush administration to send a heavyweight ambassador to the UN, John Negroponte. Negroponte was a professional US diplomat who had worked closely together with Holbrooke when they had been in Vietnam together from 1964 to 1968. It helped that Negroponte was also a friend of mine, since our paths had crossed several times in my diplomatic career.

The first act of the United States was to push for the adoption of a resolution that would legitimise the US invasion of Afghanistan to remove the Taliban regime and eliminate the forces of Osama bin Laden. After the terrorist attacks on the United States, this UNSC resolution won immediate and unanimous support. One of the first presidents to contact President George W. Bush was President Jiang Zemin of China. Since the United States and China had had a major confrontation over the crash landing of a US spy plane on Hainan Island on April 1, 2001, just a few months earlier, relations between them could have been tense. But they weren't. Instead, the attack by Osama bin Laden on the United States proved to be a huge blessing for China, as the Bush administration focused its attention on the Islamic threat rather than the Red China threat for its entire term in office.

You could ascertain the state of the world just by observing the interactions between the ambassadors on the UNSC, especially the five ambassadors from the countries that had permanent seats: China, France, Russia, the United Kingdom, and the United States. These were the five veto-holding members. Since the veto was a powerful symbol of their global power and standing, the five countries assigned truly outstanding ambassadors to the UN: Wang Yingfan from China, Jean-David Levitte from France, Sergei Lavrov from Russia, Sir Jeremy Greenstock from the United Kingdom, and John Negroponte from the United States.

It was fascinating to watch the cut and thrust among them. And there was a lot of it, as the United States began trying to pass a resolution to authorise an invasion of Iraq to remove Saddam Hussein. As I write about the Iraq war twenty years after the US invasion in March 2003, it's clear that a consensus has developed that this was a huge mistake. Some friends of the United States, including friends in the UNSC, tried to warn that such an invasion would be a mistake. Living through the buildup to this disastrous Iraq war, I could see that the United States was totally incapable of listening to or heeding the advice of friends such as France and Germany.

Instead, France was vilified in the United States. In 2003, Republican members of the US Congress decided to rename "French fries" "freedom fries." Once, when I attended a high-powered lunch with senior American corporate executives, an American CEO told the waiter to throw away the expensive French wine that was being served. Anti-French sentiment reached a fever pitch. Twenty years later, the United States should send an apology to France and thank France for trying to save it from a disastrous war. But I doubt that such an apology will ever be sent.

What shocked me was that many thoughtful and well-informed Americans bought the narrative of the Bush administration on Iraq. I had a practice of hosting brainstorming lunches to discuss the issues of the day. I invited a distinguished international law professor, Thomas Franck from New York University, to one of these lunches. He began the conversation by asking a provocative question: What was the technical difference, under international law, between the impending US invasion of Iraq and Hitler's invasion of the Sudetenland? After he raised this question, I became very scared. I had the impression that the bright and influential New Yorkers in the room were about to lynch Prof Franck for raising this question in these terms.

This encounter with American groupthink in the buildup to the illegal American invasion of Iraq in March 2003 continues to trouble me greatly twenty years after the event. I see a similar groupthink emerging when it comes to dealing with China in 2023. Groupthink has captured the world's most educated intelligentsia twice in my lifetime. The remarkable thing about the determination to invade Iraq is that many friends of the United States, in addition to France and Germany, bluntly warned the United States of the dangers of invasion. Three months after the US/UK invasion of Iraq in March 2003, I happened to play golf with Sir Jeremy Greenstock, the British ambassador to the UN. After the golf game, we drank beer together. He said to me, "Kishore, summer is here. We're still in Iraq. So what was the hurry in mounting the invasion?" Clearly, the British would have preferred an enabling UNSC resolution that would have made the invasion of Iraq legal. But the Bush administration was determined to invade Iraq come what may.

A senior Egyptian diplomat told me about a meeting between Omar Suleiman, then the director of the General Intelligence Directorate in Egypt, and Dick Cheney, who had become vice president of the United States just before the Iraq war. Suleiman accurately and perceptively warned that while the invasion of Iraq would be easy, the US forces would then be bogged down in a painful war of attrition, and many US soldiers would be killed. His prediction proved exactly right. But Cheney brushed it aside and just said, "We will kill them all." Suleiman was known to be the "tough guy" in the then Mubarak government of Egypt, but even this hard man was shocked by Cheney's brutal retort. Clearly, the loss of Iraqi lives mattered little to Cheney, reinforcing the central lesson I learned from my two years in the UNSC: power always trumps ethical principles.

As the Bush administration, and the American elites in general, were focused on the aftermath of 9/11 and the Iraq war, none of them paid careful attention to an event of even greater significance than 9/11 that took place in 2001: China's admission to the WTO. To be honest, I didn't pay attention to this WTO admission either, yet it changed world history far more significantly than the Iraq war did. In 2001, when China joined the WTO, the GDP of the United States was US$10.6 trillion, while that of China was only US$1.3 trillion. In short, the US economy was eight times larger than the Chinese economy. By 2022, the US GDP of US$25.5 trillion was only 1.4 times larger than the Chinese GDP of US$17.9 trillion. When future historians reflect on the first two decades of the twenty-first century, they will surely note that the strategic minds of the American establishment were focused on short-term issues, like the Iraq war, while the strategic minds of the Chinese establishment were focused on long-term trends, like China's admission into the WTO. Kissinger commented on this difference in his book *On China*, and I later tried to do the same in my book *Has China Won?*

Another contentious issue that the Bush administration brought to the UNSC was the creation of the International Criminal Court (ICC) by the Rome Statute on July 1, 2002. The main fear of the Bush administration was that US soldiers could be prosecuted by the ICC for fighting in wars that were technically illegal (like the wars in Kosovo or Iraq) because they hadn't been endorsed by the UNSC. So just hours before the Rome Statute came into force,[5] the Bush administration proposed a resolution to provide "immunity" for US soldiers.

The key operative parts of the resolution said that "the ICC, if a case arises involving current or former officials or personnel from a contributing State not a Party to the Rome Statute over acts or omissions relating to a United Nations established or authorized operation, shall for a twelve-month period starting

1 July 2002 not commence or proceed with investigation or prosecution of any such case." It also "[expressed] the intention to renew the request in paragraph 1 under the same conditions each 1 July for further 12-month periods for as long as may be necessary."[6] When the debate began, the British delegation gave a high-minded speech explaining how the United Kingdom, as a state party of the ICC, couldn't support a resolution that undermined it. However, by the end of the debate, the British delegation made a complete U-turn and eloquently explained why it supported the resolution. For the British government, developing good ties with the new Bush administration was more important than fidelity to key international laws and principles.

I was shocked by this complete British U-turn on the ICC, as the British had consistently told us from the days when Singapore was a British colony that in British culture and tradition, the rule of law was paramount. No one was above the rule of law. No one could bend the rule of law. Nevertheless, the United Kingdom was able to "bend" its legal treaty obligations to the ICC and allow exceptions for US servicemen not to be prosecuted.

The five permanent members (P5) were overwhelmingly more powerful than the ten elected members (E10). In theory, the fifteen members are "equal"; in practice, there are five "members" of the council and ten "visitors" to the council. Before Singapore joined in January 2001, the Chilean delegation shared this insight with us. We discovered how true it was all through our stay, both before and after 9/11.

The P5 were more powerful because of their veto powers. In theory, the veto applied only to "substantive" issues.

Procedural issues couldn't be vetoed. But this theory was completely wrong in practice. Once when Singapore presided over the UNSC, probably in May 2002, we received a request from the president of the ICJ, also known as the World Court, to brief the council. Since the ICJ was an affiliated member of the UN family and its statute was annexed to the UN Charter, I assumed that there couldn't possibly be any objection to the president of the ICJ briefing the council. I was wrong. When I brought up this request at one of the informal consultations to secure agreement, all the delegations except the US delegation agreed.

After some discussion, it became clear that the US delegation wouldn't budge. I then told the US delegation that since the question of whether to invite the president of the ICJ was a "procedural" issue, we could resolve it with a vote. If the majority agreed, we could proceed to invite him. The US delegation had an ingenious response: they said that whether the proposed invitation to the president of the ICJ was a procedural issue was itself a substantive issue—and since they believed it to be a substantive issue, they could veto it. In short, even on procedural issues, the veto could come into play. Since virtually no delegation wanted to confront the US delegation, I worked out a compromise whereby the president of the ICJ could brief the members of the UNSC in a private closed-door session in the main chamber. No press or nonmembers could attend. The United States prides itself on being a society that welcomes public discussions so that different views can be contested in the "marketplace of ideas." Here, it preferred to keep the discussions under wraps, with no public exposure.

It is a tragedy that the United States has chosen to walk away from the ICJ, as the World Court was essentially America's gift to the world. The field of international arbitration began with the Jay Treaty of 1794 between the United States and the United Kingdom, and the United States continued to tend this field over the course of nearly two centuries.[7] However, after the ICJ ruled against the United States on Nicaragua in 1986,[8] the Reagan administration decided to withdraw from the compulsory ICJ jurisdiction. When this happened, few Americans realised that they were ditching a US creation. As the United States acquired the trappings of the sole superpower when the Cold War ended, it decided to place itself beyond any jurisdiction except its own. This prefigured a series of horrible international mistakes in which the United States showed its indifference to international legal opinions that might have caused it to moderate its behaviour. Everybody lost from its refusal to participate in the ICJ.

The United States was not the only P5 member to threaten to use its veto or its influence on procedural issues. Russia and China also did so. One of the anomalies of the UNSC is that its rules of procedure are "provisional." Many procedural matters had been agreed upon through practice since 1946. However, the council members have been averse to reopening the Rules of Procedure to codify them officially.[9] As a result, many UNSC procedures are cumbersome and outdated, and there has been no attempt to improve or update them.

When we joined the council, I asked myself how the Singaporean delegation could contribute to improving the UNSC.

Since Singapore was known for its efficiency and good governance, I thought that the Singaporean delegation could help by trying to improve the "procedures" of the council. To avoid resistance from the United States, the most powerful delegation, I managed to persuade McKinsey & Company, the best-known American consultancy firm, to agree to provide pro bono services to help bring us into the twenty-first century. Since the West was known for its belief in modern and rational policymaking, I assumed that the Western delegations would support our well-intentioned initiative. Instead, we ran into a wall of resistance from the P5. The French delegation explained this resistance in a private comment that eventually reached our ears: "Why do these 'tourists' think that they can come into our home and rearrange our furniture?"

The term "tourists" was probably apt. It captured how the P5 viewed the elected members of the council. However, while the P5 were resistant to changes suggested by the E10, it did not mean that all the P5 were complacent about improvements. In our two years on the UNSC, we discovered a major difference among the P5 members. Three of them, the United States, China, and Russia, had no doubt that they deserved to be members of the UNSC. They were confident about their "great power" status. By contrast, the United Kingdom and France were less confident. They accurately understood if a new UNSC was created that was fit for the new power configuration of the twenty-first century, it was unlikely that the United Kingdom and France would be included as veto-wielding permanent members. As the *Financial Times* columnist Martin Wolf commented in 2009, "Within a decade a world in which the UK is on the United Nations Security Council and India is not will seem beyond laughable. The old order passes. The sooner the world adjusts, the better."[10] Needless to say, a decade and more later, nothing had changed. But since the British and French delegations understood their precarious position on the UNSC, they felt an obligation to work harder than the other P5 members and to deliver results. This also explains why the United Kingdom and France have not used their veto in a solitary no vote in recent decades.

The last thing I expected was to discover that the French delegation was probably the most hardworking delegation. I discovered this when the fifteen ambassadors decided to visit fifteen African countries over ten days. The UN chartered a plane for us to ensure that we could complete the demanding itinerary. Still, we had a punishing schedule.

The ambassador of France then was Jean-David Levitte. He led the delegation, and he slept much less than the rest of us. Each night, after we went to bed, he would convene a meeting with his French officials. They would then produce notes from the day's meetings. Early the next morning, the notes of the previous day's meetings would be ready for us. Since Singapore is known for its hardworking culture, especially among its civil servants, and France is known for its thirty-five-hour work week, I was surprised and embarrassed to discover that the French ambassador to the UN worked much harder than the Singaporean ambassador to the UN.

The highlight of the African trip was the invitation to tea in the home of Nelson Mandela. He lived in a comfortable midsized bungalow in Soweto. It was a tight squeeze to get fifteen ambassadors and the UN officials into his modest living room, where he received us warmly and graciously. British ambassador Jeremy Greenstock's wife, Anne, told her husband not to wash his hands after meeting Mandela as she wanted to shake the hand of someone who had shaken hands with Mandela.

So did fifteen UN ambassadors accomplish anything on this trip to Africa on an expensively chartered aircraft? The honest answer is no, although we did gain a better understanding of some of the deeper problems of Africa (which occupied most of the agenda of the UNSC). From time to time, we also gained a sense of the precariousness of the situation there. In Bujumbura, the economic capital of Burundi, we were told to complete our work as soon as possible and to return to the aircraft before sundown because after the sun set, the airport where we had just landed would occasionally be shelled. I felt an enormous sense of relief when our aircraft took off just as the sun was setting.

Travel in some parts of the world is risky. As chairman of the Liberian Sanctions Committee, I was told that I was expected to visit the countries of West Africa to study the situation there. I travelled in a small private jet from Freetown, Sierra Leone, to Abuja, the capital of Nigeria—a somewhat tense five-hour flight, as the small plane had no toilet on board. Still, we were lucky that we took off from the Freetown airport because the only way to commute from there to the city was on Ukrainian helicopters hired by the United Nations. We made two trips in these helicopters. Two weeks after we left Freetown, one of the helicopters crashed and killed all the occupants. While my respect for the P5 in the UNSC went down (as I was turned off by their bullying tactics), my respect for UN staff went up, as they were prepared to take on risky assignments, even in dangerous places. Many lost their lives. A good friend, Sérgio Vieira de Mello, was killed in a terrorist explosion in Baghdad in August 2003.

As Singapore was on the UNSC until December 31, 2002, we also had a ringside seat to the increasingly heated debate on Iraq as it became clear that the Bush administration had already decided to invade Iraq and remove Saddam Hussein come what may, weapons of mass destruction or no weapons of mass destruction. But the United States wanted an enabling UNSC resolution to legitimise the war. The Russian and French delegations were then fiercely opposed to providing such legitimisation. This debate on the impending Iraq war also made us aware that the real discussions were taking place among the P5 members secretly and without any publicity in locations that were kept from the E10. The P5 would bargain and make trade-offs among themselves. When they finally agreed on a resolution, they would present it to the E10 as a fait accompli. That is how they presented Resolution 1441, the last resolution on Iraq to be adopted by consensus, to us for adoption in November 2002. In theory, the E10 could have rejected the P5 draft resolution, but in practice, virtually no elected member could stand up to the combined pressure from those five powers. When the P5 agreed on a resolution, it would have been politically impossible for the E10 to oppose it.

One other key lesson I learned in the UN was that the P5 had no qualms about double standards. One key human right that the West had traditionally defended for decades, especially since the promulgation of the Universal Declaration of Human Rights (UDHR) in 1948, was the principle that no human being should be subjected to torture. Indeed, the UDHR explicitly says, "No one shall be subjected to torture or to cruel, inhuman or degrading treatment or punishment." As a practical expression of this commitment to the principles of human rights, the US Congress mandated in the Foreign Assistance Act of 1961 that the US State Department should produce an annual report documenting the status of human rights in every UN member state. These reports have been dutifully produced each year.

As a diplomat from Singapore, I noticed that the reports were often critical of the human rights situation in Singapore. Since independence in 1965, the Singaporean government had detained prisoners without trial under the Internal Security Act on the grounds that ordinary people wouldn't testify against supporters of the Communist Party of Malaya for fear of reprisals. The US State Department's Country Reports on Human Rights Practices cited such detentions as instances of arbitrary arrest or imprisonment. It would also cite, without independent verification, Amnesty International's reports that Singapore carried out torture on its internal security detainees.

Using the principle of universalisability, when the US government advocated that the Singaporean government shouldn't carry out torture, it was advocating the universal principle that no government should carry out torture. The European governments supported the United States when it made such statements. Given the long-standing and categorical stand on torture taken by the US government, you can well imagine the shock that many of us, especially in the developing world, felt when the US government became the first developed government to carry out torture on the Muslim detainees in Guantanamo.

That shock was enormous. Three other aftershocks were equally significant. First, even though every European government had consistently defended the principle of "no torture," no European government spoke out against the US government carrying out torture. Both the UK and French governments remained silent. Secondly, since the US government had begun to implement torture, it had clearly lost the moral right (as an indirect consequence of the principle of universalisability) to criticise other countries for the use of torture. Logically, the US State Department should have ceased criticising other countries for carrying out torture. Amazingly, it did not. Even more amazingly, this blatant hypocrisy by the State Department was never highlighted by the leading members of the liberal establishment in the United States, who also failed to see that their silence made them silent accomplices in this massive hypocrisy. This was the third aftershock: the failure of the "liberals" to see that they were all perceived as massive hypocrites by the rest of the world.

Such events make one aware of the power of Hans Christian Andersen's fable "The Emperor's New Clothes." It took a child to say openly and clearly that the emperor was wearing no clothes. In the eyes of the rest of the world, the West had lost its moral credibility when it began to impose a double standard on the key human rights issue of torture. Yet the West continued to lecture the rest of the world on human rights despite the fact that in the eyes of the majority of the world's population—the 88 percent who live outside the West—it had lost its moral standing to do so. Indeed, while the P5 members—especially the three key Western members, the United States, the United Kingdom, and France—gave eloquent speeches on their strong commitment to key ethical principles, they were not embarrassed in any way by the double standard they practiced. To be fair, all great powers practice double standards. However, the Western powers always put themselves on moral pedestals. They now look ridiculous on these pedestals.

When Singapore served on the UNSC, one of our fellow members was Ireland. Ireland was represented by a brilliant and capable ambassador, Richard Ryan. One day, he said to me, "Kishore, I hate you." I asked him why. He replied that before he spoke on the council, every word he said had to be approved by his capital, Dublin. By contrast, for most issues, the Singaporean government gave me greater freedom of speech. The government would provide (in consultation with me and my team) a few bullet points that spelled out our position, and I was free to choose my own words to express them. Ryan resented me (in a friendly fashion) because he wasn't.

However, one day, he decided to take a risk. When we were discussing Iraq, Richard happened to speak after the French ambassador, Jean-David Levitte. Since Levitte had expressed concern about the humanitarian situation in Iraq, Richard added two words, "like France," when he expressed a similar concern. When the US diplomats in the room heard Ambassador Ryan agreeing with France, they immediately called the

US Embassy in Dublin to demand an explanation. The US Embassy immediately called the Irish Foreign Ministry to find out why Richard had said "like France." Within five minutes, the junior Irish diplomat sitting behind Richard Ryan received a phone call from the Irish Foreign Ministry asking him why Ryan had said "like France." This illustrates how closely the P5 ambassadors—especially the US ambassador—monitored the statements made by the E10 ambassadors. Still, Richard Ryan was lucky: he was only asked for an explanation. By contrast, the ambassador of Mauritius almost lost his job as a result of American pressure when he questioned US policy on Iraq. The US government applied enormous pressure on the Mauritian government to withdraw its ambassador.

It's a tragedy that the Bush administration didn't listen to the dissenting voices on Iraq. If the United States had, for example, listened to France, it would have been spared the disastrous invasion of Iraq. But the US delegation wasn't the only one that failed to listen. One of the most awkward moments I experienced as permanent representative to the UN came when the Palestinian delegation to the UN presented a resolution on Palestine. Singapore was and is a member of the NAM. Until we joined the UNSC, it was the tradition for all NAM members to automatically support all Palestinian draft resolutions. Singapore became the first NAM member to withhold support, as we thought that the resolution was unbalanced. This led the then Jamaican deputy permanent representative to quip that Singapore had become the first "elected" member of the UNSC to cast a veto since Singapore, as a NAM member, had prevented the tabling of a resolution in the name of the NAM.

Before Singapore joined the UNSC, no other NAM member had refused to cosponsor a resolution on Palestine. We were the first NAM member to refuse to do so.

Unlike many elected members to the UNSC who feel an exaggerated sense of self-importance while serving on the powerful council, Singapore never forgot that we were permanent members of the UNGA and temporary members of the UNSC. We also emphasised in our speeches that the UNSC was accountable to the UNGA, according to Article 24 of the UN Charter, which states, "The Security Council shall submit annual and, when necessary, special reports to the General Assembly for its consideration." Surely, this makes it clear that the UNSC is accountable to the UNGA and not vice versa. This is why I said at a UNSC meeting on November 30, 2001, that

> if, just after a massive debate in the General Assembly on the report of the Security Council to the Assembly, we decide to ignore the views expressed and proceed to do exactly the same thing next year as we did in previous years, then we reinforce the views of those who say the Security Council does not listen to the members of the General Assembly. If we want to show that we are listening, then it is time for us to produce some real changes.

Sadly, many UNGA members are not pushing harder for greater UNSC accountability to the UNGA.

Since Singapore did not receive development assistance or financial grants from any P5 member, we became one of the few elected members to publicly chide a P5 member. This happened in a month when the United States was presiding, May 2001. The president was then Ambassador James Cunningham. We publicly protested the speaking slot assigned to the Singaporean delegation. In theory, speaking slots were assigned on the basis of who signed up first. Since we knew that we had signed up early, we should have been assigned an early slot. Instead, we were pushed to the bottom of the list. By publicly protesting, we put on record the devious practice of the UN Secretariat always giving preference to P5 members over E10 members in allocating speaking slots.

After this unusual public chiding of a P5 member on the UNSC, we followed up with a proposal to have speaking slots for the UNSC "balloted" so that the Secretariat would no longer, through back-room deals, give preferential treatment to P5 members. Clearly, this move angered the P5 members; it became another instance of the "tourists" trying to rearrange the furniture in their living room. Nonetheless, despite their resentment, they finally agreed to our proposal.

Many people, including many of my friends in Singapore, have little idea how brutal international relations can be, especially to small states. Small states are routinely reminded of the small space they have for manoeuvre, especially among the great powers.

This situation had prompted one of my predecessors, Ambassador Chew Tai Soo, to launch an initiative in the UN to set up a Forum of Small States with the happy acronym FOSS. I call it a happy acronym because the movie *Star Wars: Episode II* had just been released in May 2002. The New Zealand ambassador and forum member, who had a good sense of humour, went around the UN saying, "May the FOSS be with you."

The year 2002 was clearly a busy and active one for me, as it was Singapore's second year on the UNSC. Yet even while I was busy, active, and thriving in my job, I developed a strange medical condition: acute back pain. Indeed, it was so painful that I had to abandon all my physical exercises. I could no longer jog every second day, and I had to suspend my golf games. Fortunately, the island of Manhattan had many excellent doctors. After doing some research, I tracked down the best surgeons in New York who worked on back pain. Two of them gave me bad news: both said that I would need invasive spinal surgery to cure my back pain. The first one merely suggested that he would have to chip off a bit of my L4 and L5 vertebrae. The second said that he would have to fuse L4, L5, and more with a metallic clasp to get rid of the pain. Reluctantly, Anne and I came to the conclusion that back surgery was the only way out since the pain had persisted for several months. We set a date for the surgery to take place.

However, before that date, I decided to fly to a small town somewhere in the United States to meet a friend of a friend who had a reputation for curing back pain through physiotherapy. I was desperately trying to avoid surgery, as I had heard the story of how the wife of the Singapore defence attaché in Jakarta, Mrs Naidu, had become paralysed after invasive spinal surgery. The physiotherapist was a nice woman. Sadly, her physical treatment didn't help. However, I spotted a book on her bookshelf titled *Healing Back Pain* and asked her if I could borrow it. Fortunately, she lent it to me.

After reading the book, I discovered that the author was a medical doctor in New York City named John Sarno. He was almost eighty years old at the time and therefore was reluctant to take on new patients. Fortunately, he agreed to see me. I appeared at his office at the appointed day and time with US$2,000 in cash.

Meeting him proved to be one of the luckiest events in my life. After examining me, he told me that any spinal surgery on me would amount to medical malpractice, as there was nothing wrong with my spine. Instead, he was convinced that my back pain was a natural result of the acute stress I was going through. I patiently attended several lectures that he gave to his students. I also followed his advice and wrote down in a book every possible issue that could have been causing me stress.

Miraculously, the treatment of focusing on and directly confronting sources of stress worked. After a few months, the back pain disappeared. I started jogging again, and I could play golf. As I reflected on this episode, I was truly shocked that I had come so close to undergoing an invasive spinal surgery that could have paralysed me. Instead, by heeding Dr Sarno, I was completely cured of back pain!

For anyone whose back pain might be stress related, I unreservedly recommend *Healing Back Pain*. Dr Sarno warned me that the pain might recur if the stress recurred, and it did a few months later, while I was still in New York. When it did, I immediately called Dr Sarno to see if I could make an appointment with him. He apologised profusely and said that he had a full schedule, but a few hours later, he called to ask the address of my office. He told me that his office at New York University

Hospital had suffered a blackout, requiring him to cancel his appointments. However, as he had to take the Third Avenue bus to his uptown home, he would come see me in my office. It was an extraordinarily generous gesture from an eighty-year-old man. I was deeply touched. And I have no doubt that his generosity of spirit helped me to get rid of this second bout of back pain.

By following his methods, I was also able to discover the real source of my stress. It proved to be obvious: in the second half of 2002, as we were approaching the end of our stint on the UNSC, the main question that haunted my subconscious was what would happen to me after Singapore left the UNSC on December 31, 2002. Returning to my previous job as permanent secretary of the MFA was not an option, nor did any other overseas posting appear likely. Most of them would have been demotions anyway because few were considered as significant as serving on the UNSC for Singapore.

Nor was I easily employable anywhere else. I looked around to see whether any American think tanks would be interested in a diplomat from Singapore. One of my good friends was Strobe Talbott, who was then serving as president of the Brookings Institution, a well-funded and prestigious think tank in Washington, DC. He said that he would be happy to take me on. However, I would have to raise my own funding to cover my salary, and Brookings would take a cut—as an administrative fee—of any funds that I raised. Since I wasn't a US citizen, raising money in the United States wouldn't be easy. Similarly, the International Peace Academy in New York, after initially expressing interest in me, turned me down.

The stress I felt was aggravated by the fact that we had very little savings—most of my salary had gone into supporting my immediate family of five and my extended family of siblings and parents. Not for the first time, it seemed that my diplomatic career had hit a dead end. I had no alternative to fall back on. Quite often, I went to bed feeling a deep sense of despair about the future.

Almost no one in New York had any sense of my inner turmoil, partly because of my mother's advice that I should put butter on my lips and smile. So that was what people saw. Indeed, my social standing in both the UN and New York circles began to soar because of a rumour—wildly unfounded—that I could be a successor to Kofi Annan as UN secretary-general. Kofi Annan had once called me to his office for a private one-on-one chat to encourage me to run for the secretary-general post.

Hence, in the second half of 2002 and first half of 2003, I led a very strange double life. Externally, I was perceived as a rising star; internally, I was in despair. The back pain came and went and came back again. I could see the end of the road coming towards me, and I saw no alternative to the dead end.

Then Lady Luck intervened.

CHAPTER 11

Back to School

I T BEGAN WITH A LUNCH IN NEW YORK IN THE MIDDLE OF 2003.

When Tony Tan, who was then DPM, was visiting New York, he invited me for lunch at the Palace Hotel. Since the hotel was owned by the Brunei government, the restaurant was appropriately named the Istana (which means "palace" in Malay). Dr Tan told me that Lee Kuan Yew would turn eighty on September 16, 2003. The Cabinet wanted to honour him and his contributions to the country on his eightieth birthday.

There was one major problem: throughout his life, Lee Kuan Yew had refused to attach his name to any building or institution, bridge, or highway (as was the universal custom in many countries). Mr Lee had several times told his Cabinet colleagues that many Third World leaders had attached their names to buildings, and then their names were scrubbed out when they died. Mr Lee said that he didn't want his name to be scrubbed out. Whenever the idea of erecting a monument to him was raised, he would respond, "Remember 'Ozymandias,'" referring to Shelley's poem about the king whose only legacy was ruins in the desert with the following words on a pedestal: "My name is Ozymandias, King of Kings; Look on my Works ye Mighty, and despair!"

On his eightieth birthday, Mr Lee finally relented and agreed to have his name attached to a school of public policy. The Cabinet managed to persuade him by telling him that his legacy to Singapore would always be associated with good governance. Hence, an institution dedicated to promoting good governance would be an appropriate means of recognising his contributions.

Setting up the institution would be the easy part. Finding the right person to run it would be a challenge. Even though Mr Lee was turning eighty, he remained a formidable political presence in Singapore. He continued to intimidate many, even senior civil servants. Hence, there would be few volunteers brave or foolish enough to take on running an institution named after him. An equally difficult challenge would be to find a name that was acceptable to Mr Lee.

It was therefore a great honour to be selected to be the dean of the new Lee Kuan Yew School of Public Policy. I sensed this when Dr Tan made the offer to me, and I accepted immediately. It was nonetheless a challenging assignment to build a world-class school of public policy in record time.

One key reason why I took the plunge was that I was inclined to leave diplomacy to enter the world of academia. That world had always attracted me. Indeed, in all my overseas assignments, I had always stayed in touch with academic institutions, especially in New York. I regularly participated in academic seminars at Columbia and New York Universities, and I had kept up my writing for international affairs journals. As of 2023, I am the most published Singaporean in *Foreign Affairs*, and few other Asians have written as regularly. Dr Tan warned me that building a good school of public policy wouldn't be easy. He said that business schools were inherently financially viable, as their students expected to be paid well after graduating and were confident that they could recoup the cost of the degree. Hence, business students could afford to pay their tuition fees. In contrast, public policy students, especially those who would go on to work with Third World governments, expected to earn little after graduating and couldn't afford to pay the fees. Hence, as Dr Tan told me, in schools of public policy, the students would have to be provided with scholarships. Without scholarships, we couldn't attract Third World civil servants to study at the school. Fortunately, about S$63 million was raised at Lee Kuan Yew's eightieth birthday party in September 2003. However, more was needed.

By the time I stepped down as dean in December 2017, the Lee Kuan Yew School of Public Policy had become the third-best-endowed school of public policy in the world, surpassed only by two much older institutions at Ivy League universities, namely, the HKS and the Princeton School of Public and International Affairs (SPIA). (Indeed, the Princeton SPIA is a strong example of what Lee Kuan Yew meant when he said, "Remember 'Ozymandias.'" The school was formerly known as the Woodrow Wilson School of Public and International Affairs, but Princeton changed its name in 2020 after a series of incidents of violence against African Americans sparked a national reckoning with the history of racial violence in the United States. Christopher Eisgruber, the president of Princeton, said, "When a university names a school of public policy for a political leader, it inevitably suggests that the honoree is a model for students who study at the school. This searing moment in American history has made clear that Wilson's racism disqualifies him from that role.") I discovered in the course of my deanship that I had a skill for fundraising. Perhaps I had inherited the Sindhi gene that had always produced good salesmen.

In my early years as dean, I would meet Lee Kuan Yew personally to brief him on the school's progress. In one conversation, we agreed that we should approach Hong Kong business magnate Li Ka-shing, the richest man in Asia, to support the school. Mr Lee kindly agreed to give me a letter of introduction. The letter had three short paragraphs. The first paragraph introduced me to Mr Li. The second paragraph noted that the Lee Kuan Yew School of Public Policy would like to name a building after Mr Li. The third paragraph said tersely, "We hope you will make an appropriate contribution." I asked the NUS Development Office how much I should ask from Mr Li. The Development Office strongly cautioned me against asking for too much. They suggested S$30 million. Since the Ministry of Education would give a matching grant, that would lead to a S$60 million increase in the endowment.

I decided to do my own research on Mr Li's philanthropic contributions. I learned that his largest donation had been to Hong Kong University for a sum of HK$1 billion (or S$200 million). Without consulting anyone (and without trying to cover my backside, per the usual Civil Service tradition), I decided that I would ask for S$100 million.

Ambassador Toh Hock Ghim, our consul general in Hong Kong, and I walked into Li Ka-shing's office armed with the letter from Lee Kuan Yew. I had, of course, prepared a thirty-minute pitch about the virtues of the Lee Kuan Yew School of Public Policy that I would deliver after Mr Li had read the letter. I sat on the edge of my seat, ready to begin as soon as Li Ka-shing had read the letter. However, Mr Li suddenly turned to me and asked, "How much?" I said, "One hundred million dollars." He asked, "Singapore or Hong Kong?" I replied, "Singapore." He frowned. Then he turned to his assistant, Amy Au, and began a discussion in Cantonese. I did not know what they were saying. I thought that I was done for.

Instead, after three minutes of discussion, Mr Li stretched out his hand to me to shake my hand and say, "Okay." I could have fainted then. I had never expected this complete and immediate agreement. I had raised S$100 million in three minutes. Even for established universities like Yale and Harvard, raising such sums usually requires weeks (if not months) of prenegotiations.

Clearly, this wouldn't have happened without the letter from Mr Lee. This success with Mr Li emboldened me to become more ambitious in my fundraising efforts. On the fifth anniversary of the Lee Kuan Yew School of Public Policy, we set a target of raising S$5 million. Instead, we managed to raise S$33 million. As a result, by the time I stepped down as dean in December 2017, the endowment of the Lee Kuan Yew School of Public Policy had grown to over S$500 million.

Fundraising is inherently difficult. It's never easy to ask people to part with their money. However, that wasn't my most difficult job as dean. The toughest part of my job was to raise the academic standing of the Lee Kuan Yew School of Public Policy and have it recognised as one of the leading schools in the world. It's no secret that academic institutions can't be built overnight. This is why the greatest universities are centuries old. Oxford was founded in 1096 or earlier. Harvard was founded in 1636.

Yet even in the area of academic reputation building, I was helped by a generous gift from Lee Kuan Yew. In early 2004, the partners of McKinsey & Company decided to hold their annual conference in Asia for the first time, choosing a location in Shanghai. Lee Kuan Yew agreed to address this meeting. As a quid pro quo, McKinsey agreed to do a pro bono study for him. Mr Lee donated this generous pro bono package of consulting services to the Lee Kuan Yew School of Public Policy.

It turned out to be a very valuable gift. Using their global resources, McKinsey studied all the great public policy schools around the world to distil the key ingredients for building a world-class school of public policy. They then presented their results to Mr Lee and a senior team of Singaporean ministers, including Tony Tan, Teo Chee Hean, and Tharman Shanmugaratnam. After they endorsed this blueprint, I was given a clear path to follow, and I had the political protection to do so.

One member of this McKinsey team was Stavros Yiannouka, who decided to join the Lee Kuan Yew School of Public Policy to help implement the plan.

His contributions to the success of the school were enormous, as were those of the other founding members of the team, like Francis Chong, Hui Weng Tat, Kenneth Paul Tan, and Scott Fritzen. On the eighth anniversary of the school in 2012, we decided to produce a book that documented how and why the school was succeeding. The book contains many nuggets of wisdom.

For example, working out the curriculum of a school of public policy isn't easy. What do future leaders in public service need to learn? McKinsey learned that an ideal curriculum would include economics, politics, and leadership and management. One life lesson I had learned from Lee Kuan Yew was the following statement he frequently made: "I check, I double-check, I triple-check, and then I check again." So I decided to double-check McKinsey's recommendation on the curriculum with Joseph Nye, the dean of the most famous school of public policy in the world, when we both attended the annual meeting of the World Economic Forum (WEF) in Davos. Prof Nye confirmed what McKinsey had recommended.

A great school ultimately rests on great faculty. Probably the hardest job I had was to recruit world-class faculty from leading schools in the world, like Harvard University, Oxford University, and the London School of Economics. It wasn't easy. However, we eventually succeeded. To be honest, we were helped by the fact that the school is part of NUS, whose academic standing has soared since the Lee Kuan Yew School of

Public Policy was established in 2004. In the QS World University Rankings, NUS ranked eighteenth in 2004. However, by 2024, it had climbed to eighth place. One of my great blessings as dean was that all three presidents of NUS whom I worked with, namely, Shih Choon Fong, Tan Chorh Chuan, and Tan Eng Chye, were enormously supportive. They were among the best bosses I have had in my life. In my early years as dean, Choon Fong gave me a great book to understand the nature of universities: *The University: An Owner's Manual* by Henry Rosovsky. This book was valuable because it made me think hard about who "owned" the Lee Kuan Yew School of Public Policy. The answer wasn't clear!

In Rosovsky's view, the primary "owners" of a university were faculty, administrators, and students. Clearly, in his view, the students came first. He wrote, "A university is a school, and without students scholarship would eventually wither away. Every social organism needs the young to replace the old in order to survive."[1] For me, one of the greatest pleasures as dean was to welcome a new batch of students and feel their energy and idealism as they entered the school. Our classrooms were highly globalised, as McKinsey had recommended that an ideal Lee Kuan Yew School of Public Policy class should comprise students in the following proportions: 20 percent from Singapore, 20 percent from other ASEAN countries, 20 percent from China, 20 percent from India, and 20 percent from the rest of the world. Very few other schools of public policy could match our diversity.

One of the greatest pleasures of my job as dean came from regular interactions with the students. Even though I didn't teach a course at the school, I regularly met and gave lectures to the students. I particularly enjoyed giving the welcome address. I would remind them that while they would learn a lot from their professors and textbooks, they would learn just as much from their classmates. In addressing a public policy problem, many students would assume that there was one obvious solution until they heard the perspective of students from other corners of the world. They would soon come to realise that there were many ways of perceiving the same problem.

I would also remind them of the well-known adage that in the early part of their careers, they would succeed on the basis of what they knew. In the later part, it would also depend on whom they know. Few students anywhere in the world would graduate with as diverse a global network as our students. Such networks could come in handy in many ways. Larry Summers once told me a story about a Russian undersea rescue submarine that had gotten stuck six hundred feet below the surface of the Pacific Ocean in 2005. The seven-member crew was fast running out of oxygen. A Russian admiral who had gone to the HKS called his old classmate, a defence attaché at the US Embassy in Moscow, requesting assistance. This phone call between two old friends from the Kennedy School led to a joint effort by the US, British, and Russian navies, which were able to rescue the crew.

One key reason why so many international students enrolled at Lee Kuan Yew School of Public Policy was that they wanted to find out the secret reasons why Singapore had done so well in governance. Hence, to every incoming class, I would give a lecture in which I freely gave away the "secret" of Singapore's exceptional success. I boiled it down to a simple, easily memorised acronym: MPH. Most people know this acronym well, as they associate it with "miles per hour." However, in my lecture, MPH stood for meritocracy, pragmatism, and honesty. I also gave the students a 100 percent guarantee: if they could ruthlessly apply MPH in their countries, their countries would succeed as Singapore had done. And I told them that I had personally applied the MPH principles in building up the Lee Kuan Yew School of Public Policy.

Meritocracy was easy to explain. It was about choosing the best people to run a firm or an organisation, a society or a country. Since Singapore's independence in 1965, Lee Kuan Yew had ensured that only the best were selected to serve in the government. Similarly, I made every effort to ensure that we selected the best possible people to serve in leadership positions in both the academic and administrative areas. Many of the people selected by us went on to assume more senior leadership positions elsewhere: Stavros Yiannouka went on to become the CEO of the World Innovation Summit for Education in Qatar, Astrid Tuminez went on to become president of Utah Valley University, and Hui Weng Tat became dean of the Nazarbayev University Graduate School of Public Policy in Astana, Kazakhstan. We also looked for talented faculty of all nationalities.

Pragmatism was about the willingness to learn best practices from any source anywhere in the world. Goh Keng Swee said to me, "Kishore, no matter what problem Singapore encounters, somebody somewhere has encountered it before. Let's find out how they solved it. Then we can adapt their solution for

Singapore." As I told the students, Singapore had succeeded by becoming the best copycat nation in the world.

The Lee Kuan Yew School of Public Policy also succeeded by copying other schools' best practices. McKinsey had kindly shared many of them with us, and we continued learning more. Quite amazingly, we succeeded so well that within less than a decade, we were admitted into the premier leagues of sister institutions like the Global Public Policy Network (GPPN) and the Association of Professional Schools of International Affairs. Getting into the GPPN wasn't easy. We had to sign "double-degree" arrangements with the founding schools of Columbia University, the London School of Economics, and Sciences Po. Before the Lee Kuan Yew School of Public Policy came along, many Singaporean university institutions had succeeded in signing double-degree programme arrangements only by paying a premium. We were probably the first to sign a double-degree programme arrangement with an Ivy League institution without paying a fee. In short, our academic standards were validated by some of the best institutions in our field.

Honesty was always the hardest principle to implement. As I had written in an essay titled "The Ten Commandments for Developing Countries in the Nineties" in 1990, "Thou shalt acknowledge that corruption is the single most important cause for failures in development." The three founding fathers of Singapore, Lee Kuan Yew, Goh Keng Swee, and S. Rajaratnam, were exceptionally incorruptible. Hence, they set very high standards of probity that we were all expected to follow.

To explain how things worked in Singapore, I told the students what had happened when I was leaving Li Ka-shing's office after securing a S$100 million donation. Per Hong Kong practice, Mr Li gave me a gift of a Mont Blanc pen. I groaned secretly. I knew that if I decided to keep it, I would have to pay NUS about S$500 for the cost of the pen. Since I didn't need a Mont Blanc pen, I was tempted to surrender it to NUS and not retain it. However, I considered the possibility that Mr Li would visit my office someday, as he did a year later. When he did, I proudly showed him the pen he had given me. I didn't tell him that I'd had to pay NUS S$500 to retain his gift.

High standards of honesty have served Singapore well. However, they are not easy to implement. I heard a sad story of what happened to a graduate of the Lee Kuan Yew School of Public Policy when he returned to his Central Asian country. He had decided to implement the principle of meritocracy in an organisation that he was chosen to lead. He promoted the best officers, and he released a few nonperformers. Unfortunately, one of the nonperformers he released was related to the country's president. As a result, this graduate of the Lee Kuan Yew School of Public Policy lost his job because he had tried to implement the "secret" formula of Singapore's success in a society that did not recognise the core principles behind it.

This story of one failure has to be balanced against the hundreds of stories of those who were able in one way or another to implement the lessons in good governance they learned at the Lee Kuan Yew School of Public Policy. By doing so, they were in turn improving the lives of thousands, if not millions, of people. One graduate of the Lee Kuan Yew School of Public Policy, for example, helped many people by using the lessons from Singapore to eliminate long queues in a Philippines hospital. Going to see a doctor became less strenuous. Knowing that my work as dean was, through the talents of the school's graduates, essentially improving the lives of many other people proved to be a source of great satisfaction.

The deanship of the Lee Kuan Yew School of Public Policy also helped to open another meaningful chapter of my life: the publication of several books, which had some impact in terms of changing global opinion. Tony Tan had said when he offered me the deanship that to improve my credibility with the academic community, I should publish a book. Fortunately, he made this comment while I was still in New York in 2003. I started right away and found a New York publisher, Public-Affairs. Indeed, PublicAffairs has published five of my books, including this one.

In some ways, it was remarkable that PublicAffairs kept publishing me after the first book, titled *Beyond the Age of Innocence*, which was not a financial success: the total royalties I received came to less than the advance, so the publisher probably lost money. The book failed probably because its goal was to offer advice, from a non-American to Americans, on how the United States could better handle its relations with the rest of the world. The advice may have been good (I believe it was, and it was certainly offered in the spirit of wanting the United States to succeed); however, I came to realise that Americans don't really want advice from non-Americans.

I assumed that my publishing career with PublicAffairs might be over. Fortunately, they gave me a second chance. *The New Asian Hemisphere* appeared in 2008 and proved to be successful. This time, the book more than earned back its advance and was translated into many languages, including Arabic, Mandarin, Dutch, French, German, Bahasa Indonesian, Italian, Japanese, Korean, Spanish, and Vietnamese. The most spectacular launch of the book took place in Cairo, Egypt, against the backdrop of the pyramids. The book also led to many speaking engagements that were quite lucrative.

With this book and the speaking opportunities that came from it, I emerged as one of the main narrators of the greatest story of our time: the return of Asia to the world stage. This in turn led to my inclusion in several exclusive lists of the world's most influential global public intellectuals: the *Financial Times* gave my global standing a huge boost when it included my name in a short, exclusive list of fifty individuals who would "shape debate on the future of capitalism" in 2009. The list included global luminaries like Barack Obama, Wen Jiabao, and Angela Merkel. Similarly, *Foreign Policy* and *Prospect* magazines included me in their 2005 lists of top one hundred public intellectuals. I was chuffed to see my works and my writings included among those of such global luminaries. I thought that only good would come from this and that the boost to my global intellectual standing would only help my work as dean of the Lee Kuan Yew School of Public Policy.

Little did I know that I was planting the seeds of my self-destruction. Some people in the Singaporean establishment were not happy with my increasingly visible profile. I should have picked up the hint from the *Straits Times*, which, if I may be permitted an understatement, is extremely sensitive to the views of the Singaporean government. It sends out accurate signals of approval and disapproval. It was therefore significant that the *Straits Times* was reluctant to report any inclusion in these multiple global lists, even though newspapers in other parts of the world, such as India, made a big splash about them.

Foreign Policy and *Prospect* magazines may have inadvertently done me a big disfavour by including me in their inaugural lists in 2005 and then including Lee Kuan Yew in their second lists in 2008. At the time, I didn't make much of this. Mr Lee was still a towering figure, both in Singapore and in the world. I was, at best, a little-known dean or author. I didn't think any of this would hurt my relationship with Mr Lee. Yet some strange things did happen. Around that time, at a small dinner hosted by Mr Lee at the Istana, Mr Lee sharply put me down when I asked him a question. My friends around the table noticed this and pointed it out to me. I was given an even sharper put-down by Mr Lee when I posed a question to him at a subsequent event. More of my friends noticed this.

Still, these appeared to be small, isolated events against a larger backdrop in which things were seemingly going swimmingly well, both for the Lee Kuan Yew School of Public Policy and for me. The global standing of the school continued to rise. Similarly, my personal standing continued to grow. I was invited to attend the annual Davos meeting of the WEF every year. The founder of the WEF, Klaus Schwab, even included me in the exclusive Global University Leaders Forum (GULF), which comprised mainly university presidents and only two deans: the dean of the HKS and me, the dean of the Lee Kuan Yew School of Public Policy.

When Larry Summers suddenly had to step down on February 21, 2006, as one of the two presidents of GULF, Klaus

Schwab had to find a replacement. Instead of turning to another Ivy League university president, Klaus asked me to become the coleader of GULF. It was a great honour to be recognised by this august group.

The admiration I received from many foreign sources seemed deep and genuine. It surfaced in many different ways. In 2008, for example, the former president of Mexico, Ernesto Zedillo (a brilliant academic who will go down in history as the most honest president of Mexico) invited me to join a Commission of Eminent Persons to review the future of the International Atomic Energy Agency, which is one of the most powerful bodies in the world, as it monitors nuclear proliferation.

I received other formal and informal signals of my high international standing. One year as I was standing in a corridor in Davos, a tall gentleman tapped my back and asked me if I was Kishore Mahbubani. I said yes and asked who he was. He said he was Jan Peter Balkenende, PM of the Netherlands. I asked how he knew me, and he told me that his mother had asked him to read the Dutch edition of *The New Asian Hemisphere*, which had become a bestseller there.

When the PM of India from 2004 to 2014, Manmohan Singh, set up a very eminent group of advisers in a council called the PM's Global Advisory Council that included luminaries like Nobel Laureate Amartya Sen; Jagdish Bhagwati of Columbia University; and Indra Nooyi, CEO of PepsiCo, he asked me to join too.

Clearly, some people in the Singaporean government were aware of my growing international stature and thought that it could be useful to Singapore. Hence, in 2010, I was invited to lunch by Mah Bow Tan, who was then head of the Ministry of National Development (MND). He told me that Lee Kuan Yew had agreed to have a second project named after him. It would be called the Lee Kuan Yew World City Prize (LKYWCP). To select and choose the winners, the LKYWCP would need a jury and a nominating committee. Joe Pillay, one of Singapore's greatest luminaries, had agreed to become the chairman of the jury. Minister Mah asked if I would agree to chair the nominating committee.

I was surprised by this invitation. Unlike Mr Pillay, who had once been permanent secretary of the MND, I had had no experience in urban planning or urban management issues. The only thing I could provide was my name. The hope was that it would encourage a suitably distinguished group to serve as the nominating committee. Fortunately, the MND managed to attract a good group to serve on the committee that included Alan Altshuler of Harvard.

I was pleased that Prof Altshuler had agreed to serve in the first round since several people at Harvard considered him one of the wisest souls in the Harvard community. I learned a lot from him and other members of this eminent group. Alan asked to stand down after the first round. I asked him why. He told me all the real hard work in the selection of the prizewinner was done by the "nominating committee." We had to short-list the applications, visit the short-listed cities, and then meet several times to nominate the winner. By contrast, the jury met only once and always endorsed the choice of the nominating committee.

Nonetheless, I enormously enjoyed working with the nominating committee. The discussions were candid and fascinating.

We made bold choices. I strongly urged this committee to consider not just established European cities that had enjoyed decades of progress. I felt we should also recognise Third World cities that had struggled to improve against all odds. I chaired the nominating committee over four rounds, and the winners were a diverse group: Bilbao, New York City, Suzhou, and Medellín.

I also developed a good relationship with two Indonesian presidents, Susilo Bambang Yudhoyono (SBY) and Joko Widodo (Jokowi). President SBY honoured me by inviting me to be the third speaker (after Bill Gates and Shaukat Aziz) to address the Indonesian Cabinet in 2012. Given the huge disparity in size between Indonesia and Singapore and some Indonesians' historical feelings of ambivalence towards Singapore, it was a special invitation. President Jokowi, then governor of Jakarta, invited me to spend a day with him in December 2013 as he was trying to raise his international profile before announcing his bid for the presidency in 2014.

In 2016, I had what would normally be described as an unfortunate development: a double bypass heart operation. In reality, it was a fortunate development. It was truly fortunate that I made it to the operating table. I could have died a couple of times before getting there.

Twice, when I was about a kilometre into my morning run, I felt a pain in my chest and stood on the road, frozen into inactivity. On both occasions, my body somehow recovered, I kept running, and I even sprinted back. This led me to believe that I was fine. A few days after this happened, I attended the wake of a former boss of mine at the MFA, Lee Khoon Choy, on a Saturday afternoon. His son, C. N. Lee, is one of the best cardiologists in Singapore. I described what had happened to C. N. He insisted that I go for a comprehensive checkup of my heart on Monday morning. Fortunately, I was able to arrange a full day of tests at the Singapore General Hospital.

At the end of the tests, the cardiologist broke the news to me that I needed a double bypass operation, as there were two significant blockages in my arteries, including a 90 percent blockage in one of them. I was shocked by the news. I told the cardiologist that I would go home and think about it. The doctor said that I could think about it, but I couldn't go home. I asked why not. He said that they were very surprised that I hadn't yet had a major heart attack. They were confident that I would soon have one. They said that it would be much easier to recover from a heart attack in the hospital than at home. Judging from what they said to me, it was clear that the blockages were serious. The doctors explained that since I had been running regularly for over fifty years, the ancillary arteries in my heart had done a natural bypass when the main artery was blocked. This was why I could keep on running after suffering a blockage twice.

All the medical doctors I consulted told me that I had no choice: I had to have the bypass operation as soon as possible. Fortunately, a slot was available on Tuesday morning. I still vividly remember waking up in the ICU that evening. It took me several weeks to recover. Anne had to slowly and patiently make me walk around the neighbourhood. In the beginning, I couldn't even walk a hundred metres. Eventually, I recovered fully and started running again. Looking back at this episode, I realised that I was extraordinarily lucky.

When I was renewed for a third five-year term as dean on July 1, 2014, it seemed to be a perfectly natural development. NUS was particularly pleased that the school had successfully recruited well-known faculty from leading universities, including Kanti Bajpai, Yuen Foong Khong, and Danny Quah. Financially, our situation could hardly have been better. We were also attracting high-quality students. Personally, my intellectual contributions continued to be recognised by leading universities. Cornell University invited me to become the Bartels World Affairs Fellow in 2013. The HKS paid me a great honour by inviting me to deliver the Albert H. Gordon Lecture in April 2015. Among the first people to deliver the lecture were Presidents Gorbachev and George H. W. Bush. The lecture, titled "What Happens When China Becomes Number One?," became exceptionally successful, with over four million cumulative views on YouTube by August 2023.

However, I didn't complete my third five-year term. Instead, by mutual agreement, the chairman of the Governing Board of the Lee Kuan Yew School of Public Policy, the president of NUS, and I agreed that I should step down on December 31, 2017. The sudden announcement of my departure in October 2017 quite naturally led to speculation that I had been asked to resign. I should admit here that I was initially a little disappointed that I couldn't complete my third five-year term. Yet, as I soon discovered after stepping down, my life then improved significantly again. It helped that NUS gave me a sabbatical, enabling me to spend time at six leading global universities: Columbia, Harvard, Fudan, Sciences Po, Georgetown, and Oxford.

When I left for my sabbatical in January 2018, heading to Columbia University, I asked myself, "How many people get to go on a sabbatical at the age of sixty-nine after having had a heart bypass operation at sixty-seven and while drawing a regular salary?" Since I love universities and I wanted to carry on with my life of learning, the sabbatical was a treat. As I had already decided then to publish a book on US-China relations, I had a clear research focus. The end result of all this research was truly satisfying, and I published *Has China Won?* in January 2020.

Not long after my return from the sabbatical, I began a new chapter in my association with NUS when I was appointed as Distinguished Fellow at the Asia Research Institute (ARI) on July 1, 2019. Even though I had turned seventy by the time of this appointment, I decided not to slow down. After *Has China Won?* came out in January 2020, I had planned to go on a tour of the United States over several weeks in mid-2020 to promote the book. Unfortunately, COVID intervened. The entire book tour had to be cancelled. This could have led to a catastrophic failure of the book. Instead, it proved to be a big success. I even received a generous compliment from Larry Summers, who said in a live *Bloomberg* interview in January 2021 that it was one of the best three books he had read in 2020.

Because Singapore is so small, domestic travel is not an option when Singaporeans need a break from their regular lives—it takes only an hour to drive from one end of the country to the other. I expected to have difficulties with the nearly two-year-long travel ban (in most of 2020 and all of 2021) since I had become addicted to regular overseas travel for both work and pleasure. Instead, I enjoyed the quiet years of not travelling. To my absolute surprise, the global footprint of my speeches and writings actually increased significantly in these two years. Since we could not meet in person, I did several speaking engagements over Zoom that were then posted by the organisers on YouTube. In several cases, they were viewed millions of times in many countries around the world. I had become a beneficiary of the explosion of social media consumption during COVID.

I also enjoyed my runs and long walks along East Coast Park. In the evenings, I would listen to podcasts on Spotify while walking. Hours would go by effortlessly. At the end of 2021, my Fitbit watch told me that I had run or walked an average of eleven kilometres a day over the 365 days. In short, I had covered four thousand kilometres in one year. Without COVID, this would never have happened.

Despite the many limitations that COVID had imposed on us all, with the approval of NUS and ARI, I managed to launch the Asian Peace Programme (APP) in July 2020. As a young man, I was an idealistic pacifist, committed to promoting peace. As a working man, especially during my diplomatic career, I became a hardheaded realist. I also shared the conviction of realists, like Lee Kuan Yew and Goh Keng Swee, that the best way to achieve peace was to be brutally realistic about the state of great power relations. Many wars, including the latest Ukraine and Gaza wars, could have been avoided if more attention had been paid to the underlying geopolitical stresses and strains in these areas. Unfortunately, even though peace is critical, we spend far more resources on studying war than on studying peace. I thought that the cause of peace could benefit from more voices, especially Asian voices, sharing their ideas on how the countries of the region could mitigate tensions and gradually resolve their differences. One of the great blessings that Asia, especially East Asia, has enjoyed is that there have been no major wars in this region since the Sino-Vietnamese war of 1979. Yet history teaches us that peace can never be taken for granted. Given the many smouldering disputes and geopolitical flash points in the region, from the Korean peninsula to the South China Sea, it would be best to work proactively to preserve peace. Indeed, the greatest danger to the achievement of the Asian century is the outbreak of a major war.

The fears with which the APP was established proved to be well-founded when a major skirmish broke out between China and India in the Galwan Valley in June 2020. Many Chinese and Indian soldiers lost their lives. This drastically set back Sino-Indian relations. Before this clash in June 2020, President Xi Jinping and PM Narendra Modi had probably spent more time talking to each other than any two major-power rivals ever had. They spent two days together in Wuhan, China, in April 2018 and two days together in Mahabalipuram, India, in October 2019. These long hours of talks proved to be fruitful. Trust between these two countries increased, as did trade, which rose from $71 billion in 2014 (when PM Modi came to power) to $85 billion in 2019.[2]

However, since the clash, there have been no bilateral meetings between Xi and Modi. The clash set back everything. The APP tried to help the situation by publishing an article by

Kanti Bajpai suggesting, inter alia, that future clashes could be prevented if both sides could agree to install a virtual system of surveillance (using cameras, sensors, drones, and satellite reconnaissance) in disputed areas to determine whether there had been any infringements. Our article was published in July 2020. In the following months, China and India both installed more surveillance equipment along the Line of Actual Control. We will never know whether these sensors were installed as a result of the suggestion by the APP. Nevertheless, if a small suggestion by the APP can help to make a difference, we would have helped to preserve or strengthen peace.

The aspiration for the APP is to be as discreetly effective as a small acupuncture needle. Inserted in the right place and at the right time, it can make a huge difference. It can relieve a lot of pain too. Fortunately, many donors have stepped up to help support our efforts, confirming that many Asians believe that a great future lies ahead.

The outbreak of the Ukraine war in February 2022 and the Gaza war in October 2023 have only reinforced the key lesson of history: we can never take peace for granted. If the APP can light a small candle that keeps these forces of darkness away from Asia, it will make a meaningful contribution to the Asian century. As I enter the last lap of my life, this seems to be a fitting and appropriate mission to which I can dedicate my remaining years.

CHAPTER 12

A Happy Ending

OFTEN, OUR DESTINIES ARE DETERMINED AT BIRTH.
When I was born in 1948 to a twenty-eight-year-old Sindhi man (who had been orphaned and had acquired self-destructive life habits) and a twenty-three-year-old Sindhi woman (isolated in Singapore), I should have had the same fate as my three sisters, who experienced the same childhood I did. I shouldn't have gone to university. Or I could have enjoyed the same fate as other young Sindhi boys who were born in Singapore around the same time. Almost none of them went to university, though some became prosperous merchants.

The great privilege I enjoyed was to imbibe a rich life of the mind. I have no doubt that my parents and my sisters had brains that could have seen them through universities, but they were never given the opportunity. I was.

Empowered by education, I overcame the challenge of having been born a "British subject," a second-class citizen in my own country. Yet if I hadn't experienced the mental colonisation myself, I wouldn't have understood what it meant. My journey was not capsized by colonialism! Without studying philosophy, I would never have thoroughly understood the era of Western domination of world history, the subject of so much of my writings. I also grew up with a deep and genuine admiration of the West, especially of the great thinkers who advanced our understanding of the human condition more than those of any other civilisation.

I was equally fortunate to experience the heady currents of postcolonial sentiment. I was never a freedom fighter. Singapore acquired self-government from the British when I was eleven years old. Yet, as my mother was also an ardent Indian nationalist, I grew to respect and admire great freedom fighters like Mahatma Gandhi and Jawaharlal Nehru. Indeed, one of the books that had a profound effect on me was Nehru's *A Discovery of India*. That book allowed me to slough off the sense of inferiority to white people and acquire a greater sense of self-confidence in my Indian heritage.

For most of my childhood, I was meek and submissive. I didn't rebel when my mother asked me to sit with her and bathe little statues of various Hindu gods in milk, although I sometimes wondered whether the traces of milk would attract ants to the altar. Nor did I rebel when my mother regularly took me with her to Indian prayer sessions. As a child, I dutifully bowed down and touched the feet of every elder who came to our house. I respected every tradition thrust upon me.

Yet I must have had a mysterious rebellious streak in my soul that was liberated when I went to study at the University of Singapore. None of my professors or peers encouraged me to rebel; it came spontaneously. I began to challenge authority in many dimensions. Fortunately, my philosophy professors welcomed dissent and liked it when I challenged them in the classrooms, as I often did. A fellow student in the philosophy department told me that he would often see me sitting with my eyes closed, apparently asleep, in the last row of the class. Yet when the lecture ended, I would often be the first to pose a question and challenge the professor.

This streak of independence could have proven to be a liability in a young Singaporean nation as the government became progressively more authoritarian. Indeed, six years after I joined government service in 1971, my best friend from childhood, Jeffery Sng, was detained by the government for his leftist tendencies. Detention wasn't a pleasant experience. He was made to sit completely naked on an ice block in an ice-cold room. This experience could have been life-threatening for him, as he had suffered from epilepsy since childhood. Other friends of mine, like Ho Kwon Ping and Arun Senkuttuvan, were also detained in similar conditions. I was strongly urged by my fellow civil servants not to intervene on Jeffery's behalf. However, my rebellious streak and sense of loyalty to my oldest friend made me throw caution to the winds, and I wrote a strong letter of defence of him. Fortunately, he was later released, and no harm befell me for defending him.

I was fortunate to be posted to Cambodia in 1973. In university, I thought that the moral thing to do was to rebel against the strong and dominant government of Singapore. In Cambodia, I discovered that there was a greater moral mission: to defend small Singapore in a world of many regional and global geopolitical bullies. This moral conviction gave me great comfort as I served in the Singaporean Foreign Service for thirty-three years, doing my part to defend and advocate for Singapore.

While I was not fully aware of it then, the experience of war in Cambodia instinctively taught me a lesson I came to grasp later in life: wars are a result of geopolitical incompetence, peace a result of geopolitical competence. Recent wars, like the Iraq war, the Ukraine war, and the Gaza war, all confirm this. All three could have been avoided if the leaders in question had paid attention to fundamental geopolitical realities. Lee Kuan Yew was always known to be a hardheaded geopolitical realist. He was a tough guy by any definition. He understood when wars were unnecessary. On the eve of the Iraq war in 2003, when I told him that President George W. Bush was likely to proceed with the invasion of Iraq, he sighed. I sensed then that he believed that the war would prove to be a disaster. His intuition proved to be correct.

Even though I inherited the "realist" geopolitical lens of Singapore's founding fathers, I also never lost my "idealist" tendencies. I continued to believe that the world could be a better place if enough goodwill was applied. Goh Keng Swee was less idealistic. When I asked Dr Goh in 1984 what my mission should be when I went as Singaporean ambassador to the UN, he replied in his usual brutal fashion, "Kishore, go and weep for the Third World." His comment was clearly cynical. However, S. Rajaratnam was less cynical. He believed that the UN and the UN Charter had made a difference. He was right.

Balancing these realist and idealist tendencies in my mind remained a constant challenge. One way of resolving the internal tensions was to write about them. In one way or another, I had to offload what I had learned from serving in several different fields of diplomacy, both bilateral and multilateral.

Having served in the UN for over a decade, I was shocked by the massive misunderstanding of this critical global organisation in the Anglo-Saxon media. Since I have been very critical of the Anglo-Saxon media, I should explain that this is a result of the great expectations that the world has of them. They claim to be fair, honest, objective, dispassionate, and accurate in their descriptions of the state of the world. This may have been true a few decades ago, but it is far from true today. Thus, the disillusionment that many other Asians and I feel towards the Anglo-Saxon media is a result of the great expectations they unleashed. This was one reason why I published *The Great Convergence* in 2013 (and I was honoured when the *Financial Times* chose it as one of the best books of 2013). An equally important mission for my books was to encourage greater self-confidence among my fellow Asians. This was clearly one of my main goals with my first book, which had the deliberately provocative title *Can Asians Think?* Most books, especially nonfiction books, go out of print after five to ten years. It's a source of great pride that this book remains in print after twenty-five years and continues to sell at airport bookstores. It provides the first glimpses of the emerging Asian century.

The explosion of cultural self-confidence among many Asian societies has been a transformative and joyous event to see and participate in. When I first visited Mumbai (then called Bombay) in 1969, it was a typical Third World city teeming with poor people. Dodging beggars became an art. Few in India believed then that their country had a great future, as two decades of independence had brought relatively few improvements in living standards. In my most recent visit to Mumbai in November 2023, I felt that I was entering a different universe. The fifty or sixty young entrepreneurs whom I spoke to (each of whom had a net worth of over US$250 million) at the Young President's Organization (an American creation) were among the most dynamic and optimistic young entrepreneurs I had met in my life. There were still poor people on the streets, but even they seemed to be infected with a new confidence, bolstered by the many new public policies whose effects they could feel directly through their cell phones. In 1990, there were probably fewer than five million cell phones among the one billion people of India. Now there are over six hundred million smartphone users. If my mother could see this, she would be astonished by this new India, brimming with new hope.

Barack Obama bravely and accurately tried to describe his early life as a mixed-race child raised by a single mother (like me) in books like *The Audacity of Hope*. I had absolutely no audacious hopes as a young person. Unlike Obama, I didn't dream of becoming a president. When I was a child, it never occurred to me that I could aspire to anything but being a textile salesman, perhaps one who read a lot. And after a few years at the University of Singapore, I dreamt only of becoming a philosophy teacher.

I never fulfilled that dream. Yet, even without the audacity of hope, I managed to fulfil far greater dreams. My life went from poverty to plenty. When I was a child, six of us lived in a one-bedroom terrace home. Now, as an adult, I live in a six-bedroom house with Anne. Never in my wildest dreams as a child did I believe that I would one day own a bungalow in land-scarce Singapore.

But the richest road I travelled was always in the field of ideas. Starting with the sparks ignited on the Bukit Timah campus by my philosophy professors, I went on to experience greater insights derived from sitting at the feet of many great men. In the world of ideas, I have had a truly privileged life. And it has been an even greater privilege to share my ideas with a large global audience and to receive feedback from them, especially from my fellow Asians.

None of my books has been on the *NYT* bestseller list. Once this would have suggested that they had missed their mark. But the *NYT* may not be the mark that matters so much anymore. When I published *The Asian 21st Century*, a volume of essays, as an open-access book (meaning that it is free of charge) in January 2022, the publisher hoped it would be downloaded twenty thousand times. As I write, there have been over 3.4 million downloads from across Asia and the world. We have begun a dialogue that does not need to be mediated through the legacy institutions of the Western media. There is a vibrant intellectual conversation going on in Asia and beyond; readers and writers are finding their way. We don't need anyone's permission or to follow a road map that is set in London or New York.

It has been my joy to live the Asian dream and perhaps contribute a little to the realisation of the Asian century. It is truly heartening to realise that the path I have trodden from poverty to plenty, from ignorance to education and intellectual curiosity, will now be replicated by millions, if not billions, of fellow Asians. To have been a pioneer in this great Asian renaissance has been one of the greatest privileges, and fulfilments, of my life.

Acknowledgements

I dedicate this book to my late parents, Janki and Mohan. If they hadn't made the fateful decision to make Singapore my birthplace, I would not have experienced the exceptionally rich and rewarding life documented in this book. There's no doubt that my father let our family down and that my mother's steel will saved us. By passing this steel will on to me, my mother gave me an exceptional gift. Paradoxically, the poverty our father left us with also taught me the virtues of resilience and fortitude.

My second choice would have been to dedicate this book to the three key founding fathers of Singapore, Lee Kuan Yew, Goh Keng Swee, and S. Rajaratnam. Consciously and sub-consciously, I learned enormous lessons from them. Without all those lessons, I couldn't have written ten books, and this memoir would have been impoverished without their shining presence in my life.

A memoir, unlike an intellectual tome, doesn't require deep research. However, it still needs careful vetting and checking. In recent years, since I became dean of the Lee Kuan Yew School of Public Policy, I have been blessed with excellent research assistants. The two who helped me with this volume, Varigonda Kesava Chandra and Kristen Tang, have been equally exceptional. They were rigorously thorough in their research, and, amazingly, they could read my scribbles on yellow legal pads, which were the drafts of this book. I would also like to thank Bertrand Seah for his assistance in the early stages of the book.

When I stepped down as dean of the Lee Kuan Yew School of Public Policy on December 31, 2017, seven years ago, I could have become lost in trying to find my bearings. Fortunately, the NUS presidents, Tan Chorh Chuan and Tan Eng Chye, generously declared that Carol Chan Chor Eng should continue to support me as a manager and personal assistant. Everyone who has dealt with me and my office knows that Carol has been an indispensable person in my life. Her strong and dedicated support explains my continuing productivity. I am truly sorry that she stepped down on April 30, 2024, and I wish her all the best. I want to thank Fanny Chang for agreeing to step in. Both Carol and Fanny also contributed a great deal to the production of this book.

I also want to thank the exceptional team at PublicAffairs. As with my previous four books with them, they have been truly helpful in all the stages of production, from editing to copyediting, from page proofs to cover designs. Clive Priddle, with whom I have worked since my first book in 2005, has become a good friend. I am glad he visited Singapore when I was writing this book. I also want to thank Kelly Lenkevich, Connie Oehring, Amy Quinn, and Ellie Wells for their excellent work.

Acknowledgements

Several old friends, including Alan Altshuler, Tarun Kataria, and Jeffery Sng, kindly agreed to read the draft manuscript and provided me with helpful comments. I am grateful for their comments. However, I bear sole responsibility for any mistakes. I am also grateful for the generous blurbs I received from Chan Heng Chee, Meira Chand, Indra Nooyi, Anne-Marie Slaughter, Eddie Teo, Martin Wolf, and George Yeo.

I also want to thank my lifelong musical companions, Mohammed Rafi, Lata Mangeshkar, Asha Bhosle, and Kishore Kumar. I heard their songs all through my childhood. As I listened to them again while writing these memoirs (and all my other books), they ignited some childhood neurons in my brain that made me truly enjoy the journey.

Finally, any life story is enriched by family. I want to thank my siblings, my nephew and nieces, and their spouses and children for enriching my life. And all who know me know that one woman is truly responsible for my success: my wife, Anne. Anne and our children, Kishore, Shelagh, and Jhamat, and our daughter-in-law, Becky, are the very dear souls who have made my life rich and meaningful. I hope these memoirs will help my children better understand the blessed life I have experienced.

Notes

Chapter 1: Born Poor

1. Alvin Powell, "Getting to the Why of British India's Bloody Partition," April 6, 2018, https://news.harvard.edu/gazette/story/2018/04/harvard-scholars -take-fresh-look-at-the-partition-of-british-india-which-killed-millions/.

2. In Singapore, children generally enter primary school the year they turn seven. After six years of primary education, they attend secondary school from the ages of thirteen to sixteen. Students can then choose to attend a polytechnic, usually for three years (seventeen to nineteen), or a junior college for two years (seventeen to eighteen). After that, they may choose to continue their education at university.

3. Peranakan culture melds the indigenous cultures of the Malay-Indonesian archipelago with other ancestral cultures—in Singapore, most commonly Chinese culture. "About the Peranakans," Peranakan Museum, accessed February 13, 2024, www.nhb.gov.sg/peranakanmuseum/learn/about-the-peranakans.

4. Village.

5. Coffee shop.

Chapter 2: Still Poor

1. A fried noodle dish.

2. Bertrand Russell, "Nature and Origin of Scientific Method," 1948, https://users.drew.edu/~jlenz/br-on-scientific-method.html.

3. "Only 13,736 Pass S'pore Primary Leaving Test," *Straits Times*, December 22, 1960, https://eresources.nlb.gov.sg/newspapers/digitised/article /straitstimes19601222-1.2.88.

4. Bertrand Russell, "Why I Am Not a Christian," March 6, 1927, https:// users.drew.edu/~jlenz/whynot.html.

5. Ibid.

Chapter 3: Lighting Firecrackers

1. Roland Puccetti, "Authoritarian Government and Academic Subservience: The University of Singapore," *Minerva* 10, no. 2 (1972): 223–241.

2. "Statement from the Prime Minister's Office" (press release), accessed February 6, 2024, www.nas.gov.sg/archivesonline/data/pdfdoc/lky19680309.pdf.

3. John R. Searle, "Insight and Error in Wittgenstein," *Philosophy of the Social Sciences* 46, no. 6 (December 2016): 527–547.

Chapter 4: Explosive Lessons in Geopolitics

1. Wok-fried rice noodles.

Chapter 5: Studying Philosophy in the Cold

1. The practice of splitting secondary school students into different courses in order to cater to their different paces of learning.

Chapter 6: Kuala Lumpur

1. *Directory of Officials of the People's Republic of China*, April 1975, p. 142, https://books.google.com.sg/books?id=hShUPtnVz5gC&pg=PA142.

2. International Court of Justice, "Case Concerning Sovereignty over Pedra Branca/Pulau Batu Puteh, Middle Rocks and South Ledge (Malaysia /Singapore)," March 25, 2004, www.icj-cij.org/public/files/case-related/130 /130-20040325-WRI-02-06-EN.pdf.

3. "SM Lee: Strong Reserves Will Deter Currency Raiders," *Business Times*, January 13, 2001.

Chapter 7: The Rome of the Twentieth Century

1. "White House Diaries," Thursday, March 17, 1983, Ronald Reagan Presidential Foundation and Institute, www.reaganfoundation.org/ronald-reagan /white-house-diaries/diary-entry-03171983/.

2. Hedrick Smith, "Reagan and O'Neill: Each One Needs the Other," *New York Times*, March 17, 1983, www.nytimes.com/1983/03/17/us/reagan-and -o-neill-each-one-needs-the-other.html.

3. Chris Matthews, "When the President and the Speaker Were a Team," NBC News, September 30, 2013, www.nbcnews.com/id/wbna53150184.

4. Atomic Heritage Foundation, "Strategic Defense Initiative (SDI)," July 18, 2018, https://ahf.nuclearmuseum.org/ahf/history/strategic-defense-initiative-sdi.

5. Strobe Talbott, "Reagan and Gorbachev: Shutting the Cold War Down," August 1, 2004, www.brookings.edu/articles/reagan-and-gorbachev-shutting-the-cold-war-down/.

6. David Smith, "Gorbachev and Reagan: The Capitalist and Communist Who Helped End the Cold War," August 32, 2022, www.theguardian.com/world/2022/aug/31/gorbachev-and-reagan-the-capitalist-and-communist-who-helped-end-the-cold-war.

7. Jack Foust Matlock Jr., interview by Mary Marshall Clark, "The Reminiscences of Jack Foust Matlock Jr.," Harriman Institute, Columbia University, February 2, 2017, https://oralhistory.harriman.columbia.edu/interview/18.

8. Ronald Reagan, "Address to the Nation and Other Countries on United States–Soviet Relations," Ronald Reagan Presidential Library and Institute, January 16, 1984, www.reaganlibrary.gov/archives/speech/address-nation-and-other-countries-united-states-soviet-relations.

9. Hedrick Smith, "The Right against Reagan," *New York Times*, January 17, 1988, www.nytimes.com/1988/01/17/magazine/the-right-against-reagan.html.

10. "Punch Coomaraswamy to Be Appointed Supreme Court Judge," *Singapore Monitor*, May 6, 1984, https://eresources.nlb.gov.sg/newspapers/Digitised/Article/singmonitor19840506-1.2.4.5.

11. "The Situation in Kampuchea: Resolution/Adopted by the General Assembly," United Nations Digital Library, October 27, 1983, https://digitallibrary.un.org/record/278340?ln=en.

Chapter 8: New York, New York

1. United Nations Programme of Action for African Economic Recovery and Development, 1986–1990: Resolution/Adopted by the General Assembly," United Nations Digital Library, July 1, 1986, https://digitallibrary.un.org/record/118877?ln=en.

2. Paul Lewis, "United Nations Journal; Acres of Paper, and a World of Good Intentions," *New York Times*, December 6, 1988, www.nytimes.com/1988/12/06/world/united-nations-journal-acres-of-paper-and-a-world-of-good-intentions.html.

3. The main opposition party in Singapore in the 1960s.

4. "Statement by Singapore's Permanent Representative to the UN in New York, Prof T T B Koh, before the UN Security Council, on the Situation in Grenada on 28 October 1983," Singapore Government Press Release, October 29, 1983, www.nas.gov.sg/archivesonline/data/pdfdoc/kt19831028s.pdf.

Notes

5. "Text of Statement by U.S. on Its Withdrawal from UNESCO," *New York Times*, December 20, 1984, www.nytimes.com/1984/12/20/world/text-of-statement-by-us-on-its-withdrawal-from-unesco.html.

6. Joanne Omang, "UNESCO Withdrawal Announced," *Washington Post*, December 20, 1984, www.washingtonpost.com/archive/politics/1984/12/20/unesco-withdrawal-announced/b9c6dc92-a31f-443a-977b-f3468faf44fe/.

7. Arthur Richards, "UNESCO Loses Another Member," UPI, December 16, 1985, www.upi.com/Archives/1985/12/16/UNESCO-loses-another-member/5939503557200/.

8. "Toast by Prime Minister Lee Kuan Yew at the Dinner Hosted by President and Mrs Reagan on 8 Oct 85 at the White House," National Archives of Singapore, October 8, 1985, www.nas.gov.sg/archivesonline/data/pdfdoc/lky19851008c.pdf.

9. "Transcript of an Interview with Prime Minister Lee Kuan Yew by Mr Louis Kraar, Asian Editor of the 'Fortune' Magazine on 23 November 1984 at the Istana Annexe," National Archives of Singapore, November 23, 1984, www.nas.gov.sg/archivesonline/speeches/record-details/742325ea-115d-11e3-83d5-0050568939ad.

10. "Congressmen Concerned over Arrests," *Straits Times*, July 4, 1987, https://eresources.nlb.gov.sg/newspapers/Digitised/Article/straitstimes19870704-1.2.41.2.1.

11. "Singapore Government Press Statement," Release No. 14, National Archives of Singapore, May 7, 1988, www.nas.gov.sg/archivesonline/data/pdfdoc/831-1988-05-07.pdf.

12. "4,000 Protest against US Interference," *Straits Times*, May 12, 1988, https://eresources.nlb.gov.sg/newspapers/Digitised/Article/straitstimes19880512-1.2.27.4.

13. Kenneth Whiting, "Singapore Protests U.S. 'Interference' after Diplomat Withdrawn," Associated Press, May 12, 1988.

14. Parliamentary Debates, Singapore Official Report, Sixth Parliament, June 1, 1988, https://sprs.parl.gov.sg/search/#/report?sittingdate=1-6-1988.

15. International Law Commission, Vienna Convention on Diplomatic Relations, April 18, 1961, p. 13, https://legal.un.org/ilc/texts/instruments/english/conventions/9_1_1961.pdf.

16. World Bank, "GDP (current US$)—Singapore," accessed February 6, 2024, https://data.worldbank.org/indicator/NY.GDP.MKTP.CD?locations=SG. data.

Chapter 9: The Sweet Life of a CEO

1. Jayendra Menon, "Chirac: Europe Must Look at Asia with New Eyes," *Straits Times*, March 1, 1996, https://eresources.nlb.gov.sg/newspapers/Digitised/Article/straitstimes19960301-1.2.5.

2. Peh Shing Huei with Han Fook Kwang, *Neither Civil nor Servant: The Philip Yeo Story* (Singapore: Straits Times Press, 2016).

3. "Caught in the Middle over Michael Fay," *Straits Times*, September 18, 2011, www.straitstimes.com/politics/caught-in-the-middle-over-michael-fay.

4. George Yeo, *Musings: Series Three, with Woon Tai Ho* (Singapore: World Scientific, 2024), 266.

5. "Tunnelling Works Completed for Phase 2 of Singapore's Sewage 'Super-highway,'" Channel News Asia, August 21, 2023, www.channelnewsasia.com/singapore/deep-tunnel-sewerage-system-used-water-superhighway-tunnelling-works-completed-phase-2-3708366.

6. Lee Hsien Loong, "PM Lee Hsien Loong at the Official Opening of the Changi Water Reclamation Plant," Prime Minister's Office of Singapore, June 23, 2009, www.pmo.gov.sg/Newsroom/speech-mr-lee-hsien-loong-prime-minister-official-opening-changi-water-reclamation-plant.

Chapter 10: The UN Security Council

1. Sara Getman, "Graduation Speaker Announced: Ambassador Richard Holbrooke Will Speak on May 21," *Trinity Tripod*, May 2, 2000, https://digitalrepository.trincoll.edu/cgi/viewcontent.cgi?article=1335&context=tripod.

2. "Text of Hillary Clinton's Statement," *Politico*, December 13, 2010, www.politico.com/story/2010/12/text-of-hillary-clintons-statement-046345.

3. "Statement by the President of the Security Council," Security Council Report, January 31, 2001, www.securitycouncilreport.org/atf/cf/%7B65BFCF9B-6D27-4E9C-8CD3-CF6E4FF96FF9%7D/PKO%20SPRST%202001%203.pdf.

4. Kishore Mahbubani, *The Great Convergence: Asia, the West, and the Logic of One World* (New York: PublicAffairs, 2013).

5. Martijn Groenleer, "The United States, the European Union, and the International Criminal Court: Similar Values, Different Interests?," *International Journal of Constitutional Law* 13, no. 4 (October 2015): 923–944.

6. United Nations Security Council Resolution 1422, July 12, 2002, https://digitallibrary.un.org/record/468885.

7. "History," International Court of Justice, accessed February 6, 2024, www.icj-cij.org/history.

8. "Case Concerning Military and Paramilitary Activities in and against Nicaragua (Nicaragua v. United States of America)," International Court of Justice, June 27, 1986, www.icj-cij.org/files/case-related/70/070-19860627 -JUD-01-00-EN.pdf.

9. Loraine Sievers, "Why Are the Council's Rules of Procedure Still 'Provisional' and What Does That Mean in Practice?," *Procedure of the UN Security Council*, 4th ed., September 12, 2019, www.scprocedure.org/chapter -1-section-4.

10. Martin Wolf, "What India Must Do If It Is to Be an Affluent Country," *Financial Times*, July 8, 2009, www.ft.com/content/dc1a9462-6b1c -11de-861d-00144feabdc0.

Chapter 11: Back to School

1. Henry Rosovsky, *The University: An Owner's Manual* (New York: W. W. Norton, 1991).

2. World Bank, World Integrated Trade Solution (WITS) database, accessed February 6, 2024, https://wits.worldbank.org/.

Index

Index

Index

Index

Index

Index

Index

Index

Mahbubani, Jhamat (son of KM), 202

Mahbubani, Kishore Richard (son of KM), 170

Mahbubani, Mohandas Detaram. *See* father of KM

Mahbubani, Shelagh (daughter of KM), 191

Mahbubani family (extended family), 3–4, 12

Malays and Malay-Chinese in Singapore, 17, 34–35

Malaysia
  Pedra Branca island dispute, 117–119
  political transition in 1970s, 116–117
  relations with China, 115
  relations with Singapore, 112–113, 116–117, 124, 125–126, 222–223
  separation from Singapore, 35, 109, 112
  Singapore as part of, 33–35, 116
  trip of KM with friends, 58–59
  See also Kuala Lumpur

Mandela, Nelson, 254–255

Mantaha, Zainal Arif, 242

Marican family (neighbours), 15

Marschall, Walther von, 77, 86

Marshall, David, 63, 71–72, 174–175

Marx, Karl, in master's thesis of KM, 94–96, 97–98

Marxism, 104, 105, 122

Marxists, in Singapore, 105, 176–177

MAS (central bank of Singapore), 123

Mauritius, at UNSC, 260

McCoy, Dr, 121

McKinsey & Company, 253, 272–273

meritocracy, in MPH as recipe for success, 276, 278

Middle East policy at UN, and Singapore, 164–166

Miller, Robert Hopkins, 114

Ministry of Defence (Mindef), 63–64, 104, 122

Ministry of Foreign Affairs (MFA)
  bond of KM, 102–103
  and Cabinet papers, 225–226
  career planning and development in, 134–135

criticism of government and PAP by KM, 71

"current estimated potential" (CEP) of staff, 134–135

diplomatic training of KM, 72–75

expansion of Foreign Service, 206

financial aspect for KM, 67–68, 104

geopolitics start for KM, 52, 67, 68–69, 89

home posting of KM, 127–128, 132–135

KM as desk officer, 68–70

KM as DS, 191, 199

KM as permanent secretary (1993–98), 203–204, 205–211, 214, 224–225, 229–231

leave for Dalhousie and return to work, 102–104

negative comments sharing, 203–205

offices description and location, 68, 69, 132

start and friends of KM at, 64, 67, 68–69

team at UNSC, 242

valedictory report of KM, 124–125, 222

See also postings, appointments, and positions of KM

Ministry of National Development (MND), 283

Modi, Narendra, 290

Moscow, visit of KM, 92

mother of KM (Janki Mahbubani)
  disputes in family, 20–21
  flight from Pakistan, 1–2
  life with husband, 8–9, 37
  marriage and divorce, 4–5, 10–11
  and marriage of KM, 102
  move to Singapore, 2, 5
  name for grandson, 171
  new home, 101
  Phnom Penh visit, 76–77
  prejudices towards Muslims, 15
  raising of children, 13–15, 204
  Sindhi life in Singapore, 24–26

Index

Index

318

Index

Russell, Bertrand, as influence on KM, 27, 38
Ryan, Richard, 259–260

Salcedo, Luis Moreno, 154–155
Sanctions Committees of UNSC, 243–244, 255
Sarno, John, 264–265
Sartre, Jean-Paul, 39
Sathiah, Renji, 80
Savetsila, Siddhi, 148
School of Public and International Affairs (SPIA) at Princeton, 269–270
Schwab, Klaus, 281–282
Searle, John, 48
Senkuttuvan, Arun, 293
Seraya School (primary school), 23
Shanmugaratnam, Tharman, 176–177, 200
Shih Choon Fong, 274
Shultz, George, 141, 172
Sihanouk, King, overthrow of, 79, 88
Sind region, 2–3, 154
Sindhis (Hindus from Sind)
  as heritage of KM, 24, 26–27
  marriage custom, 102
  mercantilist streak, 3, 24
  in Singapore, 16, 24–27
Sindhu House (Singapore), 24, 25
Singapore
  Cabinet papers, 225–226, 227–229
  City Hall building, 68
  conservative values, 146
  corruption lack in, 277
  decision-making in politics, 221–222, 227
  detainment and torture of prisoners, 257
  favourable governance for children, 12
  financial reserves, 123–124
  founding fathers, 108, 109, 188–189
  generational transition in politics, 169–170, 180–181, 194–195
  in geopolitics, 78, 89, 181–182, 189
  growth in 1980s, 190–191
  and human rights, 211–212, 257

  leaders' challenge of authority, 64–65
  minorities, 16–17
  nation building as focus, 170
  as part of, and separation from, Malaysia, 33–35, 109, 112, 116
  PM handover, 194–195
  political and racial tensions in 1960s, 17, 34–35
  political tensions at top, 106–108
  press freedom, 183
  property market, 190
  public policies and public good, 225–228
  "self-governing" status after British rule, 23–24
  as small state in geopolitics, 89
  strengthening of UN by, 172–173
  toilets, 19–20
  tree cover and greenery, 227
  and UNESCO, 174–175
  See also specific topics, countries, and organizations
Singapore Armed Forces, 189
Singapore-Australia New Partnership, 210
Singapore Planning Urban Research (SPUR) Group (NGO), 71
Singapore Undergrad, KM as editor, 61–62
Singh, Manmohan, 282
Singh, Prem, 217
Sirik Matak, Prince Sisowath, 88
Siv, Sichan, 82–84
small states, in geopolitics, 78–79, 89, 158, 180, 181, 189, 262–263
Sng, Jeffery
  arrest, 177, 293–294
  and books, 11, 22
  as friend of KM, 5, 17–18, 55
  memories of KM's family, 5–7, 20–21
  memories of Singapore, 18
  travel with KM, 58–59
  at university, 11
Snyder, Joe, 114–115
Somare, Michael, 228–229
Soviet bloc, and Cambodia, 129–131

Index

Index

Index

Kishore Mahbubani is a veteran diplomat, student of philosophy, and celebrated author. He is currently a Distinguished Fellow at the National University of Singapore's Asia Research Institute. Mahbubani is also a former president of the UN Security Council (January 2001 and May 2002) and the founding dean of the Lee Kuan Yew School of Public Policy (2004–2017). Mahbubani writes and speaks prolifically on the rise of Asia, geopolitics, and global governance. His nine books and numerous articles in the *New York Times*, *Washington Post*, *Financial Times*, and *Foreign Affairs* have earned him global recognition as "the muse of the Asian century." He was inducted into the American Academy of Arts and Sciences in October 2019. More information can be found at www.mahbubani.net.

PublicAffairs is a publishing house founded in 1997. It is a tribute to the standards, values, and flair of three persons who have served as mentors to countless reporters, writers, editors, and book people of all kinds, including me.

I. F. STONE, proprietor of *I. F. Stone's Weekly*, combined a commitment to the First Amendment with entrepreneurial zeal and reporting skill and became one of the great independent journalists in American history. At the age of eighty, Izzy published *The Trial of Socrates*, which was a national bestseller. He wrote the book after he taught himself ancient Greek.

BENJAMIN C. BRADLEE was for nearly thirty years the charismatic editorial leader of *The Washington Post*. It was Ben who gave the *Post* the range and courage to pursue such historic issues as Watergate. He supported his reporters with a tenacity that made them fearless and it is no accident that so many became authors of influential, best-selling books.

ROBERT L. BERNSTEIN, the chief executive of Random House for more than a quarter century, guided one of the nation's premier publishing houses. Bob was personally responsible for many books of political dissent and argument that challenged tyranny around the globe. He is also the founder and longtime chair of Human Rights Watch, one of the most respected human rights organizations in the world.

· · ·

For fifty years, the banner of Public Affairs Press was carried by its owner Morris B. Schnapper, who published Gandhi, Nasser, Toynbee, Truman, and about 1,500 other authors. In 1983, Schnapper was described by *The Washington Post* as "a redoubtable gadfly." His legacy will endure in the books to come.

Peter Osnos, *Founder*